# The Curious Researcher

EIGHTH EDITION

# The Curious Researcher

## A Guide to Writing Research Papers

**Bruce Ballenger**

*Boise State University*

PEARSON

Boston   Columbus   Indianapolis   New York   San Francisco   Upper Saddle River
Amsterdam   Cape Town   Dubai   London   Madrid   Milan   Munich   Paris   Montréal   Toronto
Delhi   Mexico City   São Paulo   Sydney   Hong Kong   Seoul   Singapore   Taipei   Tokyo

*For Rebecca, who reminds me to ask, Why?*

**Senior Sponsoring Editor:** Katharine Glynn
**Vice President, Marketing:** Roxanne McCarley
**Executive Digital Producer:** Stefanie Snajder
**Digital Editor:** Sara Gordus
**Content Specialist:** Erin Jenkins
**Senior Supplements Editor:** Donna Campion
**Project Manager:** Rebecca Gilpin
**Project Coordination, Text Design, and Electronic Page Makeup:**
   Integra Software Services
**Cover Design Manager:** Barbara Atkinson
**Cover Designer:** Tamara Newman
**Cover Photo:** *Visitors in the Museum of Modern Art*, Daniel Schoenen/Glow Images
**Senior Manufacturing Buyer:** Roy L. Pickering, Jr.
**Printer/Binder:** Edwards Brothers Malloy
**Cover Printer:** Lehigh-Phoenix Color/Hagerstown

Credits and acknowledgments borrowed from other sources and reproduced, with permission, in this textbook appear on the appropriate page within text or on page 344.

**Library of Congress Cataloging-in-Publication Data is on file with the Library of Congress.**

10 9 8 7 6 5 4 3—V031—17 16 15

**www.pearsonhighered.com**

Student Edition ISBN 10:      0-321-99296-2
Student Edition ISBN 13: 978-0-321-99296-3
A la Carte ISBN 10:      0-321-97822-6
A la Carte ISBN 13: 978-0-321-97822-6

# Contents

# Chapter 1
# The First Week    21

# Chapter 2
# The Second Week    49

# Chapter 5
# The Fifth Week    187

# Appendix C
# Guide to APA Style    297

# Preface

## Features of the New Edition

Writing a textbook is like discovering an aunt you never knew you had. She arrives unexpectedly one summer and stands at your door beaming and expectant. Naturally, you welcome her in. How charming she is, and as you get to know her, you get to know yourself. This is her gift to you. At some point, many months later, you see her luggage by the door, and with a certain sadness, you send her off. "Come again," you yell as she ambles away. "Come again anytime. I'll miss you!" And you do. Your fondness for this newly discovered relative grows as you learn that other people who aren't even blood related like her too.

If a textbook is successful, the aunt returns again and again, and you get to know her well. Though you may wish, especially in the beginning, that she wouldn't visit so often, after a few weeks there are new conversations and new discoveries. That's the way it has always been for me with *The Curious Researcher*, and the eighth edition is no different. Here are some of the new features of the book that make me feel that way:

- *Focus on learning outcomes.* For the first time, each chapter opens with a list of what I hope students will learn from the chapter. I've attempted to describe these outcomes in ways that will help students grasp the aims of each chapter and also help instructors assess students' progress.

- *More attention to plagiarism.* A new section—"A Taxonomy of Copying"—should help students better understand when their borrowing from sources crosses the line.

- *New assignments.* The new edition features culminating assignments for each chapter that lead to the drafting of a research essay. These include an exercise on developing a multimedia infographic at the end of week two and an annotated bibliography assignment when students finish the third week.

- *Expanded treatment of online research routines.* Drawing from recent research on how undergraduates conduct online research, the new edition helps students identify—and reflect on—the routines they habitually use to find information on the Web.

- *New student examples.* The new edition also includes engaging and instructive examples of work by students who used the book to help them with their inquiry projects.

# Placing Inquiry at the Heart of the Course

For many of my college writing students, there are two kinds of school writing—"creative" writing and "academic" writing—and the two have very little in common. Creative writing is typically any personal writing assignment—a personal narrative, a reader response, or a freewriting exercise—and academic writing is almost anything that involves research. I've spent quite a few years now trying to understand this perceived gap between creative and academic writing, a distinction that I have found troubling because it short-circuits the connection I have been trying to build between the personal and the academic, especially the idea that students' own subjectivities are not only relevant to academic work but are also an inescapable part of it. I also know from my own experience as an academic that research writing is a very creative enterprise. *Why don't my students see that?* I've wondered.

The answer, in part, lies with the research paper assignment itself. It seems to encourage a very closed process of inquiry: Come up with a thesis quickly, hunt down evidence to support it, and wrap it up—all the while focusing less on learning something than on getting it right: the right number of pages, the right citations, the right margins. This isn't the way academics approach research at all, I've thought. We do research because we believe there is something to discover that we don't already know. How might I help my students understand that? I've concluded that the traditional research paper is unlikely to teach them what I want them most to learn.

I began to see the problem more clearly after I read the Boyer Commission's national report on the state of undergraduate education in America's research universities. The report was sobering. It also reminded me of what I'd already sensed: For all of our talk about student-centered learning, much of what goes on in undergraduate classrooms is lecture. The aim, above all, is to transmit information, with students as passive recipients of knowledge. But it is mostly the Boyer Commission's call for an inquiry-based curriculum, particularly in students' first and second years, that has changed my thinking. Commission members call for a "radical reconstruction" of undergraduate education. "The ecology of the university," they write, "depends on a deep and abiding understanding that inquiry, investigation, and discovery are the heart of the enterprise....Everyone at a university should be a discoverer, a learner." The freshman year, in particular, should provide "new stimulation for intellectual growth and a firm grounding in inquiry-based learning."

*The Curious Researcher* answers that call. The college research paper, probably the most common writing assignment in the university, presents an ideal opportunity to encourage inquiry-based learning and the kinds of thinking it demands. When students wrestle with sources, listening in on the never ending conversation among experts on a topic, the drama of inquiry can unfold for students with questions like these: *What questions does this raise that interest me? How do I decide what's true? What gives me the authority to speak?* Unfortunately, much research paper instruction mostly raises other, less compelling questions: *How many pages does it have to be? How many sources do I have to use? How do you want this structured?* These are all reasonable questions, of course, but they are certainly not the most important ones if we want students to genuinely understand what it means to engage in academic inquiry. While it definitely answers questions about the formal conventions of the research paper like any other research guide, *The Curious Researcher* tries to inspire students to ask those questions that will shape their thinking well after they leave school. But how does it do that?

# Teaching the Spirit of Inquiry

Over the years, I've refined *The Curious Researcher*'s approach to teaching inquiry, but it still rests on these premises:

1. **Students should have the experience of investigating a topic in an open-ended way, at least initially.** An important first motive to do research is *to find out,* not *to prove,* and the research *essay,* as opposed to the conventional research paper, is more likely to encourage exploration.
2. **There can't be argument without inquiry.** Most research writing in college is argumentative, and that's certainly the approach of most research papers in the disciplines. Yet in most cases, we develop arguments inductively, through inquiry, as well as deductively. We discover our thesis either by exploring the evidence or by testing our thesis against the evidence,

including evidence that is inconvenient or contrary to what we already think.

3. **One of the most useful—and difficult—things to teach and to learn is the power of questions.** Inquiry-based approaches rest on wonder. These investigations often begin with questions of fact—*What is known about the health effects of tanning booths?*—that later flower into a question, say, of policy—*What should be done to minimize the risks of tanning booths?* The power of questions fuels the critical mind and drives the research.

4. **Writing as a way of thinking is a vital tool in discovery and learning.** What students in any discipline can learn in a writing class is how to put language into the service of inquiry. As any composition instructor knows, writing isn't just a means of getting down what you already know. It's much more interesting than that. Writing can help writers *discover* what they think. In an inquiry-based classroom, this is invaluable, and we need to teach students how to use writing not only to report the results of their research but also to think about what they're discovering *as* they do research.

## Ways of Using This Book

Because procrastination ails many student researchers, this book is uniquely designed to move them through the research process, step-by-step and week by week, for five weeks—the typical period allotted for the research paper assignment. The structure of the book is flexible, however; students should be encouraged to compress the sequence if their research assignment will take less time or ignore the sequence altogether and use the book to help them solve specific problems as they arise.

Students who follow the five-week sequence usually find that they like the way *The Curious Researcher* doesn't deluge them with information, unlike so many other research paper texts. Instead, *The Curious Researcher* doles information out week by week, when it is most needed. I've also been told by instructors who use the book for online classes that the structure of the book is particularly well suited for teaching research writing in that environment, especially because each chapter contains exercises that help students work on their own to push their projects along.

The Introduction, "Rethinking the Research Paper," challenges students to reconceive the research paper assignment. For many of them, this will challenge their long-held beliefs about what it means to do academic research, which may require substantial "unlearning" on their parts. During "The First Week," students are encouraged to discover topics they're genuinely curious about and to learn to develop a "working knowledge" of their topics through library and Web research. This working knowledge will guide them as they decide on a tentative focus for their investigations. In "The Second Week," students develop a research routine, hone their skills in evaluating sources, and then begin working to develop a "focused knowledge" of their topics by systematically searching for information in the library and on the Web. In "The Third Week," students learn notetaking techniques, the dangers of plagiarism, and tips on how to conduct a search that challenges them to dig more deeply for information. During "The Fourth Week," students begin writing their drafts; this chapter also gives tips on integrating sources and on structure, voice, and beginnings. In "The Fifth Week," students are guided through the final revision.

## Alternatives to the Five-Week Plan

It isn't necessary to follow the five-week plan, of course. You can have students dip into appropriate sections of the book to solve some of the most common problems that arise during the research process. For example, you might begin by introducing students to the Third Week (Chapter 3) techniques of paraphrase and summary, assigning some of the exercises as practice before they begin a research project. You might skip to the material in the Second Week (Chapter 2), on evaluating Internet sources and using library databases, to get them acquainted with finding good academic sources. One thing to consider is what idea you'd like to foreground in your course. This would be the idea that would be a central element of every writing assignment. Among the possibilities are the following:

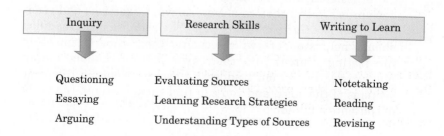

| Inquiry | Research Skills | Writing to Learn |
|---|---|---|
| Questioning | Evaluating Sources | Notetaking |
| Essaying | Learning Research Strategies | Reading |
| Arguing | Understanding Types of Sources | Revising |

Each of these would lead you to "frontload" your course with different material from *The Curious Researcher.* An emphasis on research skills, for instance, might suggest you begin with material in Chapters 1 and 2 on strategies for developing working knowledge and focused knowledge on a topic. An emphasis on how to use writing as a tool for discovery might lead you to introduce students to material on double-entry notetaking in Chapter 3 in the first few weeks.

A few other suggestions include the following:

- Research in learning theory suggests that prior beliefs about a subject or task significantly influence learning. Consider always beginning a research writing course in a way that brings to the surface students' prior beliefs about research writing and the college research paper. Exercise 1 in the Introduction of *The Curious Researcher* is one way to begin this discussion.

- Inquiry-based learning—with the approach that one begins with questions, not answers—is the concept around which the book is built. There is some evidence that one of the things students struggle with most is crafting strong questions. This is the focus of Chapter 1. But the heuristic power of questions is something you can demonstrate in virtually any writing assignment. Consider having students try Exercises 1.1, 1.2, and 1.3 early in the course, well before the research paper assignment, to get them thinking not only about possible topics but also about the importance of good questions.

- The distinction between developing working knowledge of a subject and developing focused knowledge is a major emphasis in Chapters 1 and 2. If assignments in your writing course involve research from the very beginning, you might have students focus on these chapters in the first few weeks of class.

- Finally, another way to proceed is to identify, after one or more assignments, the kinds of problems your students are encountering and then to assign relevant exercises and readings from *The Curious Researcher.* The exercises and readings should help students with focusing their papers, smoothly integrating sources into their own writing, understanding plagiarism, and so on. I address these problems in different sections of the book, and you can find them easily in the table of contents and index.

# Resources for Students and Instructors

- **MyWritingLab™ Now Available for Composition**
*MyWritingLab* is an online homework, tutorial, and assessment program that provides engaging experiences for today's instructors and students. New features designed specifically for composition instructors and their course needs include a new writing space for students, customizable rubrics for assessing and grading student writing, multimedia instruction on all aspects of composition, and advanced reporting to improve the ability to analyze class performance. For students who enter the course underprepared, *MyWritingLab* offers pre-assessments and personalized remediation so they see improved results and instructors spend less time in class reviewing the basics.

- **Pearson eText** An online version of *The Curious Researcher* brings together the many resources of *MyWritingLab* with the instructional content of this successful book to create an enhanced learning experience for students.

- **CourseSmart eTextbook** Students can subscribe to *The Curious Researcher* at CourseSmart.com. The format of the eText allows students to search the text, bookmark passages, save their own notes, and print reading assignments that incorporate lecture notes.

- **Android and iPad eTextbooks** Android and iPad versions of the eText provide the complete text and the electronic resources described above.

# Acknowledgments

I began working on the first edition of this book back in 1991, and in the many years since then, I've been fortunate to have great students who tutored me on what worked and what didn't. Over the years, these have included many more students than I can name here, but I'd like to single out a few who have been particularly helpful: Andrea Oyarzabal, Amanda Stewart, and Patricia Urbick. I'd also like to thank my extraordinary daughter, Becca Ballenger, who collaborated with me, for the first time, on this new edition. When she was little, I dedicated this book to her because of her insatiable curiosity. Now things have come full circle, and she joins me as a collaborator. Becca's curiosity has not dimmed, and her spirit is an even more inspiring presence now than it was 23 years ago, when, as a two-year old, she interrupted my work on the first edition to ask, "Why?"

The strong support from the Pearson team is key to this book's success. My editor at Pearson, Katharine Glynn, demonstrated such confidence in the book and its author that she made it much easier to do the work. My former editor, Joe Opiela, took a risk on *The Curious Researcher* back in the early nineties, and for that I'm grateful. I also appreciate the enormous contribution that Randee Falk made to the book's evolution in the last few editions. Her editorial guidance was instrumental in reorganizing several of the chapters. Copyediting is not my strong suit, and Valerie Iglar-Mobley came to my rescue. Her meticulousness helped make a book on writing avoid the kind of mistakes it shouldn't make. Thanks, too, to Rebecca Glipin who ushered the project through to completion without a hitch. Finally, I've met quite a few of the company's sales staff around the country, and, without exception, these wonderful and hardworking people have treated me with kindness and expressed enthusiasm for the book. Their dedication is key to *The Curious Researcher*'s success.

A number of my colleagues at different institutions have been unflagging in their support of *The Curious Researcher* over the years. Among these are Deborah Coxwell-Teague, at Florida State University, and Nancy DeJoy, at Michigan State University. There are many others I've met traveling to campuses around the country who have been generous in their support and have said very kind things to me about the book. These visits are great learning opportunities for me, and they've been instrumental to an evolution in my thinking about how to teach writing and inquiry to all kinds of students in many different contexts. Thanks to all of you.

Most of all, I'm grateful to my wife, Karen, and my two daughters, Becca and Julia, for always leaving the light on to guide me home.

I would like to thank those individuals who have reviewed my book. Reviewers for the seventh edition include the following: Kathleen J. Cassity–Hawaii Pacific University; Sydney Darby–Chemeketa Community College; Holly DeGrow–Mt. Hood Community College; Tom Hertweck–University of Nevada, Reno; Nels P. Highberg–University of Hartford; Elizabeth Imafuji–Anderson University; and Shevaun Watson–University of Wisconsin, Eau Claire. I would also like to extend my thanks to the reviewers of this edition: Shanti Bruce, Ph.D., Nova Southeastern University; Julia Combs, Southern State University; Jordan Curtis, Bryant & Stratton College, Syracuse; Michael Delahoyde, Washington State University; Martha Silano, Bellevue College; Dr. Ann Spurlock, Mississippi State University; and Jennifer Wetham, Clark College.

BRUCE BALLENGER

# About the Author

Bruce Ballenger, a professor of English at Boise State University, teaches courses in composition, composition theory, the essay tradition, and creative nonfiction. He's the author of seven books, including the three texts in the Curious series: *The Curious Researcher*, *The Curious Reader*, and *The Curious Writer*, all from Pearson Education. His latest book is *Crafting Truth: Short Studies in Creative Nonfiction*, from the same publisher. Ballenger lives with his wife and two daughters in Boise, Idaho.

# Rethinking the Research Paper

---

**IN THIS CHAPTER, YOU'LL LEARN TO...**

■ Recognize the differences between reporting information and *using* it to explore a question or make an argument.

■ Reevaluate your assumptions about the research paper genre and ways of knowing.

■ Distinguish between a research *essay* and a conventional research *paper* and describe the similarities and differences between them.

---

Unlike most textbooks, this one begins with your writing, not mine. Open a fresh page in your notebook, computer, or tablet and spend 10 minutes doing the following exercise.

## EXERCISE 1

### This I Believe

Most of us were taught to think before we write, to have it all figured out in our heads before we compose. This exercise asks you to think *through* writing rather than *before,* letting the words on the page lead you to what you want to say. With practice, that's surprisingly easy using a technique called *fastwriting.* Basically, you just write down whatever comes into your head, not worrying about whether you're being eloquent, grammatically correct, or even very smart. If the writing stalls, write about that; or write about what you've already written until you find a new trail to follow. Just keep your fingers moving.

**STEP 1:** Following is a series of statements about the research paper assignment. Choose one that you believe is true or one that you believe is false. Then, in your notebook or on your computer—wherever

1

you can write faster—write for 3 minutes without stopping about the belief you chose. Why do you think it's true or false? Where did you get these ideas? Is there a logic behind your beliefs? What might that be? Whenever you feel moved to do so, tell a story.

- You have to know your thesis before you start.
- You have to be objective.
- You can't use the pronoun *I*.
- You can use your own experiences and observations as evidence.
- You can use your own writing voice.
- There is always a structure you must follow.
- You're supposed to use your own opinions.

**STEP 2:** Now consider the truth of the following statements. These statements have less to do with research papers than with how you see facts, information, and knowledge and how they're created. Choose one of these statements* to launch another 3-minute fastwrite. Don't worry if you end up thinking about more than one statement in your writing. Start by writing about whether you agree or disagree with the statement, and then explore why. Continually look for concrete connections between what you think about these statements and what you've seen or experienced in your own life.

- There is a big difference between facts and opinions.
- Pretty much everything you read in textbooks is true.
- People are entitled to their own opinions, and no one opinion is better than another.
- There's a big difference between a *fact* in the sciences and a *fact* in the humanities.
- When two experts disagree, one of them has to be wrong.

## Learning and Unlearning 101

By the time we get to college, most of us have written research papers, beginning as early as the eighth grade. Whenever we've done something for a long time—even if we don't think we're

*Part of this list is from Marlene Schommer, "Effects of Beliefs About the Nature of Knowledge on Comprehension," *Journal of Educational Psychology* 82 (1990): 498–504.

very good at it—we have assumptions about how it's *supposed* to be done. For example,

> "Whenever you can, use big words in your school writing to sound smart."
> "The best research is in books."

Dig a little deeper, and you'll discover that these assumptions are often based on beliefs about how things work in the world. For example, the importance of using "big words" and relying on "book facts" both arise from beliefs about authority in academic writing—where it comes from, who has it, and who doesn't. This might seem like overthinking things, but it *really matters* what implicit beliefs are at work whenever someone is trying to learn to do new things. Our assumptions, frankly, are often misleading, incomplete, or downright unhelpful. But how do you know that? By flushing those birds from the underbrush and taking a good look at them from time to time. That was the purpose of Exercise 1. The first part of Exercise 1 focused on a few beliefs you might have about writing academic research papers. Maybe you had a discussion in class about it. From my own research on common beliefs about research writing, I once discovered that one of the most common assumptions first-year college students share is this one: You have to know your thesis before you start a research paper—which obviously implies the belief that discovery is not the point of research.

The second part of Exercise 1 might have gotten you thinking about some beliefs and attitudes you hadn't thought much about— what a "fact" is, the nature and value of "opinions," and how you view experts and authorities.

Both sets of assumptions—one about the research paper genre and the other about how we come to know things—have a huge effect on how you approach the assignment. No doubt many beliefs have some truth to them. Other beliefs, however, may need to be *unlearned* if you're going to take your research writing to the next level. Keep these beliefs out in the open, where you can see and evaluate them to determine if you have some unlearning to do.

# Using This Book

## The Exercises

Throughout *The Curious Researcher*, you'll be asked to do exercises that either help you prepare your research paper or actually help you write it. You'll need a research notebook in which you'll do the exercises and perhaps compile your notes for the paper. Any notebook will do, as long as there are sufficient pages and left margins. Your instructor may ask you to hand in the work you do in response to the exercises, so it might be useful to use a notebook with detachable pages. You may also choose to do these exercises on a computer rather than in a notebook. If you do, just make sure that it feels good to write fast and write badly.

Write badly? Well, not on purpose. But if the notebook is going to be useful, it has to be a place where you don't mind lowering your standards, getting writing down even if it's awkward and unfocused. The notebook is where you have conversations with yourself, and what's important is not the beauty of a sentence or airtight reasoning but breathlessly chasing after language that threatens to run away from you. Many of the exercises in this book, including the one that started it, invite you to write badly because in doing so, you can use writing to discover what you think.

## The Five-Week Plan

If you're excited about your research project, that's great. You probably already know that it can be interesting work. But if you're dreading the work ahead of you, then your instinct might be to procrastinate, to put it off until the week it's due. That would be a mistake, of course. It's likely that the paper won't be very good. Because procrastination is the enemy, this book was designed to help you budget your time and move through the research and writing process in five weeks. But there's another reason, too, that you should think about how your research project will develop over time: You will start out not knowing very much about your topic, and how much you know impacts how much you can do. You will not, for example, be able to come up with a very strong research question until you have some working knowledge of your topic. Behind the five-week plan is the idea that research is developmental—your abilities will develop over time.

It may take you a little longer, or you may be able to finish your paper a little more quickly. But at least initially, use the book sequentially, unless your instructor gives you other advice.

## Alternatives to the Five-Week Plan

Though *The Curious Researcher* is structured by weeks, you can easily ignore that plan and use the book to solve problems as they arise. Use it when you need to find or narrow a topic, refine a thesis, do advanced searching on the Internet, organize your paper, take useful notes, and so on. The overviews of Modern Language Association (MLA) and American Psychological Association (APA) research paper conventions in Appendixes A and B, respectively, provide complete guides to both formats and make it easier to find answers to your specific technical questions at any point in the process of writing your paper.

# The Research Paper Versus the Research Report

In high school, I wrote a research "paper" on existentialism for my philosophy class. I understood the task as skimming a book or two on the topic, reading the entry on "existentialism" in the *Encyclopaedia Britannica,* putting notes on some notecards, and writing down everything I learned. That took about six pages. Did I start with a question? No. Was I expressing an opinion of some kind about existentialism? Not really. Did I organize the information with some idea about existentialism that I wanted to relay to readers? Nope. Was I motivated by a question about the philosophy that I hoped to explore? Certainly not. What I wrote was a research *report,* and that is a quite different assignment than almost any research paper you'll be asked to write in college.

## Discovering Your Purpose

For the paper you're about to write, the information you collect must be used much more *purposefully* than simply reporting what's known about a particular topic. Most likely, you will define what that purpose is and, in an inquiry-based project, it will arise from the question that is driving your investigation. In the beginning, that question may not be very specific. For example, why do dog trainers seem so polarized about the best way to make Spot sit? Later, as you refine the question, you'll get even more guidance about your purpose in the essay. A question like, "What is the evidence that domestic dogs behave like wild animals, and how does this influence theories of training?" might lead you to make an argument or explore some little-known aspect of the issue.

Whatever the purpose of your paper turns out to be, the process usually begins with something you've wondered about, some itchy question about an aspect of the world you'd love to know the answer to. It's the writer's curiosity—not the teacher's—that is at the heart of the college research paper.

In some ways, frankly, *research reports* are easier. You just go out and collect as much stuff as you can, write it down, organize it, and write it down again in the paper. Your job is largely mechanical and often deadening. In the *research paper,* you take a much more active role in *shaping and being shaped by* the information you encounter. That's harder because you must evaluate, judge, interpret, and analyze. But it's also much more satisfying because what you end up with says something about who you are and how you see things.

## How Formal Should It Be?

Whenever I got a research paper assignment, it often felt as if I were being asked to change out of blue jeans and a wrinkled oxford shirt and get into a stiff tuxedo. Tuxedos have their place, such as at the junior prom or the Grammy Awards, but they're just not me. When I first started writing research papers, I used to think that I *had* to be formal, that I needed to use big words like *myriad* and *ameliorate* and to use the pronoun *one* instead of *I.* I thought the paper absolutely needed to have an introduction, body, and conclusion—say what I was going to say, say it, and say what I had said. It's no wonder that the first college research paper I had to write—on Plato's *Republic* for another philosophy class—seemed to me as though it were written by someone else. I felt I was at arm's length from the topic I was writing about.

What we're usually talking about when we talk about formality in research writing is trying to locate ourselves in the final product. How is locating ourselves possible if we can't use first person or can't draw on our personal experiences and observations? If the best research is "objective," aren't we supposed to vacate the building? The simple answer to the last question is "no." Even in the most scientific articles, writers have a presence, though it's often ghostly. They are present in the questions they ask, the things they emphasize, and the words they choose. Academic researchers work within *discourse communities* that may limit their movements somewhat but do not ever bind their feet. "Discourse community" is a term academics use to describe certain identifiable ways in which people with expertise talk to each other, ask questions, or evaluate evidence they consider convincing. We all belong to discourse communities; any time you have a feeling that there are certain things that might be said and certain ways to say them, you're probably thinking of a particular discourse community.

Although you've been going to school for years, you're still fairly new to the academic discourse communities. You don't yet know how they work; that's something you'll learn later as you begin to specialize in your academic major. What's far more important as you begin academic research is developing the habits of mind that will help you know what might be a researchable question and how to see patterns in the information you collect, along with skills like knowing where to find the information you need. Most important of all, you should feel—no matter what you end up writing about—that you're part of an ongoing conversation about your topic: speculating, asking questions, offering opinions, pointing to gaps, making connections. In short, you must not vacate the building but occupy it, and the easiest way to do this, at least at first, is to worry less about the "rules" of the research paper than the process of discovering what you want to say.

# The Question Is You

Okay, so how do you have a strong presence in a research paper aside from talking about yourself? More than anything else, you are present in the questions you ask, particularly the inquiry question that is at the heart of your investigation of a topic. An inquiry question both makes you curious about a topic and suggests what might lead to answers in which other people have a stake, too. A good question is a wonderful thing. As kids, my friends and I used to mess with magnets and iron filings. We would scatter iron filings on a steel pot lid and move the magnet around underneath, marveling at the patterns it produced in the filings. Good questions have the same power. They help you to see patterns in information and to organize it in a way that makes scattered information easier to make sense of. Finding the question, particularly the one *key* question about your research topic that most interests you, is how any project becomes *your* project. In an inquiry-based investigation, questions power the process, and learning to ask good ones may be the most essential skill.

## Thinking Like an Academic Writer

What does it mean to *think* like an academic writer? These are some habits of mind that are typical:

1. Academic inquiry begins with questions, not answers.
2. Because genuine inquiry must be sustained over time, it's essential that researchers suspend judgment and even tolerate some confusion. You do research not because you know what you think already but because you want to discover what you think.

3. Insight is the result of *conversation* in which the writer assumes at least two seemingly contrary roles: believer and doubter, generator and judge.
4. Writers take responsibility for their ideas, accepting both the credit for and the consequences of putting forth those ideas for dialogue and debate.

# A Method of Discovery

If college research assignments don't simply report information on a topic, what do they do? They are organized around what you think—what you believe is important to say about your topic—and there are three ways you can arrive at these ideas:

1. You can know what you think from the start and write a paper that begins with a thesis and provides evidence that proves it.
2. You can have a hunch about what you think and test that hunch against the evidence you collect.
3. You can begin by not knowing what you think—only that you have questions that really interest you about a topic.

Academic inquiry rarely begins with item 1. After all, if you already know the answer, why would you do the research? It's much more likely that what inspires research would be a hunch or a question or both. The motive, as I've said before, is discovery. *The Curious Researcher* promotes a method of discovery that probably isn't familiar to you: essaying.

*Essay* is a term used so widely to describe school writing that it often doesn't seem to carry much particular meaning. But I have something particular in mind.

The term *essai* was coined by Michel Montaigne, a sixteenth-century Frenchman; in French, it means "to attempt" or "to try." For Montaigne and the essayists who follow his tradition, the essay is less an opportunity to *prove* something than an attempt to *find out*. An essay, at least initially, is often exploratory rather than argumentative, testing the truth of an idea or attempting to discover what might be true. (Montaigne even once had coins minted that said *Que sais-je?*—"What do I know?") The essay is often openly subjective and frequently takes a conversational, even intimate, form.

Now, this probably sounds nothing like any research paper you've ever written. Certainly, the dominant mode of the academic research paper is impersonal and argumentative. But if you consider writing a *research essay* instead of the usual *research paper,* four things might happen:

1. *You'll discover that your choice of possible topics suddenly expands.* If you're not limited to arguing a position on a topic, then you can explore any topic that you find puzzling in interesting ways, and you can risk asking questions that might complicate your point of view.
2. *You'll find that you'll approach your topics differently.* You'll be more open to conflicting points of view and perhaps more willing to change your mind about what you think. As one of my students once told me, this is a more honest kind of objectivity.
3. *You'll see a stronger connection between this assignment and the writing you've done all semester.* Research is something all writers do, not a separate activity or genre that exists only on demand. You may discover that research can be a revision strategy for improving essays you wrote earlier in the semester.
4. *You'll find that you can't hide.* The research report often encourages the writer to play a passive role; the research essay doesn't easily tolerate passivity. You'll probably find this both liberating and frustrating. While you may likely welcome the chance to incorporate your opinions, you may find it difficult to add your voice to those of your sources.

As you'll see later in this Introduction, the form a research essay can take may be a bit different from the usual thesis-proof research paper. But even if you write a more conventional (and frankly more common) paper that makes an argument, the method of essaying can help you discover the claims you want to argue.

## Firing on Four Cylinders of Information

Whatever the genre, writers write with information. But what kind? There are essentially four sources of information for nonfiction:

1. Memory and experience;
2. Observation;
3. Reading; and
4. Interview.

A particular type of writing may emphasize one source over another. For example, literary analysis obviously leans very heavily on reading. The information largely comes from the text you're studying. A personal essay is often built largely from memory. The research essay, however, is a genre that typically fires on all four cylinders, powered by all four sources of information. For example, for an essay exploring the behavior of sports fans, you may observe the behavior of students at a football game, read critiques of unruly soccer fans at the World Cup or theories about group behavior, and remember your own experience as a fan of the Chicago Cubs (God help you!) when you were growing up.

What makes research writing "authoritative" or convincing is less whether you sound objective than whether you are able to find *varied* and *credible* sources of information to explore your research question. Credible to whom? That depends on your audience. The more specialized the audience (the more expertise they have on your topic), the more demanding their standards for evidence.

## "It's Just My Opinion"

In the end, *you* will become an authority of sorts on your research topic. I know that's hard to believe. One of the things my students often complain about is their struggle to put their opinions in their papers: "I've got all these facts, and sometimes I don't know what to say other than whether I disagree or agree with them." What these students often *seem* to say is that they don't really trust their own authority enough to do much more than state briefly what they feel: "Facts are facts. How can you argue with them?"

Perhaps more than any other college assignment, research projects challenge our knowledge beliefs. These can reach pretty deeply: things like how we feel about the value of our ideas, our relationship to authority, and most profoundly, whether we think that knowledge is fixed and certain or is something that is constantly shifting. Step 2 of Exercise 1, which began this Introduction, may have started you thinking about these questions. Are facts unassailable? Or are they simply claims that can be evaluated like any others? Is the struggle to evaluate conflicting claims an obstacle to doing research, or the point of it? Are experts supposed to know all the answers? What makes one opinion more valid than another? What makes *your* opinion valid?

I hope you write a great essay in the next five or so weeks. But I also hope that the process you follow in doing so inspires you to reflect on how you—and perhaps all of us—come to know what seems to be true. I hope you find yourself doing something you may not have done much before: thinking about thinking.

# Facts Don't Kill

When my students comment on a reading and say, "It kinda reads like a research paper," everybody knows what that means: It's dry and it's boring. Most of my students believe that the minute you start having to use facts in your writing, the prose wilts and dies like an unwatered begonia. It's an understandable attitude. There are many examples of dry and wooden informational writing, and among them, unfortunately, may be some textbooks you are asked to read.

But factual writing doesn't have to be dull. You may not consider my essay, "Theories of Intelligence" (see the following exercise), a research paper. It may be unlike any research paper you've imagined. It's personal. It tells stories. Its thesis is at the end rather than at the beginning. And yet, it is prompted by a question—Why is it that for so many years I felt dumb despite evidence to the contrary?—and it uses cited research to explore the answers. "Theories of Intelligence" may not be a model for the kind of research essay you will write—your instructor will give you guidelines on that—but I hope it is a useful model for the kind of thinking you can do about any topic when you start with questions rather than answers.

## EXERCISE 2

### Reflecting on "Theories of Intelligence"

The following essay may challenge your "genre knowledge." That is, it may defy your expectations about what a "research paper" should be like. Before you read it, then, spend a little time jotting down the five or six features of an academic research paper, at least as you understand it. For example,

- What should it sound like?
- How should it be structured?
- How should it use information, and what kinds of information?
- What are appropriate topics for academic research?
- What kind of presence should the writer have?
- What makes a research paper authoritative?

Jot down your list of research paper conventions, and then read "Theories of Intelligence," paying attention to the presence or absence of those features. Here are the questions I hope you discuss or write about:

1. If this isn't a research paper, what is it?
2. What conventions does it share, and which doesn't it share, with academic research, at least as you understand it?
3. More generally, what (or who) determines conventions of a genre like the college research paper in the first place? Do they matter? Why are there genres anyway?

## Theories of Intelligence

*by Bruce Ballenger*

At age 55, I've finally decided I'm not as dumb as I thought. This might seem a strange confession from a professor of English, a man who has spent 25 years making his living with his intellect, working all those years in an environment where being "smart" was a quality valued above all others. This revelation—that I'm not as dumb as I thought—is a relief, of course. More and more, I can sit in a meeting of my colleagues and feel okay when I'm unmoved to speak. It pains me less when I can't quite follow someone's argument or sort out the arcane details of a curriculum proposal. Now, more than ever before, I can stand in front of my classes and say, without shame, "That's a good question. I don't really know the answer."

It's quite possible—no, likely—that I'm not nearly as smart as many of the people around me; but I've learned, at last, not to care. Self-acceptance may simply be one of the few blessings of late middle age. I was watching the news the other day and learned of a report on happiness that suggests the midlife crisis is a universal phenomenon. The study, with the straightforward title "Is Well-Being U-Shaped over the Life Cycle?", reviewed data from two million people in 72 countries, and it concluded that American men are most miserable at around age 52, perhaps because they have the sobering realization that life did not unfold the way they hoped it would. Happiness slowly returns when they "adapt to their strengths and weaknesses, and…quell their infeasible aspirations" (Blanchflower and Oswald 20). It's a great relief for me to know that things should be looking up.

I've considered this idea—that I'm really not that smart but have finally accepted my limitations—but I'm coming around to the belief that I'm probably smarter than I thought I was—that I was *always* smarter than I thought I was. I'm pretty sure this is true for most people and, frankly, the ones who have always known they were really smart—and who behave as if they are quite sure of this—are not the kind of people I usually like very much. Yet even the self-consciously smart people deserve our sympathy because being intelligent really, really matters to most of us. We can live with being unattractive, but no one wants to feel dumb. One of the most popular videos on YouTube is a clip from the Miss Teen USA contest when, during the interview segment of the program, Caitlin Upton, the contestant from South Carolina, was asked this question: "Recent polls have shown that a fifth of Americans can't locate the U.S. on a world map. Why do you think this is?" Her response was, sadly, completely incoherent, and the relentless, often unkind ridicule Upton endured prompted her appearance on the *Today Show* a few days later. "I was overwhelmed," she said. "I made a mistake. Everyone makes mistakes. I'm human" ("Miss Teen on Today"). I'm ashamed to admit that I joined the throngs who gleefully watched the clip and enjoyed Upton's humiliation; at the time, I told myself that my response wasn't personal—it just confirmed my belief that beauty pageants are socially bankrupt. But I know that the real reason I enjoyed it was the relief that it wasn't me up there.

The YouTube clip is now painful for me to watch, not only because the humor in humiliation wears off quickly but also because I recognize in Caitlin Upton a phenomenon I see in myself: We believe that our own intelligence is a script that others author and we cannot revise. Researchers tell us that children typically have one of two theories of intelligence. Some believe that intelligence is an "uncontrollable trait," a thing they are stuck with like eye color or big ears. Others, particularly older children, believe that intelligence is "malleable," something they can alter through effort and hard work (Kinlaw and Kutz-Costes 296). I have never met any of these children, but apparently they're out there.

It is a nearly inescapable fact of American childhood that we are branded as smart or somewhat smart or not too smart or even dumb. For many of us who lack faith in our own intelligence, this branding begins in school, a sad fact that researchers say is especially true of African American kids (Aronson, Fried, and Good 113). I am white, but I can trace my own experience with this by following the scent of old resentments back to memories of school that never lose their bitter taste—even when I try to sweeten them with humor. There was the time in the second grade when I was sent to the back of the room to sit alone in a corner because I couldn't remember all the months of the year. And later, in the eighth grade, I moved from green to orange in the SRA reading packet but never moved again. In those days orangeness was a sign of mediocrity. The shame of never busting through orange to blue, the color Jeff Brickman, Mark Levy, and

Betsy Cochran achieved with ease, convinced me that reading and writing were just not my thing, a feeling that was reinforced by my teacher, Mrs. O'Neal, who spattered my essays with red marks. From then on I hated school and, ironically, especially English (a feeling I freely shared on the inside covers of my class yearbooks). I spent my high school days languishing in "Level 3" English and science classes, where I joined the working-class Italian American students from Highwood and the kids from the army base at Fort Sheridan. We found solidarity in hating Shakespeare, lab reports, and the five-paragraph theme. And we pretended to find solidarity in being dumb, though I think most of us were secretly ashamed.

In my junior year, I dated Jan, one of the "smart" kids who moved in a small herd, migrating from one AP class to another. I was awed by her intelligence, and in the twisted logic of an adolescent male, this awe translated into indifference. I pretended I didn't really care about her. Eventually, however, I found Jan's persistent kindness moving and began to write her bad poetry that she copied and bound into a book that she gave me for my birthday. For a time, I entertained the idea that I wasn't unintelligent. Not smart, exactly—not like Jan—but maybe I could hold my own in the AP crowd. Yet what I did not understand back then was that whatever small gains I was making in school could easily be undone at home.

There was never any question that I would go to college. My parents expected it, and so did I. But I knew that I was not destined to go anywhere Jan and her friends were headed—University of Michigan, Brown, Tufts, Beloit, Kalamazoo. I applied to one school, Drake, with rolling admissions, and when I was accepted early, I excused myself from the endless senior chatter about colleges. I pretended I just didn't care. "You're selling yourself short," my father said, disappointed that I wouldn't pursue more schools. My brother—who was two years older—attended my father's alma mater, the University of Rochester, a school with high academic standards. Dad never encouraged me to apply there, confirming what I had already suspected—that I was a dimmer bulb.

My father was an intelligent man, a Rhodes scholar with an interest in British literature who worked for both Chicago and New York newspapers before the booze took him down. Nothing pleased him more than an argument. When I went to college in the early seventies it was an easier time for students to believe in values and ideas without being wounded by the charge that they were being "naïve." My idealism made me an easy target, and when the vodka kicked in, my father would pick up the scent of some belief I held with uninformed fervor and go after it. Even drunk, Dad knew what he was talking about, and with a cold, ruthless logic he would pick apart whatever passion I brought to the dinner table. I felt young, stupid, and hopelessly inadequate. Dad was not a cruel man; what I know now is that his head may have been full, but his heart was empty. His intellect was one of the last things he clung to as drink became the only way to dull some unspeakable pain; in the end, of course, even intellect succumbs.

There were moments after these arguments when I sat seething and my father would turn to me, wagging his finger. "The most important thing you can be, Bruce," he said, "is an intellectual. Live the life of the mind." Oddly enough, I have become an academic, and, had he lived, my father would likely have approved. Yet the ache I feel about Dad these days is that he didn't possess the kind of knowing that might have saved him had he only valued it. One of the things my Dad's alcoholism taught me was how weak-kneed his kind of intelligence could be against the sucker punches of self-loathing. "Your Dad was just too smart for his own good," my mother would say. "Just too smart for his own good."

Theories of intelligence have evolved considerably since I was a child, a time when everyone was taking IQ tests. In the early eighties, Howard Gardener's "multiple intelligences" came as a relief to many of us whose scores on intelligence tests were not worth bragging about. Back then, I never really understood Gardener's theory but seized on the idea that being smart didn't necessarily mean being smart in one way. More recently, in response to his own bad experiences being labeled dumb in school, intelligence expert Robert Sternberg offered a "Triachic Theory of Successful Intelligence." Being smart, he said, isn't just being analytical but being creative and practical, too. Strength in one can compensate for weakness in the other two ("Robert J. Sternberg"). Yet I always sensed that, no matter what Gardener or Sternberg said, there was a kind of intelligence that really counted and that I didn't possess. It was school smarts—the ability to pick apart an argument, to recognize the logical fallacy, and to make an arresting point—all of the things, I see now, that my father could do so well. As an academic, I see these qualities in some of my colleagues, whom I admire and envy. A very few of them, however, use their intelligence to bully people like my father bullied me.

Before I entered the profession, I imagined that many professors were like these intellectual bullies, people who bludgeon others with reason, looking to wound rather than to enlighten. The literary critic Jane Tompkins once wrote that college teachers are often driven by fear, "fear of being shown up for what you are: a fraud, stupid, ignorant, a clod, a dolt, a sap, a weakling, someone who can't cut the mustard" (654), and this is what drives us to do everything we can to prove to our students and others that we're intellectually superior. In rare cases, this fear of being found out turns teachers into intellectual bullies. More often, their anxiety in the classroom leads to what Tompkins calls the "performance model" of instruction: teachers talking at their students, teachers trying desperately to demonstrate how smart they are. It probably is no surprise that this tendency moves easily from the classroom to the department faculty meeting where the stakes feel higher.

I can't recall exactly how things began to change for me, when I started to see that I might revise the script that had governed my life for so long, but I started to notice it in those department meetings. Whether I spoke or not ceased to matter. I didn't decide one day that I was just as smart as my colleagues. I didn't suddenly start believing the strong evidence that I must have some intellectual ability because I enjoyed a successful career as a college professor. There was no sudden epiphany or dramatic moment. I think I just stopped being afraid.

It has helped to know, too, that my own ideas about intelligence don't travel well. In a famous study, developmental psychologist Joseph Glick asked a Liberian Kpelle tribesman to sort 20 items—food, tools, and cooking utensils—in a way that made "sense" to him. He did this quickly enough, pairing a knife with an orange, a potato with a hoe, and other matches that reflected the practical, functional relationships between the items. "This is what a wise man would do," said the tribesman. The researchers then asked, "What would a fool do?" The Liberian then sorted the items in what we would consider "logical" categories, putting food in one pile, cooking utensils in another, tools in another, and so on (Cole, Gay, Glick, and Sharp 84–87). I live a world away, of course, where as I write this my wife, Karen, is putting away the groceries using a logic that a Kpelle tribesman might find curious. The definition of a fool, obviously, depends on who and where you are.

My self-doubts will never go away completely, but I think they have made me a better teacher. I have empathy for my own students in whom I see the same struggle. Just the other night in a graduate seminar, Greg, a particularly bright student, derailed himself in mid-sentence while interpreting a passage from a Montaigne essay we were reading. "My head just isn't working tonight," he said. "I don't know what's wrong with me." I reassured him that he was making perfect sense, but for the rest of the class Greg was solemn, his hand fixed on his forehead, concealing a brow darkened by frustration. Ironically, Montaigne, a sixteenth-century philosopher and father of the personal essay, constantly questioned his own intelligence, and in the piece we were reading that night, Montaigne writes that his "mind is lazy and not keen; it can not pierce the least cloud" (213). And yet, Montaigne's work celebrated his shortcomings as well as his strengths, the very things that make us human. Learning's highest calling, he thought, was to know oneself, and the essay seemed the best vessel into which this self-reflection might be poured, as I have done here.

On the advice of a friend, I recently took up meditation, a practice that often involves visualization. Sometimes as I listen to the slow rhythm of my breathing, there are moments when I meet myself on a beach on Nantucket Island, a place I spent a spring nearly 30 years ago. There are just the two of us there—one young version of myself, with a navy blue beret and his hands thrust in the pockets of his khaki pants, and the other the grayer, bearded man I see in the mirror these days. I am walking with that younger self on the empty beach at sunset, and I have my arm around his shoulders. I am whispering something to him meant to be comforting. I might be saying many things, but lately I imagine it is this: "You're going to be okay." I think that learning to fully believe this will be the smartest thing I'll ever do.

## Works Cited

Aronson, Joshua, Carrie B. Fried, and Catherine Good. "Reducing the Effects of Stereotype Threat on African American College Students by Shaping Theories of Intelligence." *Journal of Experimental Psychology* 38.2 (2002): 113–25. Print.

Blanchflower, David G., and Andrew J. Oswald. "Is Well-Being U-Shaped over the Life Cycle?" National Bureau of Economic Research Working Paper No. 12935. Cambridge, MA, 2007. Print.

Cole, Michael, John Gay, Joseph A. Glick, and Donald W. Sharp. *The Cultural Context of Learning and Thinking.* New York: Basic Books, 1971. Print.

Kinlaw, Ryan C., and Beth Kutz-Costes. "Children's Theories of Intelligence: Beliefs, Goals, and Motivation in the Elementary Years." *Journal of General Psychology* 34.3 (2007): 295–311. Print.

Montaigne, Michel de. *Essays.* Trans. J. M. Cohen. London: Penguin, 1958. Print.

"Robert J. Sternberg." *Human Intelligence: Historical Influences, Current Controversies, and Teaching Resources.* Indiana U., 7 Oct. 2010. Web. 22 Dec. 2010.

Tompkins, Jane. "Pedagogy of the Distressed." *College English* 52.6 (1990): 653–60. Print.

## Creative Research Papers?

**Question:** How often will I get to write a research paper like "Theories of Intelligence"?

**Answer:** Not often.

**Question:** So why should I write one now?

**Answer:**   Because writing a research *essay,* one that also uses some of the conventions of academic writing like citation, is a great introduction to the essentials of academic inquiry. These essentials include the following:

1. **Powered by questions.** In the beginning, at least, the motive behind nearly any kind of research is to answer questions or solve a problem. The research rests on a simple hope: discovery. You write about the doubts about intelligence or the habits of a housefly or the motives of a terrorist because you want to find out something. Formal academic writing shares this motive, too, but it's less apparent in the product, which focuses mostly on the persuasiveness of its conclusions. In the research essay, the process of discovery is often a visible part of the product.

2. **Extend an ongoing conversation.** The purpose of research writing is not simply to show readers what you know. It is an effort to *extend a conversation about a topic* that is ongoing, a conversation that includes voices of people who have already spoken, often in different contexts and perhaps never together. Research writers begin with their own questions and then find the voices that speak to them. They then write about what others have helped them to understand. This experience of entering into a conversation with sources is much more likely when you are visibly part of it, even if this means using the first person.

## Prose +: Alternative Forms of Research

What *form* should your research take? That's easy. You write it up, print it out, and hand it in. In most cases, that's exactly right. But the rise of digital media means there are fresh ways to "publish" researched writing and new ways to introduce interactivity into conventional documents. For example, rather than a written "paper," a research essay might be an audio documentary or podcast. You might "publish" your research as a blog or wiki. But you might also write a more conventional essay but include links or repackage it as a PowerPoint for a face-to-face presentation.

3. **Write across, not up.** Normally, when we write conventional research papers, we have a very narrow conception of audience: the teacher. In a sense, we tend to write *up* to the instructor because she knows more about the subject than we do. That's actually quite different from most academic writing, which is written to an audience of peers. You should write your research essay to an audience like that; you're trying to make your topic relevant and interesting to people who share in your own "discourse" community. As you advance in college, that community will become more specialized, and so will your writing.

No matter what form your paper takes for this class— whether it's an exploratory research essay or an argumentative one—what happens behind the scenes is similar: If the goal is to engage in genuine inquiry, the kind your professors do, then you begin with this simple question: "What can I learn from this?" From there you begin to listen in to what has already been said by others about your topic; when you know enough, you join the conversation. The process must begin, of course, with figuring out what you want to know. That's the subject of the next chapter.

# The First Week

## The Importance of Getting Curious

Despite what they say, curiosity is not dead. You know the obituary: At some point around the age of (fill in the blank), we stop wondering about things. We lose that childlike sense that the world is something to explore. Actually, we never stop being curious, especially if we feel like there's a good reason for it. More than ever, we live in an information-rich environment, and the Internet makes information more accessible than ever before. Say you're having a conversation with a friend about deodorant. "I wonder what the first deodorant was?" asks she. "That's the kind of question that the Internet was made for," says you. And within a minute, you report that the first commercial deodorant was a product called "Mum," invented in the 1880s, though noncommercial deodorants were in use 5,000 years ago. This kind of short-term curiosity—sometimes called "situational curiosity"—is incredibly common in this Internet age.

On the other hand, genuine research relies on a sustained interest in something. It can begin with situational curiosity. For example, I once wrote an entire book on lobsters, an interest that was initially triggered by childhood memories of eating them during the holidays with my family and, many years later, reading a newspaper article that reported the lobster catch was down 30 percent and some believed the lobster fishery was on the verge of collapse. I wondered, will lobster go the way of caviar and become too expensive for people like me?

That was the question that triggered my research, and it soon led to more questions. What kept me going was my own curiosity. If your research assignment is going to be successful, you need to get curious, too. If you're bored by your research topic, your paper will almost certainly be boring as well. By chapter's end, you'll make a proposal about what you want to investigate. But begin by simply wondering a little.

## Seeing the World with Wonder

Your curiosity must be the driving force behind your research paper. It's the most essential ingredient. The important thing, then, is this: *Choose your research topic carefully. If you lose interest in it, change your topic to one that does interest you, or find a different angle.*

In most cases, instructors give students great latitude in choosing their research topics. (Some instructors narrow the field, asking students to find a focus within some broad, assigned subject. When the subject has been assigned, it may be harder for you to discover what you are curious about, but it won't be impossible, as you'll see.) Some of the best research topics grow out of your own experience (though they certainly don't have to), as mine did when writing about lobster overfishing. Scholars tell us that a good way to sustain your curiosity in a topic is to find something to research that has some personal relevance. Begin searching for a topic by asking yourself this question: *What have I seen or experienced that raises questions that research can help answer?*

## Getting the Pot Boiling

A subject might bubble up immediately. For example, I had a student who was having a terrible time adjusting to her parents' divorce. Janabeth started out wanting to know about the impact of divorce on children and later focused her paper on how divorce affects father-daughter relationships.

Kim remembered spending a rainy week on Cape Cod with her father, wandering through old graveyards, looking for the family's ancestors. She noticed patterns on the stones and wondered what they meant. She found her ancestors as well as a great research topic.

Manuel was a divorced father of two, and both of his sons had recently been diagnosed with attention deficit disorder (ADD). The boys' teachers strongly urged Manuel and his ex-wife to arrange drug therapy for their sons, but they wondered whether there might be any alternatives. Manuel wrote a moving and informative research essay about his gradual acceptance of drug treatment as the best solution for his sons.

For years, Wendy loved J. D. Salinger's work but never had the chance to read some of his short stories. She jumped at the opportunity to spend five weeks reading and thinking about her favorite author. She later decided to focus her research paper on Salinger's notion of the misfit hero.

Accidental topics, ideas that you seem to stumble on when you aren't looking, are often successful topics. My research on Maine lobsters was one of those. Sometimes one topic triggers another. Chris, ambling by Thompson Hall, one of the oldest buildings on his school's campus, wondered about its history. After a little initial digging, he found some 1970s news clips from the student newspaper describing a student strike that paralyzed the school. The controversy fascinated him more than the building did, and he pursued the topic. He wrote a great paper.

If you're still drawing a blank, try the following exercise in your notebook.

## EXERCISE 1.1

### Building an Interest Inventory

**STEP 1:** From time to time I'll hear a student say, "I'm just not interested in *anything* enough to write a paper about it." I don't believe it. The real problem is that the student simply hasn't taken the time to think about everything he knows and everything he might want to know. Try coaxing those things out of your head and onto paper by creating an "interest inventory."

Start with a blank journal page or word processing document. Create three columns per page with the words below:

PLACES, TRENDS, THINGS, TECHNOLOGIES,
PEOPLE, CONTROVERSIES, HISTORY,
JOBS, HABITS, HOBBIES

Under each title, brainstorm a list of words (or phrases) that come to mind when you think about *what you know and what you might want to know* about the category. For example, for TRENDS, you might be aware of the use of magnets for healing sore muscles, or you might know a lot about extreme sports. Put both down on the list. Don't censor yourself. Just write down whatever comes to mind, even if it makes sense only to you. This list is for your use only. You'll probably find that ideas come to you in waves—you'll jot down a few things and then draw a blank. Wait for the next wave to come and ride it. But if you're seriously becalmed, start a new column with a new word from the list above and brainstorm ideas in that category. Do this at least four times with different words. Feel free to return to any column to add new ideas as they come to you, and don't worry about repeated items. Some things simply straddle more than one category. For an idea of what this might look like, here's what one student did with the exercise (Figure 1.1).

Allot a total of 20 minutes to do this step: 10 minutes to generate lists in four or more categories, a few minutes to walk away from it and think about something else, and the remaining time to return and add items to any column as they occur to you. (The exercise will also work well if you work on it over several days. You'll be amazed at how much information you can generate.)

**STEP 2:** Review your lists. Look for a single item in any column that seems promising. Ask yourself these questions: Is this something that raises questions that research can help answer? Are they potentially interesting questions? Does this item get at something I've always wondered about? Might it open doors to knowledge I think is important, fascinating, or relevant to my life?

Circle the item.

**STEP 3:** For the item you circled, generate a list of questions—as many as you can—that you'd love to explore about the subject. This student's interest inventory turned up a topic she didn't expect: teeth whitening. Here are some of her opening questions:

> Are tooth whiteners safe?
>
> What makes teeth turn browner over time?
>
> How has society's definition of a perfect smile changed over time?
>
> Are whiter teeth necessarily healthier than darker teeth?
>
> Is it true that drinking coffee stains your teeth?
>
> How much money is spent on advertising tooth-whitening products each year?
>
> What percentage of Americans feel bad about the shade of their teeth?

## PLACES

Freedom Tower (WTC)
Syria
Subway tunnels
Mines and caves
South Africa
Rural Western America (Wyoming, Idaho, Montana)
Galapagos
Venice (sinking?)
Guantanamo Bay

## CONTROVERSIES

Westboro Baptist Church
LDS and FLDS
Scientology
Racism—Trayvon Martin
Marriage equality
Paparazzi and celebrities (Kanye assault charge)
Teen suicide
The Millennial generation
Sugar addiction
Diversity in the fashion industry
Rights issues and copyright
NSA and security

## JOBS

Police officer
Public office (mayor, comptroller, governor, borough president)
Wedding planner
Stylist
Nutritionist/personal trainer
Animal trainer
Computer hacker
Postal worker
Publisher
Schoolteacher
Marine biologist
Weapons manufacturer
Drug dealer
Soldier

## TRENDS

3-D printing
Stupid baby names (North West, Blue Ivy)
Hip diets (paleo, gluten-free, intermittent fasting)
TV on the Internet vs. live TV
Cats on the Internet (Grumpy Cat, Lil' Bub)
Internet memes
Vampires/zombies
Mustaches
Micro-apartments

**FIGURE 1.1**   **Interest Inventory: A Student Example**

Do dentists ever recommend that people whiten their teeth?

Is there any way to keep your teeth from getting darker over time?

Can teeth get too white?

Why do I feel bad that my teeth aren't perfect?

Do other cultures have the same emphasis on perfectly white teeth as Americans do?

Are there the same standards for men's teeth and women's teeth?

What judgments do we make about people based simply on the color of their teeth?

How does America's dental hygiene compare with that of other countries? Is the "Austin Powers" myth really true?

The kinds of questions she came up with on her tentative topic seem encouraging. Several already seem "researchable." What about you? Do any of your questions give you a hunger to learn more?

## Other Ways to Find a Topic

If you're still stumped about a tentative topic for your paper, consider the following:

■ *Surf the Net.* The Internet is like a crowded fair on the medieval village commons. It's filled with a range of characters—from the carnivalesque to the scholarly—all participating in a democratic exchange of ideas and information. There are promising research topics everywhere. For instance, you might even scour Tweets that you've received from a person or organization you're following. Follow the Tweets from news organizations and major magazines, which often provide summaries of their major articles.

■ *Search a research database.* Visit your library's Web site and check a database in a subject area that interests you. For example, suppose you're a psychology major and would like to find a topic in the field. Try searching PsycINFO, a popular database of psychology articles. Most databases can be searched by author, subject, keyword, and so on. Think of a general area you're interested in—say, bipolar disorder—and do a subject or keyword search. That will produce a long list of articles, some of which may have abstracts or summaries that will pique your interest. Notice the "related subjects" button?

Click that and see a long list of other areas in which you might branch off and find a great topic.

■ *Browse Wikipedia.* While the online "free content" encyclopedia isn't a great source for an academic paper, Wikipedia is a warehouse of potential research topic ideas. Start with the main page, and take a look at the featured or newest articles. You can also browse articles by subject or category.

■ *Consider essays you've already written.* Could the topics of any of these essays be further developed as research topics? For example, Diane wrote a personal essay about how she found the funeral of a classmate alienating—especially the wake. Her essay asked what purpose such a ritual could serve—a question, she decided, that would best be answered by research. Other students wrote essays on topics like the difficulty of living with a depressed brother and an alcoholic parent, which yielded wonderful research papers. A class assignment to read Ken Kesey's *One Flew Over the Cuckoo's Nest* inspired Li to research the author.

■ *Pay attention to what you've read recently.* What articles or Web sites have sparked your curiosity and raised interesting questions? Rob, a hunter, encountered an article that reported the number of hunters was steadily declining in the United States. He wondered why. Karen read an account of a particularly violent professional hockey game. She decided to research the Boston Bruins, a team with a history of violent play, and examine how violence has affected the sport. Don't limit yourself to articles or Web sites. What else have you read recently—perhaps magazines or books—or seen on TV that has made you wonder?

■ *Consider practical topics.* Perhaps some questions about your career choice might lead to a promising topic. Maybe you're thinking about teaching but wonder about current trends in teachers' salaries. One student, Anthony, was being recruited by a college to play basketball and researched the tactics coaches use to lure players. What he learned helped prepare him to make a good choice.

■ *Think about issues, ideas, or materials you've encountered in other classes.* Have you come across anything that intrigued you, anything that you'd like to learn more about?

■ *Look close to home.* An interesting research topic may be right under your nose. Does your hometown (or your campus community) suffer from a particular problem or have an intriguing history that would be worth exploring? Jackson, tired of dragging himself from his dorm room at 3:00 A.M. for fire alarms that always proved false, researched the readiness of the local fire department to respond to such calls. Ellen, whose grandfather worked in the aging woolen mills in her hometown, researched a crippling strike that took place there 60 years ago. Her grandfather was an obvious source for an interview.

■ *Collaborate.* Work together in groups to come up with interesting topics. Try this idea with your instructor's help: Organize the class into small groups of five. Give each group 10 minutes to come up with specific questions about one general subject—for example, American families, recreation, media, race or gender, health, food, history of the local area, environment of the local area, education, and so forth. Post these questions on newsprint as each group comes up with them. Then rotate the groups so that each has a shot at generating questions for every subject. At the end of 40 minutes, the class will have generated perhaps 100 questions, some uninspired and some really interesting. You can also try this exercise on the class Web site using the discussion board or group features.

## What Is a Good Topic?

A few minutes browsing the Internet convinces most of my students that the universe of good research topics is pretty limited: global warming, abortion rights, legalization of pot, same-sex marriage, and the like. These are usually the topics of the papers you can buy with your Visa card at sites like freeessays.com (yeah, right). These are also often topics with the potential to bore both reader and writer to death because they inspire essays that are so predictable.

But beginning with a good question, rather than a preconceived answer, changes everything. Suddenly subjects are everywhere: What is with our cultural obsession about good teeth? Is it true that lawnmowers are among the most polluting engines around? What's the deal with the devastation of banana crops, and how will that affect prices at Albertson's down the street? Are "green" automobiles really green? Even the old, tired topics get new life when you find the right question to ask. For example, what impact will the availability of medical marijuana vending machines in California have on the legal debate in that state?

What's a good topic? Initially, it's all about finding the right question and especially one that you are really interested in (see box below). Later, the challenge will be limiting the number of questions your paper tries to answer. For now, look for a topic that makes you at least a little hungry to learn more.

## What Makes a Question "Researchable"?

- It's not too big or too small.
- It focuses on some aspect of a topic about which something has been said.
- It interests the researcher.
- Some people have a stake in the answer. It has something to do with how we live or might live, what we care about, or what might be important for people to know.
- It implies an approach or various means of answering it.
- It raises more questions. The answer might not be simple.

## *Where's Waldo?* and the Organizing Power of Questions

For a long time, I thought school writing assignments were exclusively exercises in deduction. You start by coming up with a thesis and then try to find examples to support it. This kind of writing starts with an idea and supports it with evidence, moving from the general to the specific. There's nothing wrong with this. In a lot of writing situations—say, the essay exam or SAT writing test—this approach makes a great deal of sense. But much academic research, at least initially, works inductively. You look for patterns in information that raise interesting questions, and it is these questions that redirect the researcher's gaze back to the information, this time more selectively and purposefully.

In other words, you start with a lot of data, form a question or hypothesis about the patterns in what you see, and then return to the data again, this time focusing on what is relevant. In this way, you get control of the information by looking at less of it.

The visual puzzles in the *Where's Waldo?* series of children's books are a great example of the power of good questions to manage information. As you know, Waldo, with his red-and-white-striped stocking cap and jersey, is hidden in a picture among hundreds of other people, many of whom look a lot like him. The challenge, quite simply, is to find Waldo in all of this data. Imagine, though, if the game didn't ask, "Where's Waldo?" but "Where are the men?" or "Where are the women?" in the picture. Suddenly, much more information is relevant and the search isn't nearly as focused. A better question might be, "Where are the people wearing yellow?"

That eliminates some of the data but still leaves a lot to work with. Obviously, "Where's Waldo?" is the best question because you know what you're looking for and what you can ignore.

Similarly, a good inquiry question will focus your investigation of any topic. Starting with an answer—a thesis or main point—before you do any research is efficient; it sets you on a steady march to a destination you already know. But beginning with questions, while sometimes a messier process, is a much more powerful way to see what you don't expect to see. Try the following exercise, and you'll see what I mean.

## EXERCISE 1.2

### The Myth of the Boring Topic

This exercise requires in-class collaboration. Your instructor will organize you into four or five small groups and give each group a commonplace object; it might be something as simple as a nail, an orange, a pencil, a can of dog food, or a water bottle. Whatever the object, it will not strike you as particularly interesting—at least not at first.

**STEP 1:** Each group's first task is to brainstorm a list of potentially interesting questions about its commonplace object. What questions do you have about this thing, or, even more importantly, this *category* of thing (i.e., not just this particular water bottle but water *bottles*)? Choose a recorder who will post the questions as you think of them on a large piece of newsprint taped to the wall. Inevitably, some of these questions will be pretty goofy ("Is it true that no word rhymes with orange?"), but work toward questions that might address the *history* of the object, its *uses,* its possible *impact on people,* or *the processes* that led to its creation in the form in which you now see it.

**STEP 2:** After 20 minutes, each group will shift to the adjacent group's newsprint and study the object that inspired that group's questions. Spend 5 minutes thinking up additional interesting questions about the object that didn't occur to the group before yours. Add these to the list on the wall.

**STEP 3:** Stay where you are or return to your group's original object and questions. Review the list of questions, and choose *one* you find both interesting and most "researchable" (see the box "What Makes a Question 'Researchable'?"). In other words, if you were an editorial team assigned to propose a researched article that focuses on this object for a general interest magazine, what might be the starting question for the investigation? The most interesting question and the most researchable question may or may not be the same.

In Idaho where I live, there are stones called geodes. These are remarkably plain-looking rocks on the outside, but with the rap of a hammer they easily break open to reveal glittering crystals in white and purple hues. The most commonplace subjects and objects are easy to ignore because we suspect there is nothing new to see or know about them. Sometimes it takes the sharp rap of a really good question to crack open even the most familiar subjects, and then suddenly we see that subject in a new light. What I'm saying is this: A good question is the tool that makes the world yield to wonder, and knowing this is the key to being a curious researcher. Any research topic— even if the instructor assigns it—can glitter for you if you discover the questions that make you wonder.

## Making the Most of an Assigned Topic

Frequently, you'll be encouraged to choose your own topic for a research essay. But if your instructor either assigns a topic or asks you to choose one within a limited subject, recall that Exercise 1.2,

"The Myth of the Boring Topic," suggests that writers can write about nearly any topic—assigned or not—if they can discover good questions. Alternatively, examine your assigned topic through the following "lenses." One might give you a view of your topic that seems interesting.

■ *People*. Who has been influential in shaping the ideas in your topic area? Is there anyone who has views that are particularly intriguing to you? Could you profile that person and her contributions?

■ *Trends*. What are the recent developments in this topic? Are any significant? Why?

■ *Controversies*. What do experts in the field argue about? What aspect of the topic seems to generate the most heat? Which is most interesting to you? Why?

■ *Places*. Can you ground a larger topic in the particulars of a specific location that is impacted by the issue? For example, controversies over wolf management in the West can find a focus in how the debate plays out in Challis, Idaho, where some of the stake holders live.

■ *Impact*. What about your topic currently has the most effect on the most people? What may have the most effect in the future? How? Why?

■ *Relationships*. Can you put one thing in relationship to another? If the required subject is Renaissance art, might you ask, "What is the relationship between Renaissance art and the plague?"

## Developing a Working Knowledge

In inquiry-based research, you often begin a project not knowing much about the topic. But in order to find the questions that will sustain your investigation, you have to quickly listen in to what other people have said about it. For example, take Jacky's interest in reality TV (see Figure 1.2). She certainly knows *something* about reality TV since she is addicted to the show "Hoarders." She knows enough to ask a preliminary question: Why do people watch programs like this? But Jacky needs to have working knowledge of her topic before she will be ready to pose an inquiry question that might work. But what kinds of things do you need to know in order to ask a good question?

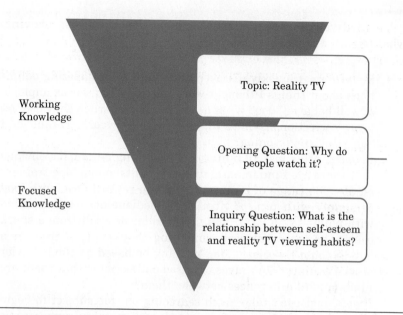

Working
Knowledge

Topic: Reality TV

Opening Question: Why do
people watch it?

Focused
Knowledge

Inquiry Question: What is the
relationship between self-esteem
and reality TV viewing habits?

**FIGURE 1.2   Steps for Developing an Inquiry Question.** You need
some background (or working) knowledge on your topic before you can settle
on a researchable inquiry question. In this example, Jacky begins with a
very general question, and after learning enough about her topic (focused
knowledge), is able to craft the inquiry question that will guide her research for
the next few weeks.

Consider the follow example on the question, *Which theory of
dog training works best?*

## Case Study on Developing Working Knowledge: Theories of Dog Training

A few years ago, we took our Lab puppy, Stella, to eight weeks of
dog training. We thought things went well: She learned a "down stay,"
she would come when we called, and she wouldn't pull on her leash.
Recently, we took our new golden retriever, Ada, to a different trainer,
and the first thing he said was that the method we used with Stella
"simply wouldn't work" with Ada. It was clear that he disapproved of
our first trainer's approach. "I don't know how she stays in business,"
he said. The experience confirmed the feeling I already had: that
despite advances in the study of animal behavior, there is little agreement on the best way to make Fido sit on command. Dog trainers are
a particularly contentious lot.

If I develop a working knowledge on theories of dog training, what might I discover?

1. *Definitions.* I quickly discover that there are competing definitions about things I thought were settled. What, for example, is a "well-behaved" dog? What do trainers mean when they use the term "correction"? What's the difference between "operant" and "classical" conditioning?

2. *Debates.* After just 10 minutes of searching online, it's obvious that there are fundamental disagreements among dog trainers on a whole range of issues. Should you reward dogs with food or simply with praise? Should disobedient dogs be punished with pain—say, a yank on a prong collar or a jolt from a shock collar—or with removing something they want—a treat or a ball? Should theories of dog training be based on the behavior of wild canines like wolves or based on the belief that there are fundamental differences between them?

3. *People.* It doesn't take much searching on this subject to begin to recognize certain experts or advocates whose names come up again and again in the debates. There is, for example, the "Dog Whisperer" on cable TV, Cesar Milan, who applies some of the principles of the wolf pack to dog training. Then there are behaviorists like Patricia McConnell and Victoria Stilwell, who advocate positive reinforcement.

4. *Contexts.* Before long, I realize that I can understand dog training in more than just the context of debates among trainers. This is a topic that leashes together a whole range of disciplines: animal behavior, social psychology, wildlife biology, and anthropology.

## Research Strategies for Developing Working Knowledge

There are many ways to develop a working knowledge of your topic, but generally the research strategy is like many others: Work from more general information to more specialized information. Try these steps:

1. *Begin with a Google search.* Enter as many search terms as you can at one time to narrow the results, with the most important terms first. Save the relevant results (see "Using Apps to Manage Your Research" on page 16).

2. *Search general and subject encyclopedias.* I know that Wikipedia is the first thing that comes to mind, but there are other, better encyclopedias. You'll find bound versions of the venerable *Encyclopaedia Britannica* in your library; your library might also provide free online access. There are online encyclopedias galore, including the *Columbia Encyclopedia* and *Encyclopedia .com*. Subject encyclopedias (see list below) are more focused references, and they are sadly underused by students. There are subject encyclopedias on hundreds of subjects: art history, war, African American literature, nutrition—you name it. (My favorite

## SUBJECT ENCYCLOPEDIAS

### HUMANITIES

*Dictionary of Art*
*International Dictionary*
   *of Films and Filmmakers*
*Encyclopedia of World Art*
*Encyclopedia of Religion*
*Encyclopedia of Philosophy*
*Encyclopedia of African American*
   *Culture and History*
*Encyclopedia of America*
*Encyclopedia of Sociology*
*Social History*

### SOCIAL SCIENCES

*African-American Encyclopedia*
*Dictionary of Psychology*
*Encyclopedia of Marriage*
   *and the Family*
*Encyclopedia of Psychology*
*The Blackwell Encyclopedia*
   *of Social Psychology*
*Encyclopedia of Educational*
   *Research*
*Encyclopedia of Social Work*
*Encyclopedia of World Cultures*
*Encyclopedia of the Third World*
*Encyclopedia of Democracy*
*Guide to American Law:*
   *Everyone's Legal Encyclopedia*

### SCIENCE

*Dictionary of the History*
   *of Science*
*Dictionary of the History*
   *of Medicine*
*Encyclopedia of the Environment*
*Concise Encyclopedia of Biology*
*Encyclopedia of Bioethics*
*Encyclopedia of Science*
   *and Technology*
*Macmillan Encyclopedias*
   *of Chemistry and Physics*
*Food and Nutrition Encyclopedia*

### OTHER

*Encyclopedia of the Modern*
   *Islamic World*
*The Baseball Encyclopedia*
*Encyclopedia of Women*
   *and Sports*
*Encyclopedia of World Sport*
*The World Encyclopedia*
   *of Soccer*
*Worldmark Encyclopedia*
   *of the Nations*

is the *Encyclopedia of Hell.*) You can find these online at your university library as well as at the Internet Public Library (http://www.ipl.org).

3. *Use the Internet Public Library.* The merger of the Internet Public Library and Librarians' Internet Index created a super-site that is a boon to online researchers. This is currently the most successful effort on the Web to bring some order to the chaos that is the Internet. Here you will find specialized encyclopedias, a search portal for finding additional reliable sources on your topic, and even special collections.

4. *Try Google Scholar.* Regular Google searches will turn up all kinds of results—mostly commercial sites—but Google Scholar will get you the kind of information that you know you can count on as reliable and authoritative—journal articles and scholarly books. These publications are often "peer reviewed," so everything that sees print, online or off, passes academic muster.

5. *Start building a bibliography.* Finally, conclude your working knowledge search by collecting the basic bibliographic information on the most useful sources you found. A convenient way to do this is to use a "citation machine," a Web-based program that automatically prompts you for the bibliographic information and then magically turns it into citations in whatever citation format you want. Don't trust one of these to generate references for your final essay—they can make mistakes—but they're great as a preliminary method for collecting a list of citations. Visit Citation Machine (http://citationmachine.net), bibme (http://www.bibme.org), or another site and enter information about your best sources, choosing APA or MLA format.

## Using Apps to Manage Your Research

There are a growing number of free applications you can use to keep track of your research. These programs will not only help you organize online sources but will also help you build a bibliography. See Table 1.1 below for some of the current options.

## The Reference Librarian: A Living Source

There are compelling reasons to visit the library, even at this early stage in your research. First and foremost is that the reference desk is where reference librarians hang out, and these are people you should get to know. They can save you time by guiding you to the very

**TABLE 1.1** Software for Managing Research

|  | Zotero | Mendeley | RefWorks | EndNote |
|---|---|---|---|---|
| **Web-based or desktop?** | Web-based | Web-based, but has desktop program that syncs with Web program | Web-based | Desktop only, but Web option, EndNote Web, is available after purchase |
| **Available offline?** | Yes | Yes | No | Yes |
| **Available in app?** | Third-party apps | iPhone and iPad apps | No | No, but has mobile capability |
| **Cost** | Free | Free | $100. May be available free through your university's library | $249.99. May be available free through your university's library |
| **Import capabilities** | Can import from databases and Web pages | Can import from databases and Web pages, with Mendeley browser plug-in | Can import from databases and Web pages | Can import from databases and Web pages |
| **Citation capture from Web pages** | Yes. Can archive page and annotate | Yes, from certain sites. Can archive page and annotate | Yes | Yes, with Ref-GrabIt plug-in |
| **Citation styles** | Many available, difficult to modify | Many available, difficult to modify | Many available, and can modify and add styles | Many available. Can modify, but cannot add new styles |
| **Storage size** | Unlimited local storage. 100 MB available online (more for purchase) | Unlimited local storage. 1 GB available online (more for purchase) | Limited to 10,000 citations in Web program, but unlimited in desktop program | 100 MB per user, but can be increased to 5 GB |

*(continued)*

**TABLE 1.1** *Continued*

|  | Zotero | Mendeley | RefWorks | EndNote |
|---|---|---|---|---|
| **Sharing options** | Create groups, share references | Share references, create one three-member group free (more available for purchase) | Create groups, share references | Create groups, share references |

best sources on your topic, and they often give great advice on how to narrow your research question. Reference specialists are invaluable to college researchers; without a doubt, they're the most important resource in the library.

## Narrowing the Subject

Consider these two photographs. The first is a long shot of a school in my neighborhood. It's not particularly interesting. The shot is straight-on—the most obvious way of seeing—and while it's clear what the subject is in the photograph, there's isn't much that catches the eye.

The second image is a much closer shot of *a part of* the school—the same subject but much more narrowly focused. While it's hardly a great picture, the photo is far more visually interesting than the long shot, with the geometric shadows of the stair railings clashing with the orderly horizontal lines of the cement steps. This is what often happens in photography when you begin to look more closely at a larger subject that interests you, varying distance, angle, and light.

In writing, when we talk about narrowing your focus, this is what we mean: Maybe start with a long shot but then find some aspect of the topic to look at more closely. This is especially important with projects that involve research because they involve so much information. An investigation with too broad a focus is a hindrance to writers because it's hard to know what information *not* to include, and the result is usually a paper that is general and uninteresting. On the other hand, if you can move in for a closer shot, you'll see an *aspect* of your topic that's less obvious, more interesting, and more efficient to research. With a camera, narrowing a focus is easy: Get closer to your subject. In writing, it's a little more difficult. You have to find the right inquiry question to direct your gaze. In the exercise that follows, I'll prompt you to first generate a lot of questions about your topic to help you find your way to the inquiry questions that will drive your project.

**Other Ways to Narrow Your Subject**

1. **Time.** Limit the time frame of your project. Instead of researching the entire Civil War, limit your search to the month or year when the most decisive battles occurred.
2. **Place.** Anchor a larger subject to a particular location. Instead of exploring "senioritis" at American high schools, research the phenomenon at the local high school.
3. **Person.** Use the particulars of a person to reveal generalities about the group. Instead of writing about the homeless problem, write about a homeless man.
4. **Story.** Ground a larger story in the specifics of a "smaller" one. Don't write about dream interpretation, write about a dream *you* had and use the theories to analyze it.

## EXERCISE 1.3

### Finding the Questions

Although you can do this exercise on your own, your instructor will likely ask that you do it in class this week. That way, students can help one another. (If you do try this on your own, only do Steps 3 and 4 in your research notebook.)

**STEP 1:** Post a large piece of paper or newsprint on the wall. (In a classroom with computers, you can do this exercise in an open Word document.) At the very top of the paper, write the title of your tentative topic (e.g., "Plastics in the Ocean").

**STEP 2:** Take a few minutes to briefly describe why you chose the topic.

**STEP 3:** Spend 5 minutes or so briefly listing what you know about your topic already. This is information you harvested this week from your effort to develop working knowledge on your proposed topic. You might list any surprising facts or statistics, the extent of the problem, important people or institutions involved, key schools of thought, common misconceptions, observations you've made, important trends, major controversies, and so on.

**STEP 4:** Now spend 15 or 20 minutes brainstorming a list of questions *about your topic* that you'd like to answer through your research. Make this list as long as you can; try to see your topic in as many ways as possible. Push yourself on this; it's the most important step.

**STEP 5:** As you look around the room, you'll see a gallery of topics and questions on the walls. At this point in the research process, almost everyone will be struggling to find a focus. You can help one another. Move around the room, reviewing the topics and questions other students have generated. For each topic posted on the wall, do two things: Add a question *you* would like answered about that topic that's not on the list, and check the *one* question on the list you find most interesting. (It may or may not be the one you added.)

If you do this exercise in class, note the question about your topic that garnered the most interest. This may not be the one that interests you the most, and you may choose to ignore it altogether. But it is helpful to get some idea of what typical readers might want most to know about your topic.

You also might be surprised by the rich variety of topics other students have tentatively chosen for their research projects. The last time I did this exercise, I had students propose papers on controversial issues such as the use of dolphins in warfare, homelessness, the controversy over abolishment of fraternities, legalization of marijuana, and censorship of music. Other students proposed somewhat more personal issues, such as growing up with an alcoholic father, date rape, women in abusive relationships, and the effects of divorce on children. Still other students wanted to learn about historical subjects, including the role of Emperor Hirohito in World War II, the student movement in the 1960s, and the Lizzie Borden murder case. A few students chose topics that were local. For example, one student recently researched the plight of nineteenth-century Chinese miners digging for gold in the mountains just outside of Boise. Another did an investigation of skateboard culture in town, a project that involved field observation, interviews, and library research.

## Crafting Your Opening Inquiry Question

What do you do with the gazillion questions you've generated on your research topic? Throw most of them away. But not yet! If you look carefully at the list of questions you (and your peers) generated in Exercise 1.3, you will likely see patterns. Some of your questions will clump together in more general categories. Perhaps a group of questions is related to the history of your topic, trends, processes, local relevance, and so on. Look for these patterns, and especially questions that might be combined or that inspire new questions.

**TABLE 1.2**  Types of Inquiry Questions

| Type | Question | Example |
|---|---|---|
| **Policy** | What should be done about _____? | What might be ethical guidelines for how participants are treated in reality TV shows? |
| **Hypothesis** | What is the best explanation for _____? | Is the popularity of reality TV shows another manifestation of the breakdown of community in the United States? |
| **Relationship** | What is the relationship between _____ and _____? What might be the cause of _____? | Does watching reality crime shows affect viewers' attitudes toward the police? |
| **Interpretation** | What might _____ mean? | How might we interpret the politics of race relations on *Survivor*? |
| **Value** | How good is _____? | Which reality crime show provides the most realistic picture of police work? |
| **Claim** | What does the evidence about _____ suggest is true? | Is there evidence that shows like *Intervention* help viewers develop more sympathetic attitudes toward addiction? |

Your work this week will culminate in the crafting of a tentative inquiry question and research proposal that will guide your research and writing next week. This question will constantly evolve as you learn more; but for now, create the one question around which you will launch your project. Remember, your inquiry question should be the kind of question that will ultimately lead you to make some judgment: a claim, thesis, interpretation, theory, or evaluation. But what kinds of questions are these? As I mentioned earlier, questions of fact or definition are great for developing working knowledge, but they often lead to reporting information rather than making a judgment about what you discovered. But there are questions that do lead you to claims, and these are the type of inquiry questions you're working to find. In Table 1.2, you can see six categories of questions that often do lead to judgment and can sustain inquiry over time.

In Exercise 1.3, you probably generated a whole raft of fact and definition questions. Now the challenge is to use those questions to develop some working knowledge of your topic, and then to craft a tentative inquiry question that will guide your research project. Don't rush the process. You need to know something about your topic before you will land on a good inquiry question.

## Methods for Focusing Your Paper: An Example

A clear, narrow research question is the one thing that will give you the most traction when trying to get your research project moving. It's also one of the hardest steps in the process. Like gulping air after a dive into the deep end of a pool, our natural instinct at the beginning of a research project is to inhale too much of our subject. We go after the big question— why is poverty a problem?—and quickly wonder why we are submerged in information, struggling to find a direction. That's why I've spent so much time on giving you a range of methods to craft a workable research question.

In Table 1.2, I offered one approach to finding a strong inquiry question using policy, interpretation, hypothesis, claim, value, and relationship questions. Here's another approach based on time, person, place, and story, which is described in the "Other Ways to Narrow Your Subject" on page 20. Any one of these questions would be a good starting place for an inquiry into fad diets.

*Topic: Fad diets*

*Opening question: What is the basis for our culture's current obsession with fad diets?*

1. *Time — How does human gastronomic history play a role in the popularity of the "Paleo" diet?*

*(continued)*

2. *Person*—How did Dr. Atkins' low-carb diet launch the dieting industry, which is now so powerful today?

3. *Place*—Where is each diet the most popular? What do cost and accessibility have to do with popularity?

4. *Story*—What were the effects of the 1944–1945 Minnesota Starvation Experiment? How have these findings influenced dieting strategy and healthfulness today?

# Possible Purposes for a Research Assignment

As you're considering your inquiry question, think a bit about the motive behind your project. Are you primarily interested in exploring what you think or making an argument? While any essay can have more than one purpose, which would you say is your *main* motive in writing your paper—at least at this moment?

1. *To explore.* You pose the question *because* you're unsure of the answer. This is what draws you to the topic. You're most interested in writing an essay, not a paper; that is, you want to write about what you found out in your research and what you've come to believe is the best or truest answer to the question you pose. Your essay will have a thesis, but it will probably surface toward the end of the paper rather than at the beginning. This is what I would call a *research essay* rather than a research paper, and it's the most open-ended form for academic inquiry. Exploratory essays often begin with sense-making or relationship-analyzing questions.

2. *To argue.* You know you have a lot to learn about your topic, but you have a very strong hunch about what the answer to your research question might be. In other words, you have a hypothesis you want to test by looking at the evidence. Inspired by a hypothesis question ("Is it true that...?"), you report on your investigation. However, you may quickly move from a hunch to a conviction; and then you move immediately into arguing your claim, trying to influence what your readers think and even how they behave. Your thesis is a statement—for example, *Muslim religious schools in Pakistan are not to blame for Islamic extremism*—that you can probably roughly articulate at the beginning of your project. It may very well change as you learn more, but when

you write your paper, your purpose is to state a central claim and make it convincing. Frequently, that claim is stated near the beginning of the paper.

## EXERCISE 1.4

### Research Proposal

This is an important moment in the research process. How well you've crafted your research question will significantly influence the success of your project. You can change your mind later, but for now, jot down a brief proposal that outlines your research plan in your research notebook or to turn in to your instructor. It should include the following:

1. Inquiry question
2. Primary purpose
   - *Explore:* What are additional questions that most interest you and might help you discover the answers to your research question?
   - *Argue:* What theory or hypothesis about your topic are you testing? What is your tentative main claim or thesis?
3. What, if any, prior beliefs, assumptions, preconceptions, ideas, or prejudices do you bring to this project? What personal experiences may have shaped the way you feel? Before you began developing working knowledge on the topic, what were you thinking about it? What are you thinking about it now?

# Reading for Research

For this assignment, and many others in your other college classes, you will have to read things that you find difficult. Maybe they seem really boring or full of jargon or hard to follow, or perhaps they seem to be all of those things. Aside from procrastinating, how do you deal with that?

Researchers who study reading say that the best readers are guided by a strong sense of purpose—they know why they are reading something and what they hope to get from it. They also have some knowledge of the *type* of text they're reading. They know where to look for what they need to know. More than anything, though, the strongest readers are those who already have some prior knowledge about the subject. Yet even in situations where you have little prior knowledge of the subject you're reading about, you can still read effectively if you read "rhetorically."

## Reading Rhetorically

When you're reading to write, three things will influence how you read:

1. Your motive for reading
2. Your prior knowledge of the topic
3. Your experience with the genres you read

When you're researching a topic for a college class, especially a topic about which you may know little, #2 becomes a problem immediately. Because you don't know much about your topic—the key arguments and people involved, the accepted facts and discredited claims, and so on—you're already at a disadvantage. Then there are the unfamiliar genres you're likely to confront, especially academic journal articles, with their sometimes dense language and formal conventions. These challenges prompt many students to change topics, sidestep scholarly sources, or lean on just a few sources that they *do* seem to understand, usually familiar genres like Web pages and popular articles.

And what's wrong with that? Mostly this: You'll end up with less interesting things to say. If you're always mining the surface for information, ignoring the deeper veins below, you'll discover pretty quickly that you're reading the same stuff over and over again about your subject.

Earlier in this chapter, you began developing your working knowledge of your topic, and that knowledge will help you immensely as you tackle more challenging reading. The other thing you need to develop is your genre knowledge. What does that mean? You become a *rhetorical reader* who is skilled at recognizing how certain kinds of texts are organized and where to look for the information you need. Rhetorical readers also know the intended audience for a certain kind of text and what kinds of evidence are most persuasive for that audience. They quickly make adjustments when they encounter unfamiliar genres and change their reading strategies to make the most of those genres.

## How to Read an Academic Article

Recent studies on the research routines of college students are mostly unsurprising: Students rely heavily on Google and largely skim off the top of the search results. They also tend to avoid using library databases. Naturally, one explanation for this is that students simply don't know how to use them (see the next chapter for help with that). Another is that they simply don't want to deal with scholarly articles. Since these are genres that are often crucial to academic research, let's explore how they might be read by a nonexpert.

An article in the biological sciences is different from an article in political science, which is different from one in criminology. But there are some basic similarities. This describes the structure of a lot of academic articles:

1. This is the problem or question I propose to explore.
2. This is what people have already said about it.
3. This is my claim or hypothesis.
4. This is how I propose to test the hypothesis or argue the claim.
5. Here are my results or here are the reasons and evidence that support the claim.
6. This is what is significant about what I found.
7. Here are a few things that merit further study.

Knowing that this is roughly the structure of most academic articles, you know where to look for the things you want to know. For example, you know to look about a third of the way in an article to find the hypothesis or claim, and just before that you can often find a review of the literature. Unless the article is directly relevant to your research question, you probably won't actually read the whole article in most cases but will "skim and scan."

## Rhetorical Reading Strategies

The table below offers suggestions about how to put your genre knowledge of academic articles to work.

| First Look | Second Look |
|---|---|
| To determine relevance | Mining material in a relevant article |
| ▪ Read the abstract, if there is one.<br>▪ Skim the introductory material. Do the literature review and discussion of the research question seem to point in your chosen direction?<br>▪ Check titles and subtitles. Do they include terms or concepts you've seen before? | ▪ Subtitles, if present, are often signposts for content.<br>▪ The "discussion" section in some articles provides a rich analysis of the findings.<br>▪ Scan the first few sentences of every paragraph in relevant sections. |

*(continued)*

| First Look | Second Look |
|---|---|
| To glean the basic argument or hypothesis | Harvest key phrases and terms |
| ■ The abstract, if present, will often state this.<br>■ Toward the end of the introductory material, you'll often find the phrase "this paper will argue" or "we predicted" or "we hypothesize." | ■ The introductory material, particularly the literature review, will provide you with the terms and phrases experts typically use to discuss the topic. Collect these to use as keywords in subsequent searches. |
| Peruse the bibliography | To find quotable material |
| ■ The review of literature in the introduction will summarize other studies, books, or articles that address the topic. Harvest relevant citations for follow-up.<br>■ Scan the bibliography. Do any titles seem promising? | ■ Avoid the tendency to quote a statistical discussion (paraphrase instead).<br>■ Look for well-put explanations or summaries of the findings or argument. These can be found anywhere but are often in the final sections. |

---

## Reading Strategies for Research Writers

- First develop a working knowledge.
- Let your own purposes guide you: example, context, challenge.
- Anticipate your own resistance.
- Learn the organizing principles of articles.
- Read with a pen in your hand.

# CHAPTER 2

# The Second Week

**IN THIS CHAPTER, YOU'LL LEARN TO...**

- Identify your typical research routines and adapt them to college-level research.
- Apply keyword and index search techniques to find sufficient information.
- Understand different types of information and apply this knowledge to finding varied sources on your topic.
- Distinguish between sources that have more or less authority in academic writing, and practice a method of evaluating online sources.
- Illustrate a finding, process, trend, or argument relevant to your topic using an infographic.

## What Are Your Research Routines?

Most of us have a research strategy, and it's simple: Google it. One scholar describes this as a kind of affliction. "Google dependence," she writes, has the following symptoms: The afflicted one "always returns to Google when confused; repeatedly asserts that 'Google is my friend'; demonstrates the belief that Google has everything; uses Google as an all-inclusive tool." I'm as addicted as anyone to Google's powerful search engine, and one of my purposes in this chapter is to help you use it better (see "Google Tips and Tricks" on page 56).

But even if you use it well, Google alone won't cut it for academic research. We'll explore other options. However, what databases you search is only part of the story; *what you do* with what you find is even more important. Let's begin by thinking about your current habits as an academic researcher. Look at the following table. Which of the terms—"fast surfer," "broad scanner," or "deep diver"—applies to your typical school research routines?[1]

---

| **Fast surfer** | • I'd prefer to read only the sources that are written so that I can understand them.<br>• If I don't find much on my topic when I search, I usually assume that there isn't much written about it.<br>• I always feel under a lot of time pressure when I do research.<br>• I pretty much limit myself to searching for the kinds of sources that I'm familiar with.<br>• I just look for what I need and little more. |
|---|---|
| **Broad scanner** | • I search for a range of sources on my topic, a process that I don't necessarily plan but that develops slowly as I work.<br>• I often find my best sources accidentally.<br>• I'm pretty careful about evaluating the reliability of the relevant sources I do find. |
| **Deep diver** | • I'm more interested in getting the highest-quality sources than in finding a lot of sources.<br>• I'm very open to changing my mind about what I think on my topic.<br>• I spend some time planning my research because I want to be thorough. |

---

Depending on what and why we're researching—and for whom—any one of these profiles might apply. That doesn't make you a lousy researcher. But because academic research needs to be *authoritative*—presenting the strongest evidence and solid reasoning—and because, as a student, you need to be *efficient* with your time, it pays to be a "deep diver."

Deep divers possess a quality we've already talked about: *the willingness to suspend judgment.* I can't overstate how important this is to academic inquiry—and to maximizing your learning. But you also need to plan your research rather than proceed haphazardly, hoping for happy accidents.

---

[1]See Heinstrom, Jannica. "Fast Surfing, Broad Scanning, and Deep Diving: The Influence of Personality and Study Approach on Students' Information-seeking Behavior." *Journal of Documentation* 60.2 (2005): 228–47.

# Planning for the Dive

A research strategy is built from a good inquiry question. We spent considerable time on that last week. With a tentative question in place, a working knowledge of your topic, and perhaps a research proposal, you're ready to plunge more deeply into relevant sources. There's you and an ocean of information. What are you after?

1. Enough information to fully explore a narrowly focused topic
2. Varied sources
3. Quality sources

To accomplish these goals, you'll need to cast a wide net for information. Simply surfing the web won't be enough. Use a complementary research strategy that drills down into information from three sources: the internet, the library, and people (see Figure 2.1). The deeper you drill, the more specialized (and often authoritative) the sources you'll find.

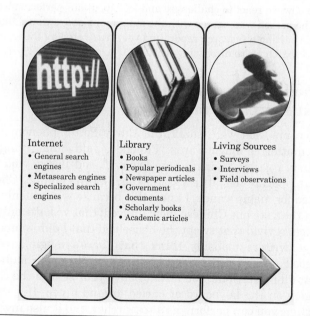

Internet
- General search engines
- Metasearch engines
- Specialized search engines

Library
- Books
- Popular periodicals
- Newspaper articles
- Government documents
- Scholarly books
- Academic articles

Living Sources
- Surveys
- Interviews
- Field observations

**FIGURE 2.1**    Maximize coverage of quality sources by investigating on three fronts.

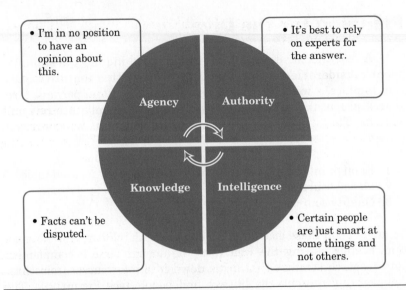

**FIGURE 2.1A**   Our knowledge beliefs include how we feel about our agency, or ability to contribute, our attitude towards authority, our view about intelligence and learning, and most importantly, our ideas about the nature of knowledge. Is it certain or uncertain? When we do research, these beliefs figure into how we react to challenges and feel about our performance. For example, the person who agrees with the statements above would likely be comfortable writing a research report and very frustrated by the kind of academic research we're discussing here.

## Find Enough Information by Using the Best Search Terms

When my kids were small, the Harry Potter phenomenon had everyone muttering magic words. "Flipendo," said Julia, trying to turn the dog into a gerbil. "Wingardium leviosa," said Becca, who was determined to elevate her little sister six feet off the ground. Chopsticks substituted for magic wands. I knew this because we suddenly had too few when the take-out Chinese meal arrived; that was the only part of this magical revival that swept the household that I didn't much like.

Some writers foolishly think that there's magic involved in getting good words on the page when it's really much more simple and not at all mysterious: You have to have your seat in the chair and your fingers on the keyboard or curled around a pen. But there is a kind of magic you can perform as a researcher, and it also involves the right words uttered in the right order. *How* you phrase your search of a library database or the World Wide Web makes an enormous difference in the results. I've come to believe that this ability, almost more than any other, is the researcher's most important skill.

You can harvest more and better results by understanding and effectively using three search tactics:

- *Index searches* deploy the language that librarians use to catalog books and other materials in university libraries.
- *Keyword searches* in library databases use relevant terms with "connectors" like AND, OR, or NOT to produce better results.
- *Keyword searches* on the Web combine a string of terms, along with exact phrases, to generate more relevant hits.

## *Index Searches Using the* Library of Congress Subject Headings

An advantage that libraries have over the Web is that information in libraries is more organized. That's the good news. The bad news is that there is so much information to organize that librarians had to develop a special language for searching it. It's not an alien language—the words are familiar—but it is a language that requires that certain words be used to reflect the way librarians organize information. These searches, called *index searches,* may therefore initially seem less straightforward than the more familiar *keyword searches.*

More specifically, reference librarians use something called the *Library of Congress Subject Headings (LCSH),* which divides all knowledge into areas. These divisions are the *index terms* that you can use for index searches, which will almost always help you to find more relevant books on your topic. How do you find out these index terms? A couple ways: There is a four-volume book in your library's reference room—sometimes called the "Red Book." These volumes are the standard reference to index terms. You can also go online to search the *LCSH* (http://authorities.loc.gov/). There you can search by subject, name, or title, and the software will tell you what subject headings to use when searching for books in the library. But the easiest method to know what Library of Congress (LOC) terms to use is to go to your library's online book database and do an initial search with terms you *think* might work. When you find relevant books, you'll likely see the relevant LOC terms in your results. For example, I did a keyword search using the term *cyberterrorism* in my library's book database and found a great book: *Cyberterrorism: The Use of the Internet for Terrorist Purposes.* The results page also suggested the following index terms as active links that would help me narrow my search:

**Cyberterrorism—Prevention**
**Computer networks—Security measures**
**Computer security—Law and legislation**

Knowing these index terms is a huge help, particularly in the early stages of a research project. Just enter the suggested terms in your library online book index, and you'll be surprised by the quality of the results.

## Keyword Searches in Library Databases

Compared to a Google search, library database searches (see a list of some of these databases on pages 76–77) rely much more on coming up with keywords and trying them in different combinations. For example, searching for books using the word "wildfires" will produce an avalanche that will quickly bury you. Efficient research requires that you maximize the number of relevant results and minimize the number of irrelevant ones. That's why searches that use careful combinations of keywords are so important. Many libraries and Internet search engines use something called "Boolean" connectors to help you when you search databases. (These connectors were invented by George Boole, a British logician, more than 100 years ago.)

The system essentially requires the use of the words AND, OR, and NOT between the search terms or keywords. The word AND, say, between "animal" and "rights" will search a database for documents that include *both* of those terms. Just keying in *animal rights* without the AND connector will often get the same results because the AND is implied. If you want to search for *animal rights* as an exact phrase, library databases ask you to put the phrase in parentheses or quotation marks.

The use of the connector OR between search terms, obviously, will produce a list of documents that contain either of the terms. That can be a lot of results. In the early stages of your project, you might want to browse a heap of results; that way you can explore different angles on your topic, see the more common treatments, and discover some alternative search terms. The NOT connector is less frequently used but really can be quite helpful if you want to *exclude* certain documents. Suppose, for example, you were interested in researching the problem of homelessness in Washington State, where you live. To avoid getting information on Washington D.C., where it's also a problem, use the connector NOT.

### Homeless AND Washington NOT D.C.

As you can see from the example above, it's possible to use the connectors between a number of terms—not just two. In fact, the art of creating keyword searches is both using the right words (those used by librarians) and using them in the right combinations (those that in combination sufficiently narrow your search and give you the best results).

One final search technique that can be very useful, especially in library database searches, is something called "nesting." This involves the use of parentheses around two or more terms in a phrase. This prompts the computer to look for those terms first. For example, suppose you were searching for articles on the ethics of animal rights, but you were particularly interested in information in two states, Idaho and Montana. You might construct a search phrase like this one:

> **(Montana OR Idaho) AND animal AND rights AND ethics**

Putting the two states in parentheses tells the software to prioritize Montana or Idaho in the results, generating a much more focused list of sources related to animal rights and ethics.

## Keyword Searches on the World Wide Web

In the last chapter, you did a subject search on the Web using popular sites, such as the Internet Public Library (http://ipl.org), that specialize in those kinds of subject searches. Far more common are searches that use so-called search engines, such as Google. As you probably know, these are remarkable software programs that in a split second "crawl" the Web, searching for documents that contain the keywords you type in. Lately, the magic of these search engines has been tarnished a bit by commercialism, allowing advertisers to purchase priority listings in search engine results and not always making that fact obvious to the searcher. But these search engines are still essential and getting better all the time.

Keyword searches are the most common method of searching the Web, used much more than subject searches. Unfortunately, there isn't consistency in search languages. Some permit Boolean searching. Some use a variation on Boolean that involves symbols rather than words. But Google, the giant of search engines, has made all of this a bit simpler through the search form provided by its Advanced Search option. You can find this on Google's search page. Once in Advanced Search, you can use the boxes provided to perform all the usual Boolean tricks but without having to use the connector words like AND, OR, or NOT.

Because of the mind-boggling amount of information on the Web, careful keyword searches are critical. Researchers waste

## Google Tips and Tricks

| If you want to... | Use... | For example... |
|---|---|---|
| Find related pages | **related:** followed by Web site address | **related:** www .epicurious.com |
| Automatically search within a specific site or type of site | **site:** followed by Web site or Web site type | microbiology **site: edu** or crime **site:** www .nytimes.com |
| Search for words or phrases in an open Web document | **Control-F (Windows)** or **Command-F (Mac)** and a search window opens | Search for the term "revision" in an article about writing |
| Search by file type | **file type:** fol- lowed by 3-letter abbreviation | Obamacare **file type: PDF** |
| Ignore words in your search | **minus sign ( – )** followed by word to ignore | pet training **– cats** |
| Include words in your search | **quotation marks** (" ") around word to include | **"the" borrowers** |
| Include results with synonyms | **tilde sign (~)** before word | eggplant **~roasting** |
| Retain stop words in phrases without quotes | **plus sign (+)** in front of stop word to retain | fish **+and** chips |
| Search for two options | capitalized **OR** be- tween two options | yellow **OR** black Labradors |
| Match any single word in a search | **asterisk (*)** to find matching word or words | "four score and * years ago" or "undergrad program pre*" |
| Search number range | **two dots (..)** between values | used laptops **$50..$1000** |
| Log and search your own search history | **Web history:** www .google.com/ history | |

more online time either not finding what they wanted or sifting through layers and layers of irrelevant documents because of thoughtless keyword searches. For example, notice in Figure 2.2 how the search on the relationship between social networks and

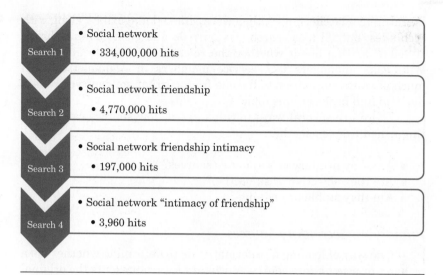

**Search 1**
- Social network
  - 334,000,000 hits

**Search 2**
- Social network friendship
  - 4,770,000 hits

**Search 3**
- Social network friendship intimacy
  - 197,000 hits

**Search 4**
- Social network "intimacy of friendship"
  - 3,960 hits

**FIGURE 2.2   How Multiple Search Terms Narrow Results**

friendship can be dramatically changed by adding terms. An initial search on Google simply using the keywords *social* and *network* produced a mind-boggling 334 million documents. Just adding *one more* keyword cut the number of hits by 6,000 percent! Finally, when combined with a phrase ("intimacy of friendship"), a search with the two terms *social* and *network* yielded significantly fewer and more focused results.

## Find Varied Sources

One of the first things I notice when I'm reading research essay drafts is whether the writer leans too heavily on a single source. Does an author or article reappear again and again on page after page, like a pigeon at a favorite roost? This is not good. It typically means that the writer has too few sources and must keep turning to these few, or one source is especially relevant to the topic, and the writer can't resist repeatedly inviting the author to reappear.

Vary your sources. This means not only using a sufficient number so that your essay is informative but also using different *kinds* of sources whenever you can. In part, the kinds of sources you rely on in preparing your paper depend on your topic. Remember my research question on competing theories of dog training? That's a current topic. There's an ongoing debate online and on cable TV about which approach is best. In addition, the topic has a history in the published literature. I'll be checking both newspapers and magazines, along with Web sites, but I'll also search the journals and books at the library. If you're writing about whether the release of secret documents by WikiLeaks endangers U.S. service members in Afghanistan, then much of your information will come from current sources; you're less likely to find books on this topic.

There are several ways to think about how sources can be distinguished from each other:

- Are they primary or secondary sources?
- Are they objective or subjective?
- Are they stable or unstable?

## Primary vs. Secondary Sources

One way of looking at information is to determine whether it's a *primary* or a *secondary* source. A primary source presents the original words of a writer—his speech, poem, eyewitness account, letter, interview, or autobiography. A secondary source analyzes somebody else's work. Whenever possible, choose a primary source over a secondary one, because the primary source is likely to be more accurate and authoritative.

The subject you research will determine the kinds of primary sources you encounter. For example, if you're writing a paper on a novelist, then his novels, stories, letters, and interviews are primary sources. Research on the engineering of the Chicago River in 1900, a partly historical subject, might lead to a government report on the project or a firsthand account of its construction in a Chicago newspaper. Primary sources for a paper in the sciences might be findings from an experiment or observations. For a paper in business, marketing information or technical studies might be primary sources. A videotape of a theatrical performance is a primary source, while the reviews in the local newspaper are secondary sources.

## Objective vs. Subjective

For now, I'm going to sidestep the debate over whether *any* source can be fully objective and simply point out that, generally speaking, we can divide all sources into those that attempt to report facts that have been gathered systematically, minimizing author bias, and those that don't pretend to be anything more than the author's opinion, perhaps supported by evidence gleaned from objective sources. You can probably guess some examples of objective sources: experiments, survey results, carefully designed studies of many kinds. The best of these are "peer reviewed" (see page 61) to double-check their accuracy. As you know, many academics prize these objective sources as the best evidence. Subjective sources are all over the map, from government propaganda to blogs to op-ed essays in the local newspaper. Of course, just because someone is pushing a point of view doesn't make a source useless. It just means that you need to consider how that point of view colors the source and read it more critically.

## Stable or Unstable?

When information went digital, a new phenomenon emerged; sometimes information simply disappears. That Web page you cited in your draft, with the great statistics on scooter fatalities, is there one day and gone the next. One of the reasons you cite sources in academic writing is so readers can consult them, making a missing Web page a serious problem. Disappearing Web pages, of course, are hard to predict, but you can make some judgments about the stability of an online source. Has it been around for a long time? Is it routinely updated? Are print versions of an online document available? Is the site associated with a reputable institution? Unstable sources are a shaky foundation for any academic essay. It's best to avoid using them.

## Find Quality Sources

The aim of your research strategy is not only to find interesting information on your topic but also to find it in *authoritative* sources. What are these? The highest-quality sources are those types found on the bottom of the upside-down pyramid in Figure 2.3. These are works that are most likely to be written by and then reviewed by experts in their fields (see the "What Does 'Peer Reviewed' Mean?" box on page 61). You find these "peer-reviewed" articles in scholarly journals, some of which are now available online as well as in the library. The downside of dealing with sources at the bottom of the authoritative pyramid is that they may be written in the *discourse* of the field; that may make the writing seem jargon-filled and hard to follow. Of course, as a nonspecialist you aren't the intended audience for the work. But the effort to make sense of an academic article really pays off. Your readers will know that you're relying on the best information available; beyond that, you're more credible because it's clear that you're willing to dig deeply to explore your research question.

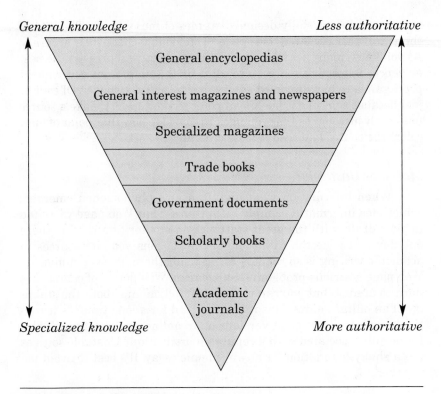

General knowledge                                    Less authoritative

General encyclopedias

General interest magazines and newspapers

Specialized magazines

Trade books

Government documents

Scholarly books

Academic
journals

Specialized knowledge                                    More authoritative

**FIGURE 2.3    Pyramid of Library Sources**

## When Was It Published?

If you're researching the treatment of slaves in nineteenth-century New Orleans, then currency is obviously less of an issue than it might be if your project were to explore the impact of the Toyota Prius on marketing practices for hybrid vehicles. Generally, in any project related to the social sciences, a recent publication date carries more weight, which is one reason APA citations emphasize date of publication. The currency of Web pages and online documents can also be important. A site that is regularly updated is obviously more likely to have the latest information on the topic.

## Why Journal Articles Are Better Than Magazine Articles

If your topic has been covered by academic journal articles, rely heavily on these sources if you can. An article on, say, suicide among college students in a magazine like *Time* is less valuable than one in the *American Journal of Psychology*. Granted, the latter may be harder to read, but you're much more likely to learn something from a journal article because it's written by an expert and is usually narrowly focused. Also, because academic articles are carefully documented, you may be able to mine bibliographies for additional sources. And, finally, scholarly work, such as that published in academic journals and books (usually published by university presses), is especially authoritative because it's often subject to peer review. Other authorities in the field have scrutinized the author's evidence, methods, and arguments; the published work has truly passed muster.

## Look for Often-Cited Authors

As you make your way through information on your topic, pay attention to the names of authors whose works you often encounter or who are frequently mentioned in bibliographies. These individuals are often the best scholars in the field, and it will be useful to become familiar with their work and use it, if possible, in your paper. If an author's name keeps turning up, use it as another term for searching the library databases or Google Scholar. Doing so might yield new sources you wouldn't necessarily encounter in other ways.

## Not All Books Are Alike

When writing my high school research reports, I thought that books were always the best sources because, well, books are thick,

### What Does "Peer Reviewed" Mean?

Broadly speaking, periodicals, books, Web sites, and magazines are one of two types: scholarly or popular. Popular publications include magazines like *Newsweek* or online sites like *Slate*, which are staff written, usually by nonexperts for a more general audience. Scholarly publications are written and edited by experts for others in their fields, and the best of these are "peer reviewed." This means that before an article is published online or in print, a group of fellow experts read and comment on its validity, argument, factual accuracy, and so on. The article doesn't appear in print until this review is completed and the journal editor is satisfied that the other scholars think the work is respectable.

What does this mean for you? It means that you can count on the authoritative muscle of a peer-reviewed source to help you make a strong point in your paper.

and anyone who could write that much on any one subject probably knows what she's talking about. Naive, I know.

One of the things college teaches is *critical thinking*—the instinct to pause and consider before rushing to judgment. I've learned not to automatically believe in the validity of what an author is saying (as you shouldn't for me) even if she did write a thick book about it.

If your topic lends itself to using books as sources, then evaluate the authority of each before deciding to use it in your paper. This is especially important if your paper relies heavily on one or two books. Consider the following:

- Is the book written for a general audience or for more knowledgeable readers?
- Is the author an acknowledged expert in the field?
- Is there a bibliography? Is the information carefully documented?
- How was the book received by critics? To find out quickly, search the Web using the author's name and title of the book as search terms.

### Evaluating Online Sources

Librarians help maintain the order, stability, and quality of information in the library. By comparison, the Internet is anarchy. Everyone knows that you have to be vigilant about trusting the accuracy, balance, and reliability of Web documents. Unfortunately, there's continuing evidence that student researchers still have a hard time assessing the quality of online sources. While the criteria for evaluating sources just mentioned apply to Web documents, Web documents also deserve special attention.

Here are some general guidelines to follow (later I'll suggest a more vigorous approach for evaluating online sources):

- *Always keep your purpose in mind.* For example, if you're exploring the lobbying methods of the National Rifle Association, then you will want to hear, and see, what this organization has to say on its Web site. In looking at the NRA Web pages, you'll know full well that they are not unbiased; however, for your purpose, they are both relevant and authoritative. After all, who knows more about the NRA than the NRA?

- *Favor governmental and educational sources over commercial ones.* There are plenty of exceptions to this, but in general you're wise to rely more heavily on material sponsored by groups without a commercial stake in your topic. How can you tell the institutional affiliation of sources? Sometimes it's obvious: They tell you. But when it's not obvious, the *domain name* provides a clue. The .com that follows a server name signifies a commercial site, while .edu, .org, or *.gov* usually signals an educational, nonprofit, or governmental entity. The absence of ads also implies that a site is noncommercial.

■ *Favor authored documents over those without authors.* There's a simple reason for this: You can check the credentials of an author. You can do this by sending an e-mail message to him or her, a convenience often available as a link on a Web page, or you can do a quick search to see if that author has published other books or articles on your topic. If writers are willing to put their names on a document, they might be more careful about the accuracy and fairness of what they say.

■ *Favor Web pages that have been recently updated over those that haven't been changed in a year or more.* Frequently, at the bottom of a Web page there is a line indicating when the information was posted to the Internet and/or when it was last updated. Look for it.

■ *Favor Web sources that document their claims over those that don't.* Most Web documents won't feature a bibliography. That doesn't mean that they're useless to you, but be suspicious of a Web author who makes factual assertions without supporting evidence.

**A Key to Evaluating Internet Sources.** As an undergraduate, I was a botany major. Among other things, I was drawn to plant taxonomy because the step-by-step taxonomic keys for discovering the names of unfamiliar plants gave the vegetative chaos of a Wisconsin meadow or upland forest a beautiful kind of logic and order. The key that follows is modeled after the ones I used in field taxonomy. This one is a modest attempt to make some sense of the chaos on the Web for the academic researcher, particularly when the usual approaches for establishing the authority of traditional scholarship and publications fail—for example, when documents are anonymous, their dates of publication aren't clear, or their authors' affiliations or credentials are not apparent.

If you're not sure whether a particular Web document will give your essay credibility, see Figure 2.4 and work through the following steps :

1. Does the document have an author or authors? If *yes,* go to Step 2. If *no,* go to Step 7.

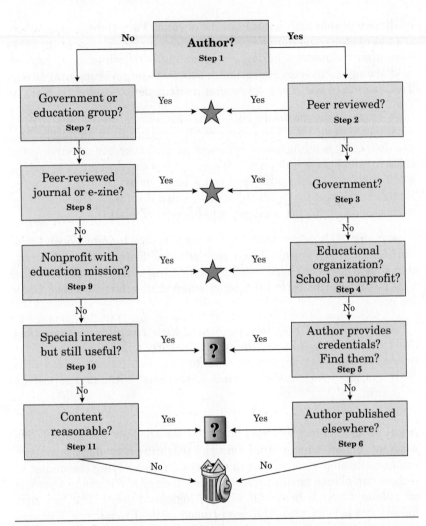

**FIGURE 2.4**   Follow the flowchart for a rigorous review of a Web document or page, beginning with whether the author is obvious or not. Sites that earn stars are generally more trustworthy. Those with question marks still may be useful, depending on the situation. Be particularly wary of information on commercial or special interest sites.

## Authored Documents

2. Does the document appear in an online journal or magazine that is "refereed"? In other words, is there any indication that every article submitted must be reviewed by other scholars in the field before it is accepted for publication? If *yes,* you've found a good source. If *no* (or you're unsure), go to Step 3.

3. Is the document from a government source? (Online, look for the .gov domain.) If *yes,* then it is likely a good source. If *no,* go to Step 4.
4. Does the document appear in an online publication affiliated with a reputable educational institution (e.g., a university) or nonprofit educational organization (e.g., the American Cancer Society)? (Online, look for the .edu or .org domain.) If *yes,* it's likely to be trustworthy. If *no,* go to Step 5.
5. If the author isn't clearly affiliated with a reputable institution, does he or she offer any credentials that help establish expertise on the topic? (For example, an advanced degree in the relevant discipline is encouraging.) If credentials are missing, can you find an author's credentials by Googling the author's name? Is there an e-mail link to the author so you can inquire about affiliations or credentials? If *no,* go to Step 6.
6. Has the author published elsewhere on the topic in reputable journals or other publications? Check this at the library by searching under the author's name in the catalog or appropriate databases. If *no,* reconsider the value of the source. You could be dealing with a lone ranger who has no expertise on your topic and no relevant affiliations.

### Unauthored Documents

7. If the online document has no author, is it from an institutional source like a university (.edu) or the state or federal government (.gov)? If *yes,* then chances are the document is useful. If *no,* go to Step 8.
8. Is the anonymous document published in an online journal or magazine? Is it refereed? (See Step 2.) If *yes,* it's likely a good source. If *no,* go to Step 9.
9. Is the document part of a publication or Web page from a non-government source whose mission is described in the document, and does it suggest that the organization's goals include research and education? Is there a board of directors, and does it include professionals and academics who are respected in the field? If *no,* go to Step 10.
10. Even if the organization offering the information represents a special interest group or business with an axe to grind, the information may be useful as a means of presenting its point of view. Make sure, if you use it, that the information is qualified to make the source's bias obvious.
11. Does the site seem reasonable? Try to apply the usual criteria for evaluating a source to this anonymous document. Does it

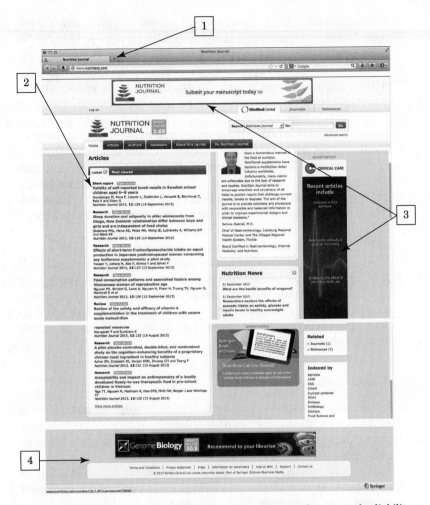

1. **Website URL:** Check the domain (.gov, .edu, .com, etc.) for type and reliability of source, though that isn't always revealing.  In this case, though the site is from a commercial domain it's an educational journal.
2. **Authors:** Do articles and features have an author(s)?
3. **Advertisements:** The presence of ads on a web page, particularly if they're tied to content, might mean it has a commercial bias.  Not the case here, though.
4. **Site and domain information:** The bottom of a web page might include invaluable information on who compiled the page, its currency, and background on the source (look for "About Us" or something similar).

**FIGURE 2.5   Scanning a Web Site.** For a cursory evaluation of a Web site, it helps to know where to look.

have a citations page, and do the citations check out? Was it published on the Internet recently? Does the argument the writer is making seem sound? Do the facts check out? If the answer is *no* to all of the above, then don't trust the document. If you can answer *yes* to more than one of these questions, the material might have some marginal value in a college paper.

A good researcher always takes a skeptical view of claims made in print; she should be even more wary of claims made in Internet documents. And while these approaches for evaluating online sources should help, it still can be pretty tricky deciding whom to take seriously in cyberspace. So to sort it all out, always ask yourself these questions: How important is this Internet document to my research? Do I really need it? Might there be a more reliable print version?

# Developing Focused Knowledge

If working knowledge equips you to sustain a 1-minute dinner conversation on your topic, then focused knowledge is enough for you to make a 15- or 20-minute presentation to the rest of the class (for more on presentations, see the box "Working Together: In-Class News Conference"). You'll probably be able to answer all of your classmates' questions. You'll hardly be an expert, but you'll probably know a lot more about your topic than any of your peers.

Focused knowledge is the product of smart research this week and the next, refining your search terms, knowing where to look for the most useful information, and using your time efficiently. As you'll see later in this section, focused knowledge also depends on what you *do* with what you find. Most important, especially at this point, are these two questions:

1. Is this information relevant to my inquiry question?
2. Does it *change* my question?

At its most basic, relevance is simply deciding whether that article or book you found is on topic. Say you're researching the disappearance of the world's frogs, and you find a *Scientific American* article titled "Extinction Countdown: World's Frogs Are Disappearing." It obviously couldn't be more relevant. But, as you develop more focused knowledge, you can make more focused judgments. *How* is a source relevant? With some traditional research papers, this question may simply mean, how does it support my point? But genuine academic

## Working Together: In-Class News Conference

By the end of this week, you should be ready to make a presentation to your class on your topic. Imagine that it's a press conference similar to the ones shown on television. You will give a 15-minute talk on your topic to your classmates, who will later, like veteran newspaper reporters, follow up with questions. Your presentation will be carefully timed. It shouldn't be any longer than the allotted time limit; any less than the allotted time suggests that you haven't yet developed a focused knowledge of your topic.

Plan your presentation with the following things in mind:

- *Rather than simply report everything you've learned about your topic, try to give your talk some emphasis.* For example, focus on what you've learned so far that most surprised you and why. Or present the most common misconceptions about your topic and why they miss the mark. Or provide some background about why the question you're exploring is important and share some of the answers you've discovered so far. If your topic has a personal dimension, tell that story, and share how your research has helped you understand your experience differently.
- *Don't read a speech.* It's fine to have notes with you—in fact, it's a good idea—but try to avoid reading them. Make your presentation as interesting as you can. After all, this is a chance to discover what other people think about your topic—what interests them about it and what doesn't. This talk is a great chance to try out some approaches to your topic that you may later use to make your essay more compelling.
- *Consider visuals.* PowerPoint or Prezi (see http://prezi.com) presentations are great because they help you organize the talk. Also think about using photographs, graphs, charts, and other visuals to present your information.
- *Begin by stating your focusing question.* Every presentation should start by establishing what question is driving your investigation. You might even put this on the board when you begin.

> While you listen to your peers' presentations, think about what questions they raise that interest you. These might be questions of clarification, questions about an assertion the presenters or one of their sources made, or areas that the speakers didn't cover but that you wonder about. Imagine that you're a hard-nosed reporter anxious to get the story right.

inquiry is about discovery, and because it begins with questions, information isn't just used to line up ducks in the service of a preconceived point. The relevant sources you encounter online and in the library can help your project in many more ways:

- *Refine the inquiry question.* Last week your question was, "Why are the world's frog's disappearing?" But you read some articles and browse some books and you realize that a more focused and interesting question is this: "What is the relationship between climate change and the decline in amphibians?"

- *Help the literature review.* A very common move in most academic research is establishing what has already been said about the question you're posing. Which scientists have published on frogs and climate change? What do they agree on? What are their disagreements? What don't they know?

- *Reveal interesting patterns.* Scholars who study the differences between how experts and novices do research often notice this: Experienced researchers see patterns in data that novices don't notice. Experts *expect* patterns, and you should look for them, too. Does the information you find seem to tell a story? Does the most persuasive information suggest a particular answer to your research question? Are there relationships among facts, theories, or claims that surprise you? Are there any unexpected contradictions, causes, or connections? For example, in Figure 2.6, I've created a "word cloud" of the last 320 words you just read. A "word cloud" takes some text and creates an image that represents word frequency in the text. The visually bigger words are repeated more than the smaller ones. Note the pattern of emphasis on certain subjects and relationships— questions and information, relevance and research, change and focus. In a sense, when you develop focused knowledge on your topic, you gather a cloud of information much like this one, except richer and more complicated. Constantly analyze the relationships in what

**FIGURE 2.6**   **Looking for Patterns**

you're finding—what are the most frequent arguments, which ideas seem connected, what facts stick out?

## What About a Thesis?

Ultimately, you must have a thesis, something you are saying about your research question. But when should you know what that is?

### Are You Suspending Judgment?

Should you have a thesis at this point? That depends on the purpose of your project. If it's exploratory, if your motive is to discover what you think, then it's too early to make any bold statements that answer the question you're researching. It might even be counterproductive. Inquiry-based investigations depend on your willingness to *suspend judgment* long enough to discover what you think.

### Are You Testing Assumptions?

If, however, you feel that you have developed some ideas about what you want to say, now might be an excellent time to make a list of your theories, assumptions, or beliefs about your topic. They will be invaluable guides for your research this week because you can examine these beliefs against the evidence and potentially break through to new understandings about your research question.

## What Are You Arguing?

In some cases, you know that what you think is the best answer to your research question even before you've done much investigation of the topic, and your motive is to build a convincing argument around that claim. For example, consider this claim: *Lawnmowers make a significant contribution to $CO_2$ emissions in the United States.* Maybe this is something you heard or read somewhere from a reputable source, and it's something you strongly suspect is true. Maybe your instructor asked you to make that argument, or you're writing an opinion piece for an assignment. Conventional research papers are frequently organized from the beginning around a thesis or claim. If that's the kind of project you're working on, now would be a good time to craft a sentence that states your most important assertion or main idea. This may well be refined or even discarded later on as you learn more, but it will help with your research this week.

To generate a *tentative* thesis statement at this point, try finishing one of the following sentences:

1. While most people think _____ about _____, I think _____.
2. The most convincing answer to my research question is _____.
3. The main reason that _____ is a problem is _____, and the best solution is _____.
4. Among the causes of _____, the least understood is _____.
5. Though much has been said about _____, very little attention has been paid to _____.
6. All of the evidence so far about _____ points to _____ as a significant cause/solution/effect/problem/interpretation/factor.

You'll be implementing your research strategy this week and next, looking at sources in the library and on the Web. The exercises that follow will help guide these searches, making sure that you don't overlook some key source or reference. Your instructor may ask you to hand in a photocopy of the exercise as a record of your journey.

# Keeping Track of What You Find: Building a Bibliography

For the next two weeks, you're going to collect a lot of material on your research question: PDF copies of articles, books, bookmarked Web pages, images, and perhaps even audio and video files. You will make your life easier if you don't just collect but *record* what you find. Your options include the following:

■ *Basic bibliography.* This is the minimalist approach. You simply keep a running list, using the appropriate citation method, of information on each source you think you'll use in your essay. If you're using MLA, for example, this will become your Works Cited page. An online citation machine, like bibme (http://www.bibme.org), can help you build it. You can, of course, wait until the last minute to do this but, trust me, you will regret it.

■ *Working bibliography.* This is one step up from the basic bibliography (see Figure 2.7) and is the simplest form of what's called an "annotated bibliography." A working bibliography provides a brief *summary* of what the source says: what topics it covers and what the basic argument or main ideas are. If you're using a double-entry journal, then you can find the material you need for your summary there. Your annotation may be a brief paragraph or more, depending on the source.

■ *Evaluative bibliography.* In some ways, this is the most useful annotated bibliography of all because it challenges you not only to "say back" what you understand sources to be saying but also to offer some judgments about whether you find them persuasive or relevant. You might comment on what you consider the strengths of the source or its weaknesses. Is writing an evaluative bibliography more work? You bet. But ultimately you are writing your paper as you go because much of the material you generate for the bibliography can be exported right into your essay. Your double-entry journal provides the raw material for these annotations.

Your instructor will tell you what kind of bibliography you should build for this project, but at the very least you should consider maintaining a basic bibliography as you go. Put it on a "cloud," like Google Docs or Evernote, that will store your draft bibliography on the Web and always be available wherever you find a new source—in the library, at home, or in the campus computer lab.

**Topic:** Theories of Dog Training
**Focusing Question:** Should dogs be trained using positive reinforcement exclusively?

1. Katz, Jon. "Why Dog Training Fails." *Slate Magazine.*
   N.p. 14 Jan. 2005. Web. 22 Dec. 2010.
      Katz argues that most theories of dog training fail to take
   into account the realities of raising an animal in a "split-level,"
   not a training compound. He calls his own method the "Rational
   Theory," which he describes as an "amalgam" of techniques that
   takes into account the actual situation of both dog and owner.
2. Schilder, Matthijs B. H., and Joanne A. M. van der Borg.
   "Training Dogs with the Help of the Shock Collar: Short and
   Long Term Behavioural Effects." *Applied Animal Behaviour
   Science* 85 (2004): 319–34. Medline. Web. 23 Dec. 2010.
      Researchers had two groups of German shepherds, one
   training with shock collars and the other training without them.
   They then studied both "direct reactions" of dogs to the shock
   and their later behavior. Study found that dogs trained with
   shock collars consistently showed more signs of stress during
   and after training, including "lower ear positions." Finding "suggests
   that the welfare of these shocked dogs is at stake, at least
   in the presence of their owner."
3. Shore, Elise, Charles Burdsal, and Deanna Douglas. "Pet Owners'
   Views of Pet Behavior Problems and Willingness to Consult Experts
   for Assistance." *Journal of Applied Animal Welfare Science*
   11.1 (2008): 63–73. Print.
      Study notes that 30 percent of dogs that are given to shelters
   are there because owners complained of behavior problems;
   yet only 24 percent of owners surveyed enrolled in obedience classes.
   Researchers surveyed 170 dog and cat owners and determined
   that the highest concern was about animals who threatened
   people, and those owners were most likely to ask for assistance
   and they mostly turned to the Web unless there was a charge.

---

**FIGURE 2.7   Working Bibliography: An Example**

# Searching Library Databases for Books and Articles

Despite the appeal of the Web, the campus library remains your
most important source of information for academic research. Sure, it
can be aggravating. There's that missing book or that article that isn't

available in full text. You needed that article! Most of all, there's the sense of helplessness you might feel as a relative novice using a large, complicated, and unfamiliar reference system.

In this chapter and the last one, you were introduced to basic library search strategies, knowledge that will help give you some mastery over the university library. Now you'll expand on that knowledge, and at the same time you'll move from a working knowledge of your topic to a deeper understanding, one that will crystallize by reading and writing about what you find.

It's hard for newcomers to the university to fully appreciate the revolution the last decade brought to how we do college research. All you need to know, really, is that finding sources is infinitely easier. And with the growing availability of full-text PDFs of articles and e-books, you can end a session of searching with not just a citation but also the printout of the article.

Because there are still relatively few digital versions of books, you should use the library the old-fashioned way: Journey into the "stacks," which at big schools can be cavernous, floor-to-ceiling aisles of books. The trip is well worth it because even if you discover that the book you want isn't right for your project, that book is surrounded by 100 others on your topic or related ones. Browse like you do on Amazon.

You will save time if you know *where* to look for the book you want, and so you must be familiar with how librarians organize books.

## Finding Books

There are two systems for classifying books: the Dewey Decimal and the Library of Congress systems.

The Library of Congress system, which uses both letters and numbers, is much more common in college libraries. This is the system with which you should become most familiar. Each call number begins with one or two letters, signifying a category of knowledge, which is followed by a whole number between 1 and 9,999. A decimal and one or more Cutter numbers sometimes follow. The Library of Congress system is pretty complex, but it's not hard to use. As you get deeper in your research, you'll begin to recognize call numbers that consistently yield useful books. It is sometimes helpful to simply browse those shelves for other possibilities.

### Understanding Call Numbers

The call number, that strange code on the spine of a library book, is something most of us want to understand just well enough to find that book on the shelf. How much do you need to know? First, you should know that there is more than just the alphabet at work in

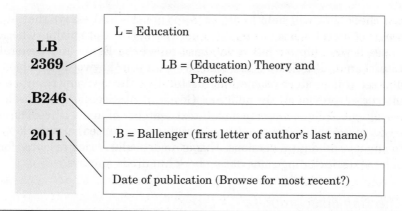

**FIGURE 2.8**    **Deciphering the Call Number Code**

arranging books by their call numbers, and that the call numbers tell you more than merely where books are shelved. Take for example the call number for *The Curious Researcher.*

The call number shown in Figure 2.8 tells you the subject area of the book, a little something about its author, and when the book was published. This is useful to know not only because it will help you find the book, but it also might prompt you to find other, possibly more recent, books on the same subject on a nearby shelf. In Figure 2.9, you can see how Library of Congress call numbers determine the arrangement of books on the shelf.

## Coming Up Empty Handed?

In the unlikely event that you can't find any books by searching directly using the online catalog, there's another reference you

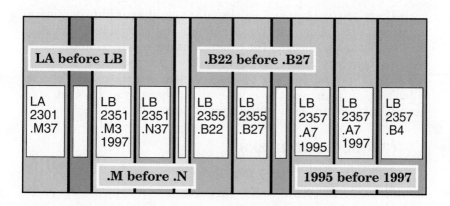

**FIGURE 2.9**    **How Books Are Arranged on the Library Shelf**

can check that will help locate relevant articles and essays that are *a part* of a book whose title may otherwise seem unpromising. Check to see if your library has a database called the Essay and General Literature Index. Search that database with your keywords or subject and see if it produces something useful. List the relevant results as instructed previously. In addition, Google Book Search (http://books .google.com) allows users to do full-text searches of many titles. Those books in the public domain (i.e., the rights have lapsed) are available to any user in digital versions. This is a particularly rich resource for older texts, including some dating back hundreds of years.

## Checking Bibliographies

One tactic that might lead to a mother lode of sources for your essay is to look at the bibliographies at the back of (mostly) scholarly books (and articles). Don't ever set aside a promising book until you've checked the bibliography! Jot down complete bibliographic information from citations you want to check out later. Keep a running list of these in your research notebook.

## Interlibrary Loan

If your library doesn't have the book (or article) you really want, don't despair. Most college libraries have a wonderful low- or no-cost service to students called interlibrary loan. The library will search the collections of other libraries to find what you're looking for and have it sent, sometimes within a week or less. Use the service by checking with the reference desk or your library's Web site.

# Article Databases

There are two kinds of article databases at your library: general databases that cover multiple disciplines and specialized databases that are discipline specific. The general databases cover multiple subjects, so their coverage is wide but shallow. The specialized databases are subject specific, so their coverage is deep but narrow. Of course, I don't know which of these general databases you have at your library, but here are some of the most common:

**GENERAL DATABASES**
Academic OneFile
Academic Search
Academic Search Premier

ArticleFirst

IngentaConnect

JSTOR

ProQuest Central

Web of Science

Many of these multidisciplinary databases index popular magazines and some newspapers, and even some scholarly journals, which makes them very useful. For example, Academic Search Premier indexes nearly 14,000 magazines and journals. Increasingly, these databases include full-text articles, an extraordinary convenience for students working from home.

## COMMON SPECIALIZED DATABASES

| HUMANITIES | SCIENCE AND TECHNOLOGY | SOCIAL SCIENCES |
|---|---|---|
| America, History and Life | AGRICOLA (Agriculture) | Anthropological Index ComAbstracts |
| Arts and Humanities Citation Index | Applied Science & Technology Index | (Communication) Contemporary Women's Issues |
| Historical Abstracts | Biological Abstracts | Criminal Justice |
| Humanities Index | CINAHL (Nursing) | Abstracts |
| Literature Resource Center | Computer Literature Index | PAIS (Public Affairs) PsycINFO |
| MLA International Bibliography (Literature and composition) | GeoRef Abstracts (Geology) Health Reference Center | Social Sciences Index Social Work Sociological Abstracts |
| Music Index | MathSciNet | Worldwide Political |
| Project Muse | Medline Web of | Science Abstracts |
| Religion and Philosophical Collection | Science (Medicine) | |

| BUSINESS | EDUCATION |
|---|---|
| ABI/Inform | Education Full Text |
| Business Source Elite | Education Index |
| FreeEDGAR | ERIC |

Specialized databases are subject specific. These are usually listed by discipline on your library's Web pages. The advantage of using these databases is that they will produce many scholarly articles that might be relevant to your research question, though they may not all be full text. For a list of some of these, see the table on page 77.

Finally, certain article databases are focused on certain *types* of publications. The most important of these are indexes to newspapers (see following list, "Newspaper Databases"). They don't index the small-town papers, but they do provide citations to the so-called national newspapers such as the *New York Times,* the *Washington Post,* the *Los Angeles Times,* the *Wall Street Journal,* and the *Christian Science Monitor.* What's good about the national newspapers is that they're among the most authoritative journalistic sources; in other words, because of their large and experienced staffs, the information they provide is more trustworthy than that of smaller newspapers and online news outlets.

If you're looking for state or local newspapers, you have a couple of options. The larger papers (and many magazines, for that matter) also have their own Web sites, where you may be able to search their archives and retrieve full-text articles. Some sites charge for this service, though you can usually request them from your campus library for free. A convenient method for searching some of these sites is to use a news search engine, which will consult thousands of papers in a few seconds. Two of the best of these search engines are Google News (http://news.google.com) and Yahoo News (http://news.yahoo.com).

Occasionally, the local papers are also indexed online by the university library, and copies are available on microfilm. More and more frequently, however, local papers, like their larger counterparts in major cities, have their own Web sites, where you can use keyword searches to scour their archives.

## NEWSPAPER DATABASES

Alternative Press Index

Ethnic Newswatch

LexisNexis Academic

National Newspaper Index

National Newspapers

Newspaper Source

ProQuest Central

## Saving Search Results

Most online book indexes and article databases allow you to save your search results. Some of these databases allow you to mark the relevant results and then print them out. Some databases and most university libraries also allow you to create an account and a file for your search results. Through the Web page at my library, I can save searches, build a list of books I want to check out, and even publish my bibliographies so others can see them (and I can see theirs). Finally, you can always e-mail your search results page to yourself and organize a bibliography on your own computer.

## EXERCISE 2.1

### Search Book and Article Databases

Develop your focused knowledge by doing a thorough search using your library's book index and article databases. Unlike in Web and database searches, in book searches it often pays off to begin with broad subject terms. I got better results, for example, when I searched for books on theories of dog training with *animal behavior-canine* than I did with *dog training theories*. Searches that begin broadly might lead you to a relevant chapter in an otherwise irrelevant book.

Choose one of the bibliographies (see pages 72–73) as a way of collecting relevant results. Your instructor may ask you to hand these in to gauge your progress. Remember that online citation machines like bibme.org can help you compile these results in the appropriate format (MLA or APA).

# Advanced Internet Research Techniques

I love the word "portal." It summons images of a little window on some vast spaceship that frames the face of an open-mouthed observer looking in wonder at the vast reaches of the universe beyond. Researching on the Internet is a lot like peeping out of that window. There is just so much out there: billions of documents, gazillions of words, each a fragment of electronic data floating in cyberspace, like dust motes in some vast sunbeam. There's useful knowledge for academic writing out there, but it's hard to find and it's easy to get lost.

You're no stranger to the Web, of course, but now, more than ever, your research on the Internet needs to be *efficient*. You need fewer, more focused results and better-quality results. To get these, you need to amp up your Internet search skills by understanding the differences among search engines and what each can do to maximize your penetration of information on the Web.

## Types of Search Engines

The most popular search engine is Google, a search engine with an enormous database that is relatively simple to use. It's easy to forget sometimes that Google is in good company; there are plenty of powerful alternatives that may generate some different results. In fact, studies in recent years consistently show that the major search engines turn up different results as much as 85 percent of the time! It obviously pays off for researchers to use more than one.

Here's a partial list of the best of these general research engines.

### POPULAR GENERAL SEARCH ENGINES

AltaVista (http://www.altavista.com)

Ask.com (http://www.ask.com)

Bing (http://www.bing.com)

Google (http://www.google.com)

Lycos (http://www.lycos.com)

Yahoo! Search (http://search.yahoo.com)

Google and the others are really quite amazing, but they do have limitations. For one thing, they only index pages on the Web that have hyperlinks pointing to them elsewhere or whose creators have requested they be indexed by a particular search tool. In addition, these databases may not be current.

There are so-called metasearch tools such as Dogpile (http://www.dogpile.com/) that are able to deploy multiple general search engines in the service of a single search (see the following list). These are very useful, particularly at the beginning of an Internet search on your topic. However, metasearch engines aren't quite as good as they sound because they skim off the top results from each individual search tool, so you won't see the range of results you would get if you focused on one of the search engines with its own large database.

### METASEARCH ENGINES

Dogpile (http://www.dogpile.com)

Mamma (http://www.mamma.com)

Search.com (http://www.search.com)

Yippy (http://yippy.com)

Finally, there are also specialized search engines (sometimes called "vertical" search engines) that focus on particular subjects such as education, politics, and psychology, as well as search engines that specialize in searching certain *kinds* of content, like finding people, images, blogs, and so on. You probably already use a specialized search engine (and might not know it) when you use a site like Pricegrabber (http://www.pricegrabber.com) to comparison shop online. In the last chapter, you were also introduced to Google Scholar, another example of a search portal that focuses on specialized content, in this case journal articles and books. There are so many of these that a list—even if it were selective—wouldn't do justice to these focused Web crawlers. One place to visit online to help you find a relevant specialized search engine for your project is Noodletools (http://www.noodletools.com/). Click on the link at the bottom of the site's page for "Choose the Best Search."

What are the keys to maximizing the efficiency of your Internet research? In the exercise that follows, you'll learn to do the following:

1. Increase your coverage by using multiple search engines, not just your favorite one.
2. If possible, exploit subject directories that allow you to drill down from general to more specific topic categories. These are often put together by people—not software—who are concerned with quality content.
3. Be thoughtful about what and how many keywords you use to search. Generally, the more words—and especially phrases—you use, the more likely you are to generate relevant hits. This contrasts with searching library databases, which respond better to more focused keywords and phrases.

## EXERCISE 2.2

### Academic Research on the Internet

**STEP 1:** You already searched on your topic on a general search engine—probably Google—and in the last chapter you tried Google Scholar. Now, using some of the keyword combinations you developed for your topic, try at least two more general search engines from the list on page 80. Remember to play around with keywords, and don't forget the search language you learned earlier in this chapter. The Help button on whatever metasearch tool you use will give you the specifics on what connectors—Boolean or others—it accepts.

**STEP 2:** Launch a search using one or more of the metasearch engines listed on page 80. Save your relevant results.

**STEP 3:** Finally, visit Noodletools (http://www.noodletools.com/) and find the link for "Choose the Best Search." Scroll down and find a search engine, perhaps a specialized one, that you haven't tried yet. As before, save relevant results.

**STEP 4:** Add to your bibliography (see "Keeping Track of What You Find" on page 72) by including Web pages that seem promising, and print copies of them for notetaking. A Web-based citation machine like bibme.org can help you with this.

# Living Sources: Interviews and Surveys

## Arranging Interviews

A few years ago, I researched a local turn-of-the-century writer named Sarah Orne Jewett for a magazine article. I dutifully read much of her work, studied critical articles and books on her writing, and visited her childhood home, which is open to the public in South Berwick, Maine. My research was going fairly well, but when I sat down to begin writing the draft, the material seemed flat and lifeless. A few days later, the curator of the Jewett house mentioned that there was an 88-year-old local woman, Elizabeth Goodwin, who had known the writer when she was alive. "As far as I know, she's the last living person who knew Sarah Orne Jewett," the curator told me. "And she lives just down the street."

The next week, I spent three hours with Elizabeth Goodwin, who told me of breakfasting with the famous author and eating strawberry jam and muffins. Elizabeth told me that many years after Jewett's death, the house seemed haunted by her friendly presence. One time, when Elizabeth lived in the Jewett house as a curator, some unseen hands pulled her back as she teetered at the top of the steep staircase in the back of the house. She likes to believe it was the author's ghost.

This interview transformed the piece by bringing the subject to life—first for me as the writer, and later for my readers. Ultimately, what makes almost any topic compelling is discovering why it matters to *people*—how it affects their lives. Doing interviews with people close to the subject, both experts and nonexperts, is often the best way to find that out.

If you'd like to do some interviews, now is the time to begin arranging them.

## Finding Experts

You may be hesitant to consider finding authorities on your topic to talk to because, after all, you're just a lowly student who knows next to nothing. How could you possibly impose on that sociology professor who published the book on anti-Semitism you found in the library? If that's how you feel, keep this in mind: *Most people, no matter who they are, love the attention of an interviewer, no matter who she is, particularly if what's being discussed fascinates them both.* Time and again, I've found my own shyness creep up on me when I pick up the telephone to arrange an interview. But almost invariably, when I start talking with my interview subject, the experience is great for us both.

So, how do you find experts to interview?

■ *Check your sources.* As you begin to collect books, articles, and Internet documents, note their authors and affiliations.

■ *Check the phone book.* The familiar Yellow Pages can be a gold mine. Carin, who was writing a paper on solar energy, merely looked under that heading and found a local dealer who sold solar energy systems to homeowners. Mark, who was investigating the effects of sexual abuse on children, found a counselor who specialized in treating abuse victims.

■ *Ask your friends and your instructors.* Your roommate's boyfriend's father may be a criminal attorney who has lots to say about the insanity defense for your paper on that topic. Your best friend may be taking a photography course with a professor who would be a great interview for your paper on the work of Edward Weston. One of your instructors may know other faculty working in your subject area who would do an interview.

■ *Check the faculty directory.* Many universities publish an annual directory of faculty and their research interests. On my campus, it's called the *Directory of Research and Scholarly Activities.* From it, I know, for example, that two professors at my university have expertise in eating disorders, a popular topic with student researchers.

■ *Check the* Encyclopedia of Associations; *the* Encyclopedia of Associations: Regional, State, and Local Organizations; *or the* Encyclopedia of Associations: International Organizations. These references (also available online through some libraries) list organizations with interests ranging from promoting tofu to preventing acid rain. Each listing includes the name of the group, its address and phone number, a list of its publications, and a short description of its purpose. Sometimes such organizations can direct you to experts in your area who are available for live interviews or to spokespeople who are happy to provide phone interviews.

■ *Check the Internet.* You can use the Internet to find the e-mail addresses and phone numbers of many scholars and researchers, including those affiliated with your own university and ones nearby. Often, these experts are listed in online directories for their colleges or universities. Sometimes you can find knowledgeable people by subscribing to a listserv or Internet discussion group on your topic. Often an expert will have her own Web page, and her e-mail address will provide a hypertext link. (For more details, see "Finding People on the Internet," later in this chapter on page 88.)

## Finding Nonexperts Affected by Your Topic

The distinction between *expert* and *nonexpert* is tricky. For example, someone who lived through 12 months of combat in Vietnam certainly has direct knowledge of the subject, though probably hasn't published an article about the war in *Foreign Affairs.* Similarly, a friend who experienced an abusive relationship with her boyfriend or overcame a drug addiction is, at least in a sense, an authority on abuse or addiction. Both individuals would likely provide invaluable interviews for papers on those topics. The voices and the stories of people who are affected by the topic you're writing about can do more than anything else to make the information come to life, even if they don't have PhDs.

You may already know people you can interview about your topic. Last semester, Amanda researched how mother-daughter relationships change when a daughter goes to college. She had no problem finding other women anxious to talk about how they get along with their mothers. A few years ago, Dan researched steroid use by student athletes. He discreetly asked his friends if they knew anyone who had taken the drugs. It turned out that an acquaintance of Dan's had used the drugs regularly and was happy to talk about his experience.

If you don't know people to interview, try posting notices on campus kiosks or bulletin boards. For example, "I'm doing a research project and interested in talking to people who grew up in single-parent households. Please call 555-9000." Also, poll other students in your class for ideas about people you might interview for your paper. Help each other out.

## Making Contact

By the end of this week, you should have some people to contact for interviews. First, consider whether to ask for a face-to-face, telephone, or e-mail interview. Though I've never tried it for this purpose,

Skype, the free online software that allows users to make a video call anywhere in the world, might be a great interview tool. The personal interview is almost always preferable; you not only can listen, but can also watch, observing your subject's gestures and the setting, both of which can be revealing. When I'm interviewing someone in her office or home, for example, one of the first things I may jot down are the titles of books on the bookshelf. Sometimes, details about gestures and settings can be worked into your paper. Most of all, the personal interview is preferable because it's more natural, more like a conversation.

Be prepared. You may have no choice in the type of interview. If your subject is off campus or out of state, your only options may be the telephone, e-mail, or regular mail.

When contacting a subject for an interview, first state your name and then briefly explain your research project. If you were referred to the subject by someone she may know, mention that. A comment like "I think you could be extremely helpful to me" or "I'm familiar with your work, and I'm anxious to talk to you about it" works well. When thinking about when to propose the interview with an expert on your topic, consider arranging it *after* you've done some research. You will not only be more informed, but you will also have a clearer sense of what you want to know and what questions to ask.

## Conducting Interviews

You've already thought about whether interviews might contribute to your paper. If there's a chance that they will, build a list of possible interview subjects and contact several of them. By the end of this week, you should begin interviewing.

I know. You wouldn't mind putting it off. But once you start, it will get easier and easier. I used to dread interviewing strangers, but after making the first phone call, I got some momentum going, and I began to enjoy it. It's decidedly easier to interview friends, family, and acquaintances, but that's the wrong reason to limit yourself to people you know.

**Whom to Interview?**  Interview people who can provide you with what you want to know. That may change as your research develops. In your reading, you might have encountered the names of experts you'd like to contact, or you may have decided that what you really need is some anecdotal material from someone with experience in your topic. It's still not too late to contact interview subjects who didn't occur to you earlier, but do so immediately.

**What Questions to Ask?**  The first step in preparing for an interview is to ask yourself, What's the purpose of this interview? In your research notebook, make a list of *specific questions* for each person you're going to interview. Often, these questions are raised by your reading or other interviews. What theories or ideas encountered in your reading would you like to ask your subject about? What specific facts have you been unable to uncover that your interview subject may provide? What don't you understand that he could explain? Would you like to test one of your own impressions or ideas on your subject? What about the subject's work or experience would you like to learn? Interviews are wonderful tools for clearing up your own confusion and getting specific information that is unavailable anywhere else.

Now make a list of more *open-ended questions* you might ask some or all of the people you're going to talk to. Frankly, these questions are a lot more fun to ask because you're likely to be surprised by some of the answers. For example:

- In all your experience with _____, what has most surprised you?
- What has been the most difficult aspect of your work?
- If you had the chance to change something about how you approached _____, what would it be?
- Can you remember a significant moment in your work on _____? Is there an experience with _____ that stands out in your mind?
- What do you think is the most common misconception about _____? Why?
- What are significant current trends in _____?
- Who or what has most influenced you? Who are your heroes?
- If you had to summarize the most important thing you've learned about _____, what would it be?
- What is the most important thing other people should know or understand?

As you develop both specific and open-ended questions, keep in mind what you know about each person—his work in the field and personal experience with your topic. You may end up asking a lot of the same questions of everybody you interview, but try to familiarize yourself with any special qualifications a subject may have or experiences he may have had. That knowledge might come from your reading, from what other people tell you about your subject, or from your initial telephone call to set up the interview.

Also keep in mind the *kinds* of information an interview can provide better than other sources: anecdotes, strong quotes, and sometimes descriptive material. If you ask the right questions, a live subject can paint a picture of his experience with your topic, and you can capture that picture in your paper.

**During the Interview.**   Once you've built a list of questions, be prepared to ignore it. Interviews are conversations, not surveys. They are about human interaction between two people who are both interested in the same thing.

I remember interviewing a lobsterman, Edward Heaphy, on his boat. I had a long list of questions in my notebook, which I dutifully asked, one after the other. My questions were mechanical and so were his answers. I finally stopped, put my notebook down, and talked informally with Edward for a few minutes. Offhandedly, I asked, "Would you want your sons or daughter to get in the business?" It was a totally unplanned question. Edward was silent for a moment, staring at his hands. I knew he was about to say something important because, for the first time, I was attentive to him, not my notepad. "Too much work for what they get out of it," he said quietly. It was a surprising remark after hearing for the last hour how much Edward loved lobstering. What's more, I felt I had broken through. The rest of the interview went much better.

Much of how to conduct an interview is common sense. At the outset, clarify the nature of your project—what your paper is on and where you're at with it. Briefly explain again why you thought this individual would be the perfect person to talk to about it. I find it often helps to begin with a specific question that I'm pretty sure my subject can help with. But there's no formula. Simply be a good conversationalist: Listen attentively, ask questions that your subject seems to find interesting, and enjoy sharing an interest with your subject. Also, don't be afraid to ask what you fear are obvious questions. Demonstrate to the subject that you *really* want to understand.

Always end an interview by making sure you have accurate background information on your subject: name (spelled correctly), position, affiliation, age (if applicable), phone number. Ask if you can call him with follow-up questions, should you have any. And always ask your subject if he can recommend any additional reading or other people you should talk to. Of course, mention that you're appreciative of the time he has spent with you.

**Notetaking.**   There are basically three ways to take notes during an interview: Use a digital recorder, a notepad, or both. I adhere to the third method, but it's a very individual choice. I like digital recorders (smartphones work great, by the way) because I don't panic during an interview that I'm losing information or quoting inaccurately. I don't want to spend hours transcribing interviews, so I also take notes on the information I think I want to use. If I miss anything, I consult the recording later. Sometimes, I find that there is no recording—the machine decided not to participate in the interview—but at least I have my notes.

Get some practice developing your own notetaking technique by interviewing your roommate or taking notes on the television news. Devise ways to shorten often-used words (e.g., *t* for *the, imp* for *important,* and *w / o* for *without*).

## The E-Mail Interview

The Internet opens up new possibilities for interviews; increasingly, experts (as well as nonexperts interested in certain subjects) are accessible through e-mail and even Facebook. While electronic communication doesn't quite approach the conversational quality of the conventional, face-to-face interview, the spontaneous nature of e-mail exchanges can come pretty close. It's possible to send a message, get a response, respond to the response, and get a further response—all in a single day. And for shy interviewers and interviewees, an e-mail conversation is an attractive alternative.

**Finding People on the Internet.**   Finding people on the Internet doesn't have to involve a needle and hay if you have some information on the person for whom you're looking. If you know an expert's name and his organizational affiliation, several search tools may help you track down his e-mail address. You can, of course, Google the person. But there are other methods, too.

For example, an easy way to use the Internet to find someone to interview is through a Web document on your topic. These often include e-mail links to people associated with the site or document. You can also find academics by visiting the Web sites of the universities or colleges where they teach and using the online faculty/staff directories to find their addresses. If you don't know the institutions with which an academic is affiliated, you can often find these listed in their articles, books, or Web page. To find the home pages of hundreds of American universities and colleges, visit the following site: the Yahoo Education Directory (http://dir.yahoo.com/Education/). This search page allows you to find the home pages of universities in the United States. It includes links to a number of sites that also index colleges and universities, as well as their various programs.

**Making Contact by E-Mail.**   Once you find the e-mail address of someone who seems a likely interview subject, proceed courteously and cautiously. One of the Internet's haunting issues is its potential to violate privacy. Be especially careful if you've gone to great lengths in hunting down the e-mail address of someone involved with your research topic; she may not be keen on receiving unsolicited e-mail messages from strangers. It would be courteous to approach any potential interview subject with a short message that asks permission for an online interview. To do so, briefly describe your project and why you think this individual might be a good source for you. As always, you will be much more likely to get an enthusiastic response from someone if you can demonstrate your knowledge of her work on or experience with your topic.

Let's assume your initial contact has been successful and your subject has agreed to answer your questions. Your follow-up message should ask a *limited* number of questions—say, four or five—that are thoughtful and, if possible, specific. Keep in mind that while the e-mail interview is conducted in writing rather than through talking, many of the methods for handling conventional interviews still apply.

**The Discussion Board and Listserv Interview.**   Discussion or message boards can be good places to find people—and sometimes experts—who are passionately interested in your research topic or question. How do you find one that might be relevant to your project? Try visiting one of the following directories, which list these sites by subject.

### SEARCH ENGINES FOR DISCUSSION GROUPS
BoardReader (http://boardreader.com)

BoardTracker (http://www.boardtracker.com)

Google Groups (http://groups.google.com)

Yahoo! Groups (http://groups.yahoo.com)

A way to get some help with knowing what to ask—and what not to—is to spend some time following the discussion of list participants before you jump in yourself. You might find, for example, that it would be far better to interview one participant with interesting views than to post questions to the whole list.

But if you do want to query the discussion board, avoid posting a question that may have already received substantial attention from participants. You can find out what's been covered by consulting the list's FAQs (frequently asked questions). The issue you're interested in may be there, along with a range of responses from list participants, which will spare you the need to ask the question at all.

## Planning Informal Surveys

Christine was interested in dream interpretation, especially exploring the significance of symbols or images that recur in many people's dreams. She could have simply examined her own dreams, but she thought it might be more interesting to survey a group of fellow students, asking how often they dream and what they remember. An informal survey, in which she would ask each person several standard questions, seemed worth trying.

You might consider it, too, if the responses of a group of people to some aspect of your topic could reveal a pattern of behavior, attitudes, or experiences worth analyzing. Informal surveys are decidedly unscientific. You probably won't get a large enough sample size, nor do you likely have the skills to design a poll that would produce statistically reliable results. But you probably won't actually base your paper on the survey results, anyway. Rather, you'll present specific, concrete information about some patterns in your survey group or, perhaps, use some of your findings to help support your assertions.

## Defining Goals and Audience

Begin planning your informal survey by defining what you want to know and whom you want to know it from. Christine suspected that many students have dreams related to stress. She wondered if there were any similarities among students' dreams. She was also curious about how many people remember their dreams and how often and whether this might be related to gender. Finally, Christine wanted to find out whether people have recurring dreams and, if so, what those were about. There were other things she wanted to know, but she knew she had to keep the survey short.

If you're considering a survey, make a list in your research notebook of things you might want to find out and specify the group of people you plan to talk to. College students? Female college students? Attorneys? Guidance counselors? Be as specific as you can about your target group.

## Paper or Electronic?

After you mull over the purpose of your survey, you need to decide whether you'll distribute it electronically or on paper. These days, free online software like the popular SurveyMonkey (see Figure 2.10) allows users to easily create basic digital surveys. You can distribute the survey to a targeted list of recipients by e-mail or post it on a blog, Web site, or even on social media like Facebook and Twitter. In addition, a program like SurveyMonkey helps you analyze the results and filter, compare, and summarize the data with charts and graphs. Web-based surveys are also cheaper than paper surveys.

Why *wouldn't* you want to go digital instead of using old-fashioned paper surveys? A couple of reasons:

- With paper, you can target an audience much more easily, particularly if you can actually *locate* those potential respondents in a specific time or place. For example, if you want to survey

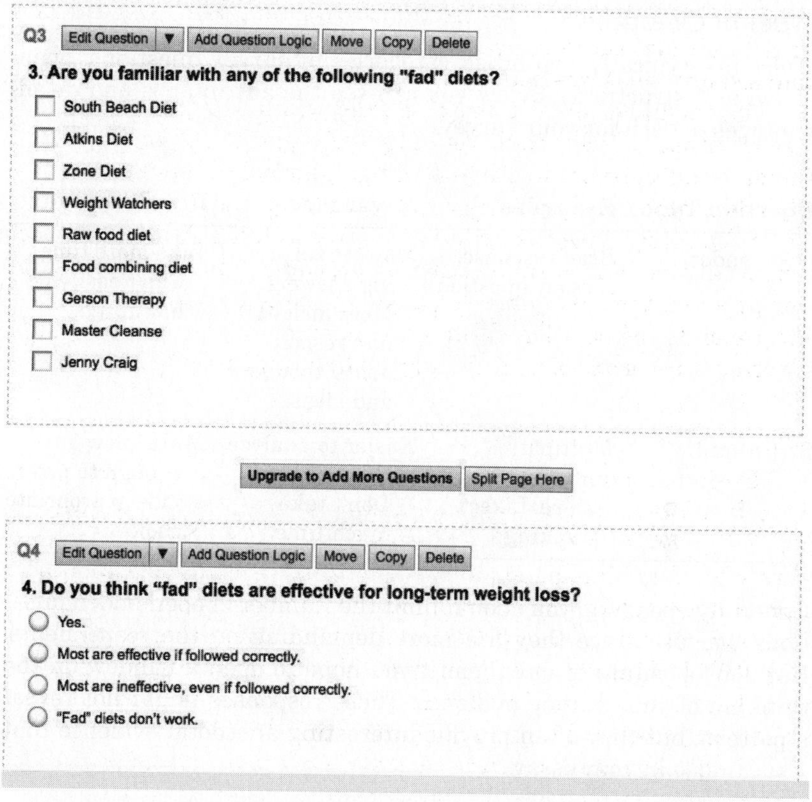

**FIGURE 2.10   A Sample Online Survey.** A student researching fad diets used SurveyMonkey to design and distribute her survey. This screen shot shows several of her questions, which are structured rather than open-ended. The key with structured questions like these is that you have to know enough about your subject to know the appropriate answers.

your school's football fans, distributing your survey on game day at the tailgate party will give you direct access to your survey audience.

- Not everyone has easy Internet access.
- The free versions of the online software may limit the number of responses you can gather.
- Response rates to electronic surveys can be lower than response rates to paper surveys.

Despite these drawbacks, a Web-based survey is often the best choice for an undergraduate research project, particularly if you can find ways to target your audience, make a personal appeal for a response, and send out a reminder or two.

## *Types of Questions*

There are typically two broad categories of survey questions: open-ended and structured. Below you can see the advantages and disadvantages of each for your survey.

| Question Type | Examples | Advantage | Disadvantage |
|---|---|---|---|
| Open-ended | Brief response, essay question | May get surprising answers. More insight into respondents' thoughts and ideas. | Take more time. Can't easily be measured. |
| Structured | Multiple choice, true/false, Likert, ranking | Easier to analyze responses. Don't take much time. | Must know enough to provide appropriate choices. |

Generally speaking, you should limit the number of open-ended questions you use since they are more demanding on the respondents. But don't hesitate to use them if you hope to open a window on the thinking of your survey audience. These responses might not reveal a pattern, but they often provide interesting anecdotal evidence that you can use in your essay.

## *Crafting Questions*

A survey shouldn't be too long (probably no more than six or seven questions, and fewer if you rely mostly on open-ended questions), it shouldn't be biased (questions shouldn't skew the answers), it should be easy to score (especially if you hope to survey a relatively large number of people), it should ask clear questions, and it should give clear instructions for how to answer.

As a rule, informal surveys should begin (or end) as polls often do: by getting vital information about the respondent. Depending on the purpose of your survey, you might also want to know whether respondents are registered to vote, whether they have political affiliations, what year of school they're in, or any number of other factors. Ask for information that provides different ways of breaking down your target group.

**Avoid Loaded Questions.**   Question design is tricky business. Biased questions should be avoided by altering language that is charged and presumptuous. Take, for example, the question *Do you think it's morally wrong to kill unborn babies through abortion?* This wording is charged and is also presumptuous (it is unlikely that all respondents believe that abortion is killing). One revision might be *Do you support or oppose providing women the option to abort a pregnancy during the first 20 weeks?* This is a direct and specific question, neutrally stated, that calls for a yes or no answer.

Controversial topics, like abortion, are most vulnerable to biased survey questions. If your topic is controversial, take great care to eliminate bias by avoiding charged language, especially if you have strong feelings yourself.

**Avoid Vague Questions.**　Another trap is asking vague questions. One such question is *Do you support or oppose the university's alcohol policy?* This wording assumes that respondents know what the policy is, and it ignores the fact that the policy has many elements. A revised question might ask about one part of the policy: *The university recently established a policy that states that underage students caught drinking in campus dormitories are subject to eviction. Do you support or oppose this policy?* Other equally specific questions might ask about other parts of the policy.

**Drawbacks of Open-Ended Questions.**　Open-ended questions often produce fascinating answers, but they can be difficult to tabulate. Christine's survey on dream interpretation asked, *Please briefly describe the dream you best remember or one that sticks out in your mind.* She got a wide range of answers—or sometimes no answer at all—but it was hard to quantify the results. Almost everyone had different dreams, which made it difficult to discern much of a pattern. However, she was still able to use some of the material as anecdotes in her paper, so it turned out to be a question worth asking.

**Designing Your Multiple-Choice Questions.**　As you've seen, the multiple-choice question is an alternative to the open-ended question, leaving room for a number of *limited* responses, which are easier to quantify.

The challenge in designing multiple-choice questions is to provide choices that will likely produce results. For example, from her reading and talking to friends, a student studying fad diets came up with a comprehensive list of the most popular diets (see Figure 2.10). Design choices you think your audience will respond to, but consider giving them room to say your choices weren't theirs by including a "none of the above" option or an open-ended "other" selection that allows respondents to insert their own answers.

**Using Scaled Responses.**    The best-known of these types of questions is the Likert scale, which provides respondents with the chance to express their levels of agreement or disagreement with a statement. Typically, you'd provide a related group of statements. For example, suppose you wanted to collect some data on how students feel about rider traffic on campus. Using a Likert's scale, you might develop a series of questions like those below.

| | Strongly Agree | Agree | Undecided | Disagree | Strongly Disagree |
|---|---|---|---|---|---|
| 1. Speeding bicyclists are a problem on the quad. | 1 | 2 | 3 | 4 | 5 |
| 2. Speeding skateboarders are a problem on the quad. | 1 | 2 | 3 | 4 | 5 |
| 3. The university should consider a policy that requires bicyclists to dismount when on the quad. | 1 | 2 | 3 | 4 | 5 |
| 4. .... | 1 | 2 | 3 | 4 | 5 |

## Conducting Surveys

Once you have finalized your questions, you can make plans to distribute the survey to the target group you defined earlier. Though surveys can be distributed by phone and mail (remember that?), it's far more likely that you'll distribute your survey online or in person. We'll concentrate on those two methods.

**In-Person Surveys.**    The university community, where large numbers of people are available in a confined area, lends itself to administering surveys this way. A survey can be distributed in dormitories, dining halls, classes, or anywhere else the people you want to talk to gather. You can stand outside the student union and stop people as they come and go, or you can hand out your survey to groups of people and collect them when the participants have finished. Your instructor may be able to help distribute your survey to classes.

Although an exclusively university audience won't always be relevant, for some research questions it is exactly what's needed. Anna, writing a paper on date rape, surveyed exclusively women on campus, many of whom she found in women's dormitories. For his paper on the future of the fraternity system, David surveyed local "Greeks" at their annual awards banquet.

How large a sample should you shoot for? Because yours won't be a scientific survey, don't bother worrying about statistical reliability; just try to survey as many people as you can. Certainly, a large (say, more than 100) and representative sample will lend more credence to your claims about any patterns observed in the results.

**Internet Surveys.** You can reach respondents online in the following ways:

1. E-mail
2. Social media like Facebook
3. Listservs, discussion groups
4. Posting survey link on a blog or Web page

Of these, targeted e-mail and online discussion groups of relevant people are likely to be the most productive. Marketing specialists often buy e-mail lists, an unlikely option for the undergraduate. That's why posting a link to your survey on a relevant online forum or listserv can be so effective, since you can match the subject of your survey to people who discuss that subject online. You must, of course, first subscribe to one or more of these lists, and it always helps to listen in on the conversation before you make an appeal for survey respondents. Make sure this group is the appropriate one to answer your questions. Try searching Google Groups to find potential respondents.

Posting a link to your survey on Facebook or Twitter will get it out to potentially many more people, but you should expect a very low response rate.

# Fieldwork: Research on What You See and Hear

My daughter Julia, as a senior in high school, belonged to the school's theater group, performing in plays and taking theater classes. She enjoyed it. But she also claimed that certain qualities distinguished "theater kids" from other kinds. How did she come to these conclusions? By hanging out with the theater crowd. To use a more academic phrasing, Julia was a "participant-observer," though there was certainly no method involved. We all make judgments about social groups, inferences that come from experience. Usually there's nothing systematic about this process, and sometimes these judgments are unfair.

Yet the data that comes from observation, particularly if we take care to collect and document it, can be a rich vein to mine. This kind of data is also relevant to research in the social sciences and humanities and even to research essays in composition courses. Suppose, for instance, that your research question focuses on comparing crowd behavior at college and high school football games. How can you research that essay *without* observing a few games? If your topic has anything do to with subcultures or social groups—say, international students on your campus or the snowboarding community—fieldwork can be invaluable.

## Preparing for Fieldwork

The kind of fieldwork you're able to do for your essay simply won't be the more rigorous and methodologically sophisticated work that academic ethnographers, anthropologists, or sociologists do. For one thing, you don't have the time it requires. But you can collect some useful observations for your paper. There are three tools for this you might find useful:

1. *Notebook.* You can't do without this. For convenience, you might choose a pocket notebook rather than a full-size one.
2. *Digital camera.* Use your camera or smartphone to take pictures of the site you're observing and the people participating in an activity for later study. Also photograph objects (ethnographers call these "artifacts") that have symbolic or practical significance to the people you're observing.
3. *Digital recorder.* Use it for interviews and other recording in the field. (Remember to ask permission to record interviewees.) Smartphones these days can fulfill both your recording and your video needs.

Where you go to conduct field observations of course depends on your topic. Typically you choose a physical space in which people in particular social or cultural groups meet to participate in meaningful (to them) activities. If your research is on the high school theater group as a subculture, you might go to rehearsals, auditions, or perhaps a cast party. A researcher interested in adult video gaming addiction might spend a few evenings watching gamers do their thing at someone's home. An essay on Kwanzaa, an African American holiday tradition, might observe some families participating in its rituals.

## Notetaking Strategies

What do you look for and how do you document it? Well, that depends on your project. Generally, of course, the task is to watch what people do and listen to what they say. More specifically, though, consider the following:

■ *Look for evidence that confirms, contradicts, or qualifies the theories or assertions you've read about in your research.* Is it true that when they're not playing, adult video gamers can appear irritable and depressed? Do dogs that are punitively corrected during a training class demonstrate submissive behavior?

■ *Look and listen to what people say during moments with particular significance for participants.* How do fans behave when the referee doesn't call the foul? What does one gamer say to another when she beats him?

■ *Describe "artifacts"—things that people in the situation typically use.* A skater's skateboard. The objects in an actor's dressing room. The clothing traditionally worn by women celebrating Kwanzaa.

When you take notes, consider using the double-entry journal system that is discussed in detail in the next chapter. Use the left-facing page of your notebook to scribble your observations and the right-facing page to later freewrite about what strikes you about these observations. Make sure that you clearly indicate when you are quoting someone and when you are describing something.

## Using What You See and Hear

Unless your research topic is an ethnography—an investigation that describes and interprets the activities of a cultural group in the field—it's likely that you will use your own fieldwork in your essay in a relatively limited way. Still, it can really be worth the effort. For example, fieldwork can be especially useful to:

■ *Give your topic a face.* Nothing makes a problem or idea more meaningful than *showing* how it affects people. Can you use your descriptions of individuals (perhaps along with your interviews) to show rather than simply explain why your topic is significant?

■ *Make a scene.* Observations in the field give you the ingredients of a scene: In a particular time and place, people are *doing something.* If what they are doing is significant and relevant to your research question, you can describe the place, the people, the action, and even the dialogue. Few techniques give writing more life.

■ *Incorporate images.* Depending on the nature of your project, the digital pictures you take in the field can be powerful illustrations of what you're writing about.

■ *Develop a multimodal research essay.* Using the digital recordings you made in the field and free editing software like Audacity, you can create a podcast of your research essay, even incorporating music. You can use free software like Microsoft Photo Story to use images, text, and voice narration to present your findings.

## EXERCISE 2.3

## DataViz: Tell a Story with Facts

By week's end, you should have a learned enough about your project to be surprised. Maybe you thought something is true when you started only to discover it isn't. Maybe you encountered some information or some perspective on the problem that few people know. Maybe there's some fascinating data that highlights the need to solve the problem or answer the question. Information, when effectively selected and arranged, can turn these discoveries into stories that have the potential to not just enlighten but to surprise, and one of the most dramatic mediums for factual storytelling these days is the infographic.

Infographics help people *visualize* information. They can explain a process, highlight a trend or interesting finding, or make an argument; but they do this through *showing,* not just telling. Imagine, for example, that I want to highlight the trend of songbird declines in the United States. I could simply illustrate this with a bar graph. But I could also illustrate it using a visual metaphor. Maybe I could have a row of bird silhouettes (passenger pigeons?) that get smaller and smaller, correlating with overall population declines over time. Even without the exact data on declines, the visualization dramatizes them for an audience.

To end the week, design a simple infographic from the research you've gathered so far that uses graphics, images, graphs, and texts to dramatize a key finding, trend, process, or argument relevant to your research topic. I'm not a designer, and I'm guessing you aren't either, so these infographics likely won't be appropriate for you to Tweet to the world. But fortunately, there are some free online programs that can help you with design. The best of these is infogr.am, which provides templates, charts, and maps that might prove useful. To see what one student did using the program, see Figure 2.11.

As you design your infographic, keep the following things in mind:

1. **Keep it simple.** You're not trying to visualize your entire topic but only the small part of it that you find interesting. Less is more.

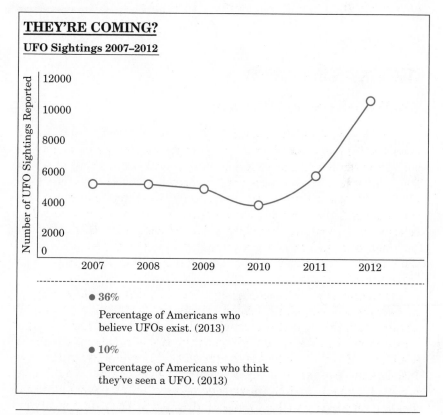

**FIGURE 2.11** A simple infographic on the trend of increased UFO sightings. This was created with the online program infogram.

2. **Minimize text.** Let the visual representations carry the load.
3. **Use metaphor.** Think about the things that typically symbolize how people see your subject. An infographic on the problem of prison overpopulation might use graphics of jail bars or prison stripes, one on the issue of American spending habits might use a pink piggy bank, and so on.
4. **Have good data.** It should be reliable, relevant, and *interesting*.
5. **Tell a story.** You're not just illustrating information, you're using it to dramatize a finding, process, trend, or argument. It should have a beginning, middle, and end and, ultimately, an implied or explicit point (e.g., songbirds are disappearing because of habitat destruction, and we have to do something about it!).

Your instructor may ask you to submit your infographic with a bibliography of sources.

# CHAPTER 3

# The Third Week

---

**IN THIS CHAPTER, YOU'LL LEARN TO...**

■ Practice notetaking as a conversation with a source.

■ Identify different types of borrowing from a source, which of these risk plagiarism, and what to do about it.

■ Understand the triad of notetaking strategies—paraphrase, summary, and quotation—and use them in your own notes.

■ Consider several techniques for notetaking that encourage written conversations with sources, and choose one that works for you as a research writer.

■ Learn some advanced methods for researching on the Web or in the library, and use them to find additional information on your inquiry topic.

■ Draft an annotated bibliography that explains and evaluates key sources on your topic.

---

## Writing in the Middle

Tim's inquiry question explores the impact that an adult's addiction to video games has on family and friends. He spends a week collecting research, mostly printing out articles from library databases and Web sites. Tim skims things, underlining a line or a passage from time to time, but for the most part he's like a bear in a blueberry patch, voraciously collecting as much information as he can. This is all in preparation for the writing, which he'll postpone until right before the paper is due.

Sound familiar? This is certainly similar to the way I always did research.

Here's how I would rewrite this scene for Tim: Tim is still hungrily collecting information about video gaming addiction, *but as he collects it, he's writing about what he's found.* Tim's notebook is open next to his laptop, and he's jotting down quotations and summaries and maybe an interesting fact or two. He's also marking up the electronic copy, highlighting passages of an article he might want to return to, or cutting and pasting relevant passages into an open Word document. Then, when he's done reading the article, Tim writes furiously in his notebook for 10 minutes or so, exploring his reaction to what he found.

I now believe that the writing that takes place in the *middle* of the research process—the notetaking stage—may be as important as, if not more important than, the writing that takes place at the end—composing the draft. Writing in the middle helps you take possession of your sources and establish your presence in the draft. It sharpens your thinking about your topic, and it is the best cure for unintentional plagiarism.

I realize I have a sales job to do on this. Writing in the middle, particularly if you've been weaned on notecards, feels like busywork. "It gets in the way of doing the research," one student told me. "I just want to collect as much stuff as I can, as quickly as I can. Notetaking slows me down." Though it may seem inefficient, writing as you read may actually make your research *more* efficient. Skeptical? Read on.

## Conversing

I went to dinner the other night at a friend of a friend's house, and while the hosts were lovely people, one of them talked too much. You know "conversations" like that? You say something like, "As a matter of fact, I'd love to go to Italy in June" or "The Chicago Cubs, what can you say about the Chicago Cubs?"; and before you can continue the thought, the person you're talking to takes your offhanded comment and runs with it for the next 10 minutes, while you smile and nod and wish you were somewhere else. That's how I think of the notes I took while writing research papers in high school. This time around, I'm hoping you'll disinvite yourself from that kind of dinner party.

*Writing as you read is a genuine conversation between you and a source.* If you imagine the qualities of a good conversation, you probably realize that they don't include just nodding and smiling while someone holds forth. On the contrary, a conversation involves a back-and-forth. You hear something that makes you think of something else, and then someone responds, and then you make a new connection with another idea or experience. It's a dialogue.

We don't often engage in a dialogue when we read to write. If we write at all, we mostly just write stuff down that the source said. This squanders some of the power of the writing process, which, yes, involves our recording things but, more importantly, allows us *to make meaning* and to follow our own words about a subject to see what we have to say about it. This is the power I hope you'll harness when you use writing to engage in conversations with what you read.

But first, let me show you how this can work for you.

## EXERCISE 3.1

### Getting into a Conversation with a Fact

Through writing, facts can ignite thought, if we let them. They can help us discover what we think and refine our point of view. But for this to happen, you have to interact with information. Rather than a monologue—simply jotting down what an author is saying— you engage in a conversation—talking *with* an author: questioning, agreeing, speculating, wondering, connecting, arguing. You can do this in your head, but it's far more productive to have this dialogue through writing.

Let's try it.

I'm going to share with you two facts—one at a time—that together start to tell an interesting story about gender, beauty, and culture. Each fact will be a prompt for about 5 minutes of fastwriting in which you explore your thinking about the fact.

**STEP 1:** How do women see men's "attractiveness"? *Harper's Magazine* recently reported the following:

**Portion of men whose attractiveness is judged by U.S. women to be "worse than average": 4/5**

What do you make of this? Does it surprise you? Assuming it's true, how would you explain it? If you doubt it's true, why? Fastwrite your response for 5 minutes.

**STEP 2:** Now that you've done 5 minutes of "thinking through writing" about how women view men, consider how men view women's "attractiveness."

**Portion of women whose attractiveness is judged by U.S. men to be "worse than average": 2/5**

What do you make of men's more generous attitude toward women? Does this surprise you? How might you explain both "facts"? Together, what does this information say to you about gender and "attractiveness"? Fastwrite for 5 minutes, exploring these questions.

As you reread your two fastwrites, do you see any consistent line of thought developing? If someone asked you what you thought about these two facts, what would you say?

In a small way, you've just practiced a method of notetaking that can help you make sense of information you encounter when you read for your research project or read any other text you want to think about. Later in this chapter, I'll show you something called the "double-entry journal," which is a system for using this technique. But in this exercise, you have practiced the essence of writing in the middle: seeing information as the beginning of a conversation, not the end of one.

Exploring your reaction to what you read during an open-ended fastwrite is only part of using information to discover what you think. You must also *understand* what you're reading. Most *good* conversations make demands on both speakers. The most important of these is simply to listen carefully to what the other person is saying, even (and perhaps especially) if you don't agree. In couples therapy there's a method to help this along called "say back"—each partner has to listen first and then repeat what he or she heard the other say. Response or reaction comes later. Researchers entering into a conversation with their sources need to engage in the same practice: You need to listen or read carefully, first making an effort to understand a subject or an author's arguments or ideas and then exploring your response to them, as you did earlier in this exercise.

The academic equivalent of "say back" is paraphrasing or summarizing, something we'll look at in more detail later in this chapter. Both are undervalued skills, I think, that require practice.

Informally writing your responses is a way to hold up your end of a conversation with a source, but when you actually *use* sources in your essay, you have an obligation to use them responsibly. Beyond quoting source material accurately, citing the right page numbers, and spelling names correctly, you're obligated to represent the source's ideas fairly. This includes making it clear which ideas and words come from the source and which come from you. Frankly, this takes practice. Give it a try in Exercise 3.2.

## EXERCISE 3.2

### "Say Back" to a Source

Read the following brief essay on "what college is for" by the President of Amherst College, and then write a paragraph summary of what it says, highlighting what you think are the main ideas. This time, leave out any comments you have about the ideas in the piece; just try to "say back" as accurately as you can what you think the writer is saying.

## What Is College For?

*Carolyn A. (Biddy) Martin*
*President of Amherst College*

College is for the development of intelligence in its multiple forms. College is the opportunity for achievement, measured against high standards. College is preparation for the complexities of a world that needs rigorous analyses of its problems and synthetic approaches to solving them. College is for learning how to think clearly, write beautifully, and put quantitative skills to use in the work of discovery. College is for the cultivation of enjoyment, in forms that go beyond entertainment or distraction, stimulating our capacity to create joy for ourselves and others. College is for leave-taking, of home and of limiting assumptions, for becoming self-directed, while socially responsible.

In his 2005 commencement speech at Kenyon College, the brilliant writer and Amherst graduate David Foster Wallace ('85), defined the value of the liberal arts in the following terms: "The real, no bullshit value of your liberal-arts education is how to keep from going through your comfortable, prosperous, respectable lives dead, unconscious, a slave to your head and to your natural default settings."

For all the tragic irony of Wallace's point, given his own premature death, his admonition holds. A spate of recent books have enjoined us to distinguish between our natural default settings and our ability to reason on the basis of evidence—between what Daniel Kahneman calls, for example, our "fast" and "slow" thinking, or the automatism housed in one part of our brain and the ability to reflect in another.

College is for finding a calling, or many callings, including the calls of friendship and love. It is for the hard work of experimentation, failure, reflection, and growth. It is about the gains we make and the losses that come with them. In an age of sound bites and indignation, college is for those who are brave enough to put at risk what they think they know in recognition of the responsibility we have to one another and to those still to come.

# A Taxonomy of Copying

My colleague Casey Keck, a linguist, studied how students paraphrase sources and ways to describe students' brushes with plagiarism. Casey notes that there are four kinds of borrowing:

- **Near copy:** About half of the borrowed material is copied from the source, usually in a string of phrases. The bolded phrases are lifted verbatim from "What Is College For?", the essay in the above exercise.

  *Example: Students shouldn't necessarily go to college just to focus on a particular job but also to prepare for **the complexities of a world that needs rigorous analyses** and to **create joy for ourselves and others.***

- **Minimal revision:** Less than half but more than 20 percent is copied from the original. Notice that the quotation marks appropriately signal at least one borrowed phrase from the original.

  *Example: Martin says David Foster Wallace **defined** what it means to go to college as learning to avoid being "a slave to your head" and being **brave enough** to **risk what they think they know.***

- **Moderate revision:** Less than 20 percent is copied from the original, and mostly individual words are mentioned only once in the source.

  *Example: Martin says that college is the search for a **calling**, but this isn't necessarily a professional one. It includes a willingness to try new things and risk both **failure** and **growth**.*

- **Substantial revision:** Though the paraphrase might include a few general words that are used a few times in the original text, there are no copies of phrases or unique words that appear in the source.

  *Example: According to Martin, college is an opportunity to reimagine ourselves—to break with old ways of thinking, and find delight in something other than the usual "distraction" and "entertainment."*

Evaluate your own summary of the "What Is College For?" essay to see if any of it involves borrowing from the original source in these four categories. Remember, this is just practice!

# Plagiarism Q & A

1. **So I can't take *any* words from the original source?** Yes, of course you can, but try to steer clear of unique words, and especially avoid using the same string of words unless you put them in quotation marks.
2. **If I add an attribution tag (e.g., "According to _____,"..., or _____ argues that...") or include a citation, does that mean I can copy things from a source?** Attribution tags and citations are really useful for your readers and are a good way to credit authors for their ideas, but they aren't licenses to use source material without the usual signals—like quotation marks—that you've copied something.
3. **Is it a problem if I paraphrase a source and follow pretty much the same structure of the original in terms of the order of ideas?** Technically, that is a form of plagiarism, and practically speaking, it's far better to restate a source in the order that reflects what *you* think are the important ideas.
4. **How do I credit the same information that I found in, say, four different books?** You may not have to. Check out the "common knowledge" exception on page 108.
5. **I've got a lot of my own ideas about my topic. Do I risk plagiarizing if someone else has the same ideas but I don't know about it?** No, you can't know what you don't know. But the point of research is that it helps *expand* your ideas about a topic. If you encounter a source that repeats an idea you already hold, look more closely to see what you didn't already know: a fresh context, a slightly different angle, a new bit of supporting evidence. Then think again. Can you revise your own ideas, discovering new insights that do reflect your own thinking?

# Why Plagiarism Matters

It may seem that concern over plagiarism is just a lot of fuss that reflects English teachers' obsession with enforcing rules. In reality, the saddest days I've ever had as a writing teacher have always

## What Is Plagiarism?

Each college or university has a statement in the student handbook that offers a local definition. But that statement probably includes most or all of the following forms of plagiarism:

1. Handing in someone else's work—a downloaded paper from the Internet or one borrowed from a friend—and claiming that it's your own.
2. Handing in the same paper for two different classes.
3. Using information or ideas from any source that are not common knowledge and failing to acknowledge that source.
4. Using the exact language or expressions of a source and not indicating through quotation marks and citation that the language is borrowed.
5. Rewriting a passage from a source, making minor word substitutions, but retaining the syntax and structure of the original.

## The Common Knowledge Exception

While you always have to tell readers what information you have borrowed and where it came from, things that are "common knowledge" are excluded from this. But what is "common knowledge"? The answer, in part, is considering what is common knowledge to *whom*. Each field makes different judgments about that. In addition, knowledge is constantly changing, so what may be accepted fact today could be contested tomorrow. What's the undergraduate researcher to do? Scholar Amy England suggests that you consider something common knowledge if you find the exact same information in four or more different sources.

been when I've talked with a student about a paper she downloaded from the Internet or borrowed from her roommate. Most instructors hate dealing with plagiarism.

Deliberate cheating is, of course, an ethical issue, but the motive for carefully distinguishing between what is yours and what you've borrowed isn't just to "be good." It's really about making

**Why Cite?**

**FIGURE 3.1**    As researchers, we're tree climbers, standing on branches that other researchers before us have grown. Citation identifies the wood we're standing on that has helped us to see further into our topic.

a gesture of gratitude. Research is always built on the work that came before it. As you read and write about your topic, I hope that you come to appreciate the thoughtful writing and thinking of people before you who may have given you a new way of seeing or thinking.

Knowledge is a living thing (see Figure 3.1), growing like a great tree in multiple directions, adding (and losing) branches that keep reaching higher toward new understandings. As researchers we are tree climbers, ascending the branches in an effort to see better. It's only natural that as we make this climb, we feel grateful for the strength of the limbs supporting us. Citing and acknowledging sources is a way of expressing this gratitude.

## The Notetaker's Triad: Quotation, Paraphrase, and Summary

Taylor is writing a paper on plastics in the ocean, and from the European Environment Commission Web site, she cuts and pastes the following text into a Word document:

> Marine litter is a global concern, affecting all the oceans of the world. Every year, approximately 10 billion tons of litter end

up in the ocean world wide, turning it into the world's biggest landfill and thus posing environmental, economic, health, and aesthetic problems. Sadly, the persistence of marine litter is the result from poor practices of solid waste management, lack of infrastructure, and a lack of awareness of the public at large about the consequences of their actions.*

She likes the passage—it succinctly states the problem of ocean pollution and even includes a powerful statistic: 10 billion tons of garbage end up in the world's oceans each year. Now, what can she do with it?

Consider her choices:

1. Do nothing. Set the passage aside and hope there will be a place in her paper where she can digitally dump the whole thing or part of it.
2. Rewrite all or part of it in her own words. Set the rewrite aside and hope to weave it into her paper later.

Student writers often face this dilemma, and in the digital age, when it's easy to cut and paste text, choice #1 is the odds-on favorite. Just collect and dump. What this usually means in the draft research essay is a quotation. In some cases, this is justified. Perhaps the material *is* so well said that you want the voice of the source to speak for itself. But more often, a cut-and-paste quotation—particularly an extended one—looks like a sign of surrender: Instead of actively guiding the reader through information, the writer opts to take a nap.

What about choice #2? How might Taylor rewrite the passage to establish herself as a reliable guide?

None of the world's oceans are spared from pollution, notes the European Environment Commission, which also reports that 10 billion tons of garbage are dumped in the world's oceans every year. They now represent "the world's biggest landfill" ("Marine Pollution Awareness").

In the rewrite, Taylor mines the original passage selectively, emphasizing what she thinks is important but without misrepresenting what was said. Here is a writer who is controlling information rather than being controlled by it.

*From http://ec.europa.eu/environment/water/marine/pollution.htm. © European Union, 1995–2011. Reproduction is authorized.

The relationship between a source and a research writer is often complex, for various reasons. Consider how difficult it can be to read someone else's words, make an effort to understand what they mean, and then find your own words to restate the ideas. What's worse is that sometimes the authors are experts who use language you may not easily grasp or use reasoning in ways you can't easily follow. And then there are those authors who write so beautifully, you wonder how you could possibly say it better. Finally, you might fear that somehow you will goof and accidentally plagiarize the source's ideas or words.

One useful, if somewhat crude, way of describing how a writer might take possession of the information she gathers is in terms of three approaches you've no doubt heard of before: paraphrase, summary, and quotation. These are useful to learn about, not only so that you know the rules for how to employ them, but, perhaps more important, so that you can see each as a different way of interacting with what you read. Ultimately, they are tools that keep you in the game.

## Paraphrasing

In Exercise 3.2, you practiced "say back," a technique that helps many married couples who may be headed for divorce. As I mentioned, *paraphrase* is the academic equivalent of this therapeutic method for getting people to listen to each other. Try to say in your own words—and with about the same length as the author said it—what you understand the author to mean. This is hard, at first, because instead of just mindlessly quoting—a favorite alternative for many students—you have to *think*. Paraphrasing demands that you make your own sense of something. The time is well worth it. Why? Because not only are you lowering the risk of unintentional plagiarism and being fair to the source's ideas, *you are also essentially writing a fragment of your draft.*

To put it most simply, at the heart of paraphrasing is this very simple idea: *Good writers find their own ways of saying things.*

## Summarizing

In order to sell a movie to Hollywood, a screenwriter should be able to summarize what it's about in a sentence. "*Juno* is a film about a smart, single, pregnant teenager who finds unexpected humor in her situation but finally finds that her wit is not enough to help her navigate the emotional tsunami her pregnancy triggers in the lives of those around her." That statement hardly does justice to the film—which is about so much more than that—but I think it basically captures the story and its central theme.

Obviously, that's what a *summary* is: a reduction of longer material into a brief statement that captures a basic idea, argument, or theme from the original. Like paraphrasing, summarizing often requires careful thought. This is especially the case when you're trying to capture the essence of a whole movie, article, or chapter that's fairly complex. Many times, however, summarizing involves simply boiling down a passage—not the entire work—to its basic idea.

While a summary can never be purely objective, it needs to be fair. After all, each of us will understand a text differently, but at the same time we have to do our best to represent what a source is actually saying without prejudice. That's particularly a challenge when you have strong feelings about a topic.

## Quoting

I'll never forget the scene from the documentary *Shoah,* an 11-hour film about the Holocaust, that presents an interview with the Polish engineer of one of the trains that took thousands of Jews to their deaths. As an old man still operating the same train, he was asked how he felt about his role in World War II. He said quietly, "If you could lick my heart, it would poison you."

It would be difficult to restate the Polish engineer's comment in your own words. But more important, it would be stupid even to try. Some of the pain and regret and horror of that time in history are embedded in that one man's words. You may not come across such a distinctive quote as you read your sources this week, but be alert to *how* authors (and those quoted by authors) say things. Is the prose unusual, surprising, or memorable? Does the writer make a point in an interesting way? If so, jot it down in your journal or cut and paste it into a digital file, making sure to signal the borrowed material with quotation marks.

There are several other reasons to quote a source as you're taking notes.

- To bring in the voice, not just the ideas, of a notable expert on your topic.
- To quote someone who says something effectively that supports a key point you're trying to make.
- When you're writing an essay that uses primary sources—a literary text, a transcript, and so on—quoted material is essential.

As a general rule, however, the college research paper should contain no more than 10 or 20 percent quoted material. This principle sometimes gets ignored because it's so easy to just copy a passage from a source and paste it into an essay. But keep in mind that a writer who quotes does not really need to think much about and take possession of the information, shaping it and allowing herself to be shaped by it. Still, you can retain a strong presence in your work even when using the words of others if you remember to do the following:

1. *Quote selectively.* You need not use all of the passage. Mine phrases or sentences that are particularly distinctive, and embed them in your own prose.
2. *Provide a context.* The worst way to use a quote is to just drop it into a paragraph without attribution or comment. If you're going to bring someone else's voice into your work, you should, at the very least, say who the source is and perhaps indicate why what this person says is particularly relevant to what you're saying.
3. *Follow up.* In addition to establishing a context for a quotation, seize the chance to analyze, argue with, amplify, explain, or highlight what is in the quotation.

As an example of effective use of quotation, consider the following excerpt from Bill Bryson's book *At Home: A Short History of Private Life*. Bryson is especially talented at telling compelling nonfiction stories using research, and here he explains the fears of people in the nineteenth century about being buried alive. In this case, Bryson incorporates a "block quotation"—that is, the passage he quotes is set off and indented, as is required in MLA style for passages of more than four [*MLA Handbook*, p. 94] lines.

> According to one report, of twelve hundred bodies exhumed in New York City for one reason or another between 1860 and 1880, six showed signs of thrashing or other postinterment distress. In London, when the naturalist Frank Buckland went looking for the coffin of the anatomist John Hunter at St. Martin-in-the-Fields Church, he reported coming upon three coffins that showed clear evidence of internal agitation (or so he was convinced)....A correspondent to the British journal *Notes and Queries* offered this contribution in 1858:
>
>> A rich manufacturer named Oppelt died about fifteen years since at Reichenberg, in Austria, and a vault was built in the cemetery for the reception of the body by his

widow and children. The widow died about a month ago and was taken to the same tomb; but, when it was opened for the purpose, the coffin of her husband was found open and empty, and the skeleton discovered in the corner of the vault in a sitting posture.

For at least a generation such stories became routine in even serious periodicals. So many people became morbidly obsessed with the fear of being interred before their time that a word was coined for it: *taphephobia*.

Notice that Bryson provides a context for his quotation—the name of the source—and then follows up the quoted passage by noting that the story it tells is typical of nineteenth-century fears of being buried alive. He also notes that the anecdote is an illustration of what was then called taphephobia. Bryson's book is not an academic work, so you don't see citations, something that you will incorporate into your own essay, but you can see how a powerful quotation can bring the work to life, especially when it's sandwiched within the commentary of a writer who chooses to allow another voice to speak.

## Notetaking

There's the skills part of notetaking—knowing how to cite, summarize, paraphrase, and quote correctly—and then there's the more interesting, harder part—making *use* of what you're reading to discover what you think. So far, we've talked about this latter process using the metaphor of conversation. In Exercise 3.1, you tried out this idea, responding in writing to facts about gender and notions of "attractiveness." This conversation metaphor doesn't originate with me. Lots of people use it to describe how all knowledge is made. One theorist, Kenneth Burke, famously explained that we might imagine that all scholarship on nearly any subject is much like a parlor conversation between people in the know (see the box "The Unending Conversation" on the following page). These are the experts who, over time, have contributed to the discussions about what might be true and who constantly ask questions to keep the conversation going.

As newcomers to this conversation, we don't really have much to contribute. It's important that we listen in so that we begin to understand what has already been said and who has said it. But at some point, even novices like us are expected to speak up. We're not

**The Unending Conversation**

Imagine that you enter a parlor. You come late. When you arrive, others have long preceded you, and they are engaged in a heated discussion, a discussion too heated for them to pause and tell you exactly what it is about. In fact, the discussion had already begun long before any of them got there, so that no one present is qualified to retrace for you all the steps that had gone before. You listen for a while, until you decide that you have caught the tenor of the argument; then you put in your oar. Someone answers; you answer him; another comes to your defense; another aligns himself against you, to either the embarrassment or gratification of your opponent, depending upon the quality of your ally's assistance. However, the discussion is interminable. The hour grows late, you must depart. And you do depart, with the discussion still vigorously in progress.

*Kenneth Burke*

there to simply record what we hear. We're writers. We're supposed to discover something to say.

Fortunately, we rarely enter the parlor empty handed. We have experiences and other prior knowledge that are relevant to the conversation we're listening in on. For example, you certainly know something about the subject of Thomas Lord's essay, "What? I Failed? But I Paid for Those Credits! Problems of Students Evaluating Faculty." After all, you've probably filled out an evaluation or two for a course you've taken. But clearly, Lord, as a science educator, has spent considerably more time than you considering whether these evaluations are useful for judging the quality of teaching. Yet college writers, even if they have limited expertise, are expected to speak up on a topic they're writing about, entering the conversation by raising questions, analyzing arguments, speculating, and emphasizing what they think is important.

## EXERCISE 3.3

### Dialogic Notetaking: Listening In, Speaking Up

Drop into the conversation that Thomas Lord has going in his essay, and, drawing on what you've learned so far, use your journal writing to listen in and speak up.

**STEP 1:**

1. Begin by listening in. Read Thomas Lord's essay once straight through. Underline and mark passages that you think are:
   a. important to your understanding of the article,
   b. puzzling in some way,
   c. surprising, or
   d. connected with your own initial ideas and experiences.

2. Reread the opening paragraph, the last few paragraphs, and all of your marked passages; then, without looking at the article, compose a three- or four-sentence summary of what you understand to be the most important thing the article is saying. Write this down on the left-hand page of your notebook.

3. Find two passages in the article that you think are good examples of what you state in your summary. Copy these on to the left-hand page of your notebook, too. Or if you're doing this on your computer, use the Table function to create two columns, and use the left one.

**STEP 2:** Now speak up. Use the right-hand side of your notebook to explore your thinking about what Lord is saying. Look on the left-hand pages to remind yourself of some of his ideas and assertions. This is an open-ended fastwrite, but here are some prompts to get you writing and thinking:

- Tell the story of your thinking:
  - *Before I read about this topic, I thought _____, and then I thought _____, and then _____, and then...but now I think _____.*
- Consider ways you've begun to think differently:
  - *I used to think _____, but now I'm starting to think _____.*
- Try both believing and doubting:
  - *The most convincing points Lord makes in his essay are _____. or Though I don't necessarily agree with Lord, I can understand why he would think that _____.*
  - And then: *The thing that Lord ignores or fails to understand is _____. or The least convincing claim he makes is _____ because _____.*
- Consider questions:
  - *The most important question Lord raises is _____.*
  - *The question that he fails to ask is _____.*

Discuss in class how this notetaking exercise worked. What went well? What was difficult? How did your initial thoughts influence your reading of the article? Did your thinking change? Which of these techniques will you continue to use in your notetaking?

## What? I Failed? But I Paid for Those Credits! Problems of Students Evaluating Faculty*
*by Thomas Lord*

Late one afternoon several days ago, I was startled by a loud rap on my office door. When I opened it, I immediately recognized a student from the previous semester clutching the grade slip he had just received in the mail. Sensing his anger and frustration, I invited him in to discuss his scores. I was surprised that he had not anticipated the failing grade because his exam scores were abysmal, his class work was marginal, and his attendance was sporadic. When I scooted my chair over to my computer to open the course's spreadsheet to review his grade, he told me he didn't have an argument with the test, class, and attendance records. His reason for coming to see me was to ask how he could get his refund. He had, after all, paid for the credits, right? I was astonished. In all my years in higher education, this was the first time I had been asked for a refund.

A day later over lunch, a colleague remarked that with the nation's troublesome economy, many universities have turned to the business model of running the institution. "The business model," he acknowledged, "focuses on financial efficiency while maintaining a quality product."

"Perhaps so," another colleague responded, "but the principal foundation of the business model is the notion of satisfying the customer. Because the products of a college are its graduates, it requires the college to meet their expectations for both a quality education and a gratifying experience. This is nearly impossible if the college wants to retain its integrity and high standards."

Furthermore, what students expect from their college experience varies greatly. A quality, highly respected education is, of course, always desirable, but that's about as common as the expectations get. Some college students relish the liberal challenges universities can provide,

*"What? I Failed? But I Paid for Those Credits! Problems of Students Evaluating Faculty" by Thomas Lord from *Journal of College Science Teaching,* November/December 2008. Used by permission of the National Science Teachers Association.

some look for a cultural experience, and others simply want to be trained for a career. A large number of undergraduates seek strong intercollegiate athletic or theater programs, and some students are most interested in an exciting social life. This diversity is where the difficulty lies. With such an assortment of demands and expectations, it's simply not possible for any institution to provide it all and maintain a student-as-consumer philosophy. Many universities have tried, and in so doing, have undercut their reputation. Several decades ago, education theorist David Reisman (1981) wrote, "This shift from academic merit to student consumerism is one of the two greatest reversals of direction in all the history of American Higher Education; the other being the replacement of the classical college by the modern university a century ago."

Despite Reisman's statement, the student-as-consumer philosophy has become more widely spread in academic institutions over the last two decades, and with it has come a tendency for students to have a stronger voice in higher education (d'Apollonia and Abrami 1997). It is common nowadays for student representatives to serve on university committees. Students are often consulted on ventures that include curriculum, discipline, regulation, and campus construction. In many schools, segments of the institution's governance are shared with students. My institution, for example, retains two students on the University Executive Board.

But by far the greatest number of student voices impacting the institution is in the evaluation of the instructors. The practice was first implemented at Purdue University in 1927, when surveys were distributed to students in a sociology class to solicit their opinions of the course (Remmers 1927). The surveys were not shared with the administration, but were retained by the professors as feedback for self-improvement. Two years later, Remmers revised the surveys to include "student ratings of their instructor's teaching and what they have learned in the course." The researcher reported his finding at a national professional meeting, and soon other universities began soliciting instructor ratings on their campuses. Course and instructor evaluations remained benign until the 1960s, when students discovered the power their united voices could make in higher education. During this time, students began vocalizing their resistance to the war in Vietnam, the ills of the environment, and the materialism of society. It was a time of student free speech about ethical, cultural, and racial issues. Suddenly, evaluations of instructors and courses became more about student satisfaction than about a professor's instructional effectiveness.

.   .   .   .   .   .   .   .   .   .   .   .   .   .   .   .   .   .   .   .   .   .   .   .

When the driving mechanism for faculty evaluations shifts from educating to pleasing, many problems occur. "Student evaluations of their professors are impacted heavily by student perception," states Professor Stanley Fish, dean emeritus at the University of Illinois (2007). "When student experiences in classes do not match their prior expectations, they react in negative ways. Students may begin to boycott classes they're unhappy with, they may write complaint letters to administrators, or they may challenge the academic integrity of their professors. Some students may become so disrespectful of the professor that they circulate their feelings in the press, on the internet, and over the airways." In 1965, for example, students at the University of California–Berkeley generated a review of teacher performance in a manual entitled *The Slate Supplement,* and sold it at the campus bookstore. "Most of the opinions in the manual were ill-informed and mean-spirited," recalls Fish. "The opinions weren't from professionals in the field but transient students with little or no stake in the enterprise who would be free (because they were anonymous) to indulge any sense of grievance they happened to harbor in the full knowledge that nothing they said would ever be questioned or challenged. The abuse would eventually affect the careers and livelihoods of faculty members especially the young, nontenured professors" (Selvin 1991). In addition, with the negative exposure, university officials became alarmed that the dissatisfaction would lead to students dropping their courses or leaving the university altogether. With the mounting anxieties, many instructors countered by lowering the expectations in their courses. A survey of faculty found 70% of professors believe that their grading leniency and course difficulty bias student ratings, and 83% admitted making their course easier in response to student evaluations (Ryan, Anderson and Birchler 1980).

This was nicely demonstrated when Peter Sacks, a young journalism instructor, was hired on a tenure track at a small northwest college. At the end of the first semester, Sacks, an accomplished writer but not yet an accomplished teacher, found himself in trouble with student evaluations. When he started, Sacks resolved to maintain a high quality in his courses by emphasizing critical thinking about issues. Although he found it extremely difficult, he stuck with his plan for the entire semester, and as a consequence, received terrible student evaluations. Fearing that he would lose his tenure-track appointment after the spring term, he decided to change his tactics and attempt to achieve higher evaluations by deliberately pandering to his students. At the end of his three-year trial, he had dramatically raised his teaching evaluations and gained tenure. Sacks shamelessly admits he became utterly undemanding and uncritical of his students, giving out easy grades, and teaching to the lowest common denominator (1986). Other researchers have confirmed that lenient grading is the most frequently used faculty strategy to counter abusive student assessment (Howard and Maxwell 1982; Greenwald 1997).

Another problem with the business model is that students truly believe they're paying for their credits and not their education. Consumers are used to paying for merchandise that can later be returned for a refund with no questions asked. The student confusion over this probably resides in the way universities charge pupils for the credits they're taking (at least for students attending part time or over the summer). If, for example, a high school biology teacher decided to upgrade his or her knowledge of wildflowers and enrolled in a three-credit course at a local college on spring flora, the teacher would be charged for the three credits. If the teacher decided to continue the learning the following semester on summer wildflowers, he or she would again pay for the three credits. It's not hard, therefore, to see how the idea of paying for credits rather than earning them came about.

A final reason why student evaluations are an unreliable way to assess faculty is that most students simply don't know what good teaching is. Undergraduates generally have a vision of how college teaching is conducted from depictions in movies or hearing tales from former students. The most common view is that professors stand before a class and recite, write on the chalkboard, or use PowerPoint slides to get across the information students should know in the lesson (McKeachie 1992).

I asked my students what they thought made a great instructor and was told the best professors move unhurriedly through their notes, speaking at a slow-to-moderate pace, explaining the information the students need to learn. One student told me that good professors don't get sidetracked by superficial chunks of information and don't waste time off the subject. Some students also suggested that competent professors are entertaining when they lecture and frequently use demonstrations and videos to back up their presentations. Many class members said the best professors repeat several times the items that are the most salient and hold review sessions before each exam to reaffirm the important content.

Most contemporary theorists, however, tell us that top instructors don't do most of those things. According to education leaders, competent teachers seldom lecture to a gallery of passive students, but provide experiences and directions that actively challenge class members to think and discover information (Handelsmen et al. 2004). Practiced professors believe understanding is the driving force for learning and spend a great amount of preclass time orchestrating team-based learning situations for the upcoming class. Proponents of student-centered instruction acknowledge that active participation in classes and discovery-based laboratories help students develop the habits of mind that drive science (Udovic et al. 2002). Furthermore, while traditional instructors create factual recall questions for their exams where students reiterate what they were told in class, contemporary teachers challenge students to discover the answers through application, synthesis, or evaluation (Huitt 2004). Quality teachers understand what agronomist George Washington Carver meant in 1927 when he wrote, "I know nothing more inspiring than discovering new information for oneself" (Carver 1998).

Students also believe that the best professors don't expect class members to know information that the professor hasn't covered in lecture. Students don't seem to realize that education is the art of using information, not the art of restating it. College graduates must understand that once they're out of school, they'll depend on their education to get them through life. Often will they have to address unfamiliar questions. As I've stated previously, "Once they're out of college, students can't fall back on the answer, 'I don't know 'cause it wasn't covered by my professor' " (Lord 2007).

Enough has been written on this matter that colleges and universities should justify why they continue to use student evaluations to assess their faculty. "The answer is already known," answers Cahn (1986). "Institutions of higher education provide faculty evaluations to students to assess student satisfaction. Not only are the evaluations easy to grade and inexpensive to administer, but they give the impression of objectivity in comparison with more subjective measures such as letters from observers since student evaluations produce definite numbers."

"The role of the university is leadership, not a servant of consumer demands as the current business model requires," states Wilson (1998). "Universities certainly have a responsibility for the safety, well-being, and satisfaction of the people they serve, but they also have a responsibility to educate the people as well. With their dignity and reputation on the line, the most important responsibility is to certify that their graduates are truly educated. Under the consumer model, the goals of satisfaction and education are sometimes in conflict. It is important, therefore, that the metaphor of students as consumers be replaced by the metaphor of students as apprentices" (Haskell 1997).

# References

Cahn, S. 1986. *Saints and scamps: Ethics in academia.* Totowa, NJ: Rowman and Littlefield.

Carver, G.W. 1998. *The all-university celebration.* Iowa City, IA: University Press.

d'Apollonia S., and P. Abrami. 1997. Navigating student ratings of instruction. *American Psychologist* 52 (11): 1198–1208.

Fish, S. 2007. Advocacy and teaching. *Academe* 93 (4): 23–27.

Greenwald, A.G. 1997. Validity concerns and usefulness of student ratings. *American Psychologist* 52 (11): 1182–86.

Handelsman, J., D. Ebert-May, R. Beichner, P. Burns, A. Chang, R. DeHann, J. Gentile, S. Luffefer, J. Stewart, S. Tukgnab, and W. Wood. 2004. Scientific thinking. *Science* 304 (5670): 521–22.

Haskell, R. 1997. Academic freedom, tenure and student evaluation of faculty: Galloping polls in the 21st century. *Education Policy Analysis Archives* 5 (6): 43.

Howard, G., and S. Maxwell. 1982. Linking raters' judgments. *Evaluation Review* 6 (1): 140–46.

Huitt, W. 2004. Bloom et al's taxonomy of the cognitive domain. *Educational Psychology Interactive*. http://chiron.valdosta.edu/whuitt/col/cogsys/bloom.html. Valdosta, GA: Valdosta University Press.

Lord, T. 2007. Putting inquiry to the test: Enhancing learning in college botany. *Journal of College Science Teaching* 36 (7): 56–59.

McKeachie, W. 1992. Student ratings: The validity of use. *American Psychologist* 52 (11): 1218–25

Reisman, D. 1981. *On higher education: The academic enterprise in an era of rising student consumerism.* San Francisco: Jossey Bass.

Remmers, D. 1927. Experimental data on the Purdue rating scale. In *Student ratings of instructors: Issues for improving practice,* eds. M. Theall and J. Franklin. 1990. San Francisco: Jossey Bass.

Ryan, J., J. Anderson, and A. Birchler. 1980. Student evaluation: The faculty responds. *Research in Higher Education* 12 (4): 395–401.

Sacks, P. 1986. *Generation X goes to college.* LaSalle, IL: Open Court Press.

Selvin, P. 1991. The raging bull at Berkeley. *Science* 251 (4992): 368–71.

Wilson, R. 1998. New research casts doubt on value of student evaluations of professors. *Chronicle of Higher Education* 44 (19): A2–A14.

Udovic, D., D. Morris, A. Dickman, J. Postlethwait, and P. Wetherwax. 2002. Workshop biology: Demonstrating the effectiveness of active learning in an introductory biology course. *Bioscience* 52 (3): 272–81.

*Thomas Lord* (trlord@grove.iup.edu) *is a professor in the Department of Biology at the Indiana University of Pennsylvania in Indiana, Pennsylvania.*

## Notetaking Techniques

In the first edition of *The Curious Researcher,* I confessed to a dislike of notecards. Apparently, I'm not the only one who feels that way. Mention notecards, and students often tell horror stories. It's a little like talking about who has the most horrendous scar, a discussion that can prompt participants to expose knees and bare abdomens in public places. One student even mailed me her notecards—50 bibliography cards and 53 notecards, all bound by a metal ring and color coded. She assured me that she didn't want them back—ever. Another student told me she was required to write 20 notecards a day: "If you spelled something wrong or if you put your name on the left side of the notecard rather than the right, your notecards were torn up and you had to do them over."

While it's true that some writers find notecards useful (and most teachers aren't finicky about their being done "correctly"), I'm convinced that notecards are too small for a good conversation. On the contrary, they seem to encourage "data dumps" rather than dialogue (see Figure 3.2).

But what's the alternative? You've already practiced one approach in the previous exercise, "Listening In, Speaking Up." There you used opposing sides of a notebook or Word document to summarize your understanding of an essay and collect relevant passages, and then you told the story of your thinking about the reading. This is *knowledge making* rather than dump truck driving—you are going beyond simply recording and collecting information to actually *doing* something with it. You'll also practice a technique called the "double-entry" journal.

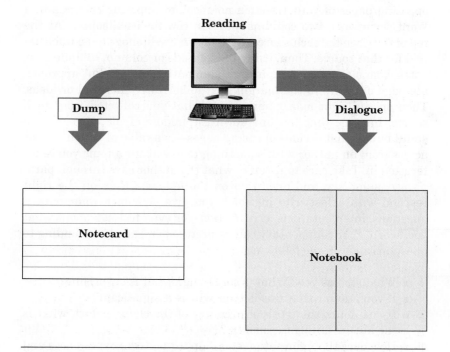

**FIGURE 3.2** **Notecards versus Notebooks**

| **Notes from Source**<br>**(left page or column)** | **Fastwrite Response**<br>**(right page or column)** |
|---|---|
| ■ Direct quotations, paraphrases, and summaries of material from the source:<br>  • of ideas that are important to project<br>  • of ideas that are surprising or puzzling or generate some emotional response<br>■ Be careful to:<br>  • include bibliographic information at the top;<br>  • include the page number from the source. | ■ Focused fastwrite in response to material at left<br>■ Tips for fastwrite:<br>  • Write as long as possible; then look left and find something else to respond to.<br>  • Try shifting between stances of believing and doubting.<br>  • Use the questions below. |

**FIGURE 3.3    Double-Entry Journal Method**

## The Double-Entry Journal

The double-entry approach (see Figure 3.3) is basically this: Use opposing pages of your research notebook or opposing columns in a Word document—two columns and one row for each source. At the top of the page for each source, write down the bibliographic information for that source. Then, using the left side or column, compile your notes from a source—paraphrases, summaries, quotes. Put appropriate page numbers in the margin next to borrowed material or ideas. Then on the right side, comment on what you collected from each source. Imagine that the line down the middle of the page—or the spiral binder that divides opposing pages—is a table at which you sit across from an author with something to say about a topic you're interested in. Take care to listen to what the author says through paraphrase, summary, and quotation on the left, and then on the right respond with a fastwrite in which you give your own commentary, questions, interpretations, clarifications, or even feelings about what you heard. Your commentary can be pretty open ended, responding to questions such as the following:

■ What strikes you? What is confusing? What is surprising?
■ If you assume that this is true, why is it significant?
■ If you doubt the truth or accuracy of the claim or fact, what is the author failing to consider?
■ How does the information stand up to your own experiences and observations?

- Does it support or contradict your thesis (if you have one at this point)?
- How might you use the information in your paper? What purpose might it serve?
- What do you think of the source?
- What further questions does the information raise that might be worth investigating?
- How does the information connect to other sources you've read?

Refer to this list of questions (and any others that occur to you) as a prompt for the writing on the right side of your journal (or right column of your Word document). There are a variety of ways to approach the double-entry journal. If you're taking notes on the printout of an article or a photocopy from a book, try reading the material first and underlining passages that seem important. Then, when you're done, transfer some of that underlined material—quotes, summaries, or paraphrases—into the left column of your journal. Otherwise, take notes in the left column *as* you read.

While you take notes, or after you've finished, do some exploratory writing in the right column. This territory belongs to you. Here, through language, your mind and heart assert themselves over the source material. Use your notes in the left column as a trigger for writing in the right. Whenever your writing stalls, look to the left. The process is a little like watching tennis—look left, then right, then left, then right. Direct your attention to what the source says and then to what *you* have to say about the source. Keep up a dialogue.

Figures 3.4 and 3.5 illustrate how the double-entry journal works in practice. Note these features:

- Bibliographic information is recorded at the top of the page. Do that first, and make sure it's complete.
- Page numbers are included in the far-left margin, right next to the information that was taken from that page. Make sure you keep up with this as you write.
- While the material from the source in the left column may be quite formal or technical, the response in the right column should be informal and conversational. Try to write in your own voice. Find your own way to say things. And don't hesitate to use the first person: *I*.
- The writers often use their own writing to try to question a source's claim or understand better what that claim might be (e.g., "What the authors seem to be missing here…" and "I don't get this quote at all…").

Prior, Molly. "Bright On: Americans' Insatiable Appetite for Whiter-Than-White Teeth Is Giving Retailers Something to Smile About." Beauty Biz 1 Sept. 2005: 36–43. Print.

Teeth are no longer just for eating with — their appearance is becoming more important as a factor in a person's image, and they need to be perfectly white. (36)

Cosmetics companies are now entering territory once reserved for dentists as more and more people care mostly about the aesthetics of their teeth and smile. (36)

"Sephora is so enthusiastic about the [tooth-whitening] category, it named 'smile' its fifth retail pillar, joining the four others (makeup, fragrance, skin care and hair care) earlier this year." (37)

"The trend has shed its clinical beginnings and assumed a new identity, smile care. Its new name has been quickly adopted by a growing troupe of retailers, who hope to lure consumers with a simple promise: A brighter smile will make you look younger and feel more confident." (37)

Instead of going to the dentist and taking care of their teeth so they function well, people are investing a cosmetic interest in their teeth. People selling tooth-whitening products hope people associate whiter, more perfect teeth with higher self-esteem and social acceptance. (40)

"What says health, youth and vitality like a great smile?" (40)

I have noticed the increasing amount of importance that people put on the whiteness of their teeth, but this also seems to have increased with the amount of advertising for whitening products on TV and in magazines. I wonder if the whole thing is profit driven: Hygiene companies wanted to make more money, so instead of just selling toothbrushes and toothpaste, they created a whitening product and then worked to produce a demand for it. I almost feel really manipulated, like everyone's teeth were fine the way they naturally existed, and then all of the sudden a big company decided it needed to create a new product and sell it by making us feel bad about our smiles, and thus bad about ourselves.

The whole thing is sad, because once something becomes the societal "norm," we start to become obligated to do it. If everyone's teeth are beige, it's no problem when yours are too. But when everyone has sparkling white teeth, then it looks funny if you let yours stay brown. It either says "I don't have the money to whiten my teeth," or "I don't care about my appearance."

Sometimes it feels people might also judge you as being dirty, because white teeth seem healthier and cleaner than brown teeth, or lazy, for not spending the time to whiten your teeth. All those things are negative, and create a negative cloud around our teeth where we once felt good, or at least ambivalent. I don't like the way I'm being told my smile isn't good enough the way it is. I feel like when I smile it should just be about showing happiness and conveying that to others, not a judgment about me as a person.

**FIGURE 3.4    Amanda's Double-Entry Journal.** Here, Amanda concentrates on thinking through the implications of the summaries and quotations she collected from an article on teeth whitening.

Greenbaum, Jessica B. "Training Dogs and Training Humans: Symbolic
Interaction and Dog Training." <u>Anthrozoos</u> 23.2: 129-141. Web. 10 Jan. 2010.

"The 'traditional' dominance-based method of training endorses obedience by using a human-centric approach that places dogs in a subordinate position in order to maintain a space in the family. The 'reward-based' behavior modification method promotes a dog-centric approach that highlights companionship over dominance. . . ." (129)

Article seems to capture the essence of the debate: Is a well-behaved dog a product of dominance or companionship? Why can't it be both? One of the things that always strikes me about these binaries—either/or—is that it ignores both/and. Dogs will always have some kind of unequal relationship with their owners. Right? They have to. And won't they try to sort out, in their own way, the question of who is in charge?

"The methods we use to train our dogs reflect our perceptions of relationships between human and non-human animals. The socially constructed status of dogs, as pet or companion, influences the philosophy, methods, and training skills used." (129)

This seems key: "the socially constructed status of dogs" has an enormous influence on how we construe our relationship with them. Greenbaum draws the distinction as between "pet" and "companion." Behind those general terms is a whole set of ways in which we "socially construct" pets. A pet can be a companion, right? It doesn't necessarily imply subservience? I keep returning to the binaries that theorists draw. This is exactly the same thing that I notice with dog trainers themselves. There is a "right" and "wrong" way, and this divide is typically described as it is here: between positive reinforcement and negative reinforcement.

Mead discounted idea that animals can engage in symbolic communication with humans: "the ability to think was the ability to say." But article, using Sanders, argues that in a sense, pet owners "speak for" their animals. Sanders's research on police dogs, however, also highlighted the "ambiguity" of dog ownership—they are both companions and "tools." Subjective beings and objective things. (130)

This idea that we "speak for animals" strikes home, and I imagine that people like me who constantly give dogs and cats a human voice are more likely to favor "human-centric" methods. How can you put a shock collar on a dog that can talk back? But I never thought about this "ambiguity" between dogs as "tools" and "companions." Though wouldn't this be mostly true of people who train dogs for particular purposes? Is this ambiguity typical of most pet owners who don't?

**FIGURE 3.5   Double-Entry Journal.** Here's a double-entry journal entry that uses Word's Table feature to respond to an article I was reading on theories of dog training. I could copy and paste quotes from the original article, a PDF file, and drop them into the left column. Also notice, however, that I rely on summaries as well. Page numbers in parentheses follow borrowed material.

Fennel argues that while the principle of modeling training on pack behavior makes sense, the method is often misapplied—correction is too harsh or effort to domesticate too extreme. She thinks this is cause of most behavior problems. "Dog guardians have failed as pack leaders." (131)

Must read Fennel's study. Seems like her argument is much like the one I'm thinking about: It may be that dogs do behave in some ways like wild pack animals, but their trainers aren't exactly alpha dogs, either.

---

**FIGURE 3.5**   (Continued)

- Seize a phrase from your source, and play out its implications; think about how it pushes your own thinking or relates to your thesis.
- In Figures 3.4 and 3.5, the writers frequently pause to ask themselves questions—not only about what the authors of the original sources might be saying but also what the writers are saying to themselves as they write. Use questions to keep you writing and thinking.

What I like about the double-entry journal system is that it turns me into a really active reader as I'm taking notes for my essay. That blank column on the right, like the whirring of my computer right now, impatiently urges me to figure out what I think through writing. All along, I've said the key to writing a strong research paper is *making the information your own.* Developing your own thinking about the information you collect, as you go along, is one way to do that. Thoughtful notes are so easy to neglect in your mad rush to simply take down a lot of information. The double-entry journal won't let you neglect your own thinking; at least it will remind you when you do.

## The Research Log

The research log is an alternative to the double-entry journal that promotes a similar "conversation" between writer and source but with a few differences. One is that, like a Tonight Show host, the researcher starts with a monologue and always gets the last word. The standard format of the research log can serve as a template, that can be retrieved whenever you're ready to take notes on another source. Those notes can then be easily dropped into a draft as needed, using the Cut and Paste feature of your word processing program.

The basic approach is this:

1. Take down the full bibliographic information on the source—article, book chapter, Web page, or whatever (see Figure 3.6).

**Project:** Belief in Alien Abduction

**Source:** Kelley-Romano. "Mythmaking in Alien Abduction Narratives." *Communication Quarterly* 54.3 (August 2006): 383-406

**Date:** 11 November 2013

**First Thoughts:**
This article argues that alien abduction stories are essentially myths, and by this she doesn't mean necessarily "untrue," but that they are stories that a growing number of people tell themselves for the same reasons we've always told myths: They are instructive. Through interviews with 130 people who claim to have been abducted, Kelley-Romano identifies four of the most common narratives. These include the "salvation" narrative (aliens are coming to save us from ourselves), the "hybridization" narrative (they need us to reproduce with them and save their own kind)....What I find so interesting about this is that instead of dismissing alien abduction stories as tales told by crazy people, the author argues that they are actually mythical stories that can tell us a lot about not only the people who believe them but also the state of our culture....

**Notes:**
"An examination of this fascinating and significant phenomenon has the potential to inform our understanding of symbolic practices—exploring what it means to believe, and how we come to know. Most importantly, unlike religions and other codified systems of belief, the alien abduction myth—the Myth of Communion—is still developing. Beginning with the supposed crash of a UFO at Roswell in 1947 and fueled by the abduction of Betty and Barney Hill in 1961, believers in the abduction phenomenon have produced a set of narratives that continues to increase in complexity in both form and function." (384)

---

**FIGURE 3.6    Research Log**

Unlike religious myth, the "alien abduction myth"
is fluid—the narrative "continues to increase in
complexity." (384)

The five elements of myth: heroes, "narrative form,"
"archetypal language," and focus on a particular
place and time. (386)

There is a difference between myths and other kinds
of stories like folk tales and fairy tales because
myths are "accepted as true" by their believers.
(387)

. . .


**Second Thoughts:**
As I think about my research question, this idea of
the "myth of communion"—the alien abduction narrative that suggests that aliens are trying to integrate
humanity into the "cosmos"—seems the most powerful
explanation of why these stories seem to cultivate
believers like religions do. As the author points out,
believers who embrace this "myth of communion" see
something "sacred" about the whole thing. Narrators
who embrace the "myth of communion" view other alien
abduction stories as relatively unenlightened, even
"transcendent." The author really emphasizes how the
need for such myths comes during certain times, and in
the case of the "communion myth," this seems to be a
time when people feel they need to be "rescued". . . .

---

**FIGURE 3.6**   (Continued)

Then read the source, marking up your personal copy in the
usual fashion by underlining, making marginal notes, and so on.

2. Your first entry will be a fastwrite that is an *open-ended response* to the reading under the heading "First Thoughts." For
example, you might begin by playing the "believing game,"
exploring how the author's ideas, arguments, or findings are
sensible, and then shift to the "doubting game," looking for gaps,
questions, and doubts you have about what the source says. You
could write a response to any or all of the questions suggested
for the double-entry journal.

3. Next, mine the source for nuggets. Take notes under the heading "Notes." These are quotations, summaries, paraphrases, or key facts you collect from the reading. They are probably some of the things you marked as you read the source initially. Make sure you include page numbers that indicate in the source where the material in your notes came from.
4. Finally, follow up with one more fastwrite under the heading "Second Thoughts." This is a second, *more focused* look at the source in which you fastwrite about what stands out in the notes you took. Which facts, findings, claims, or arguments that you jotted down shape your thinking now? If the writing stalls, skip a line, take another look at your notes, and seize on something else to write about.

## Narrative Notetaking

This is the simplest method of all. As you read, mark up or annotate your source in the ways you usually do. After you read through it carefully, you will fastwrite a rapid summary for at least one full minute, beginning with the following prompt (see Figure 3.7):

> What I understand this to be saying is....

Skip a line, and begin a second episode of fastwriting. Tell the story of your thinking, a narrative of thought that begins with what you initially might have believed about the topic covered in your source, and then how that thinking was influenced by what you read. This time, scribble (or type) for as long as you can without stopping, beginning with this prompt:

> When I first began reading this, I thought _____, and now I think _____.

Whenever your writing stalls, repeat the prompt again, inserting another discovery from your reading.

## Online Research Notebooks

These days, academic researchers frequently work with digital documents, especially PDF files. While it's always a good idea to print out hard copies of anything you use, it's also convenient to annotate and mark up electronic copies. In addition to highlighting passages, it's also possible with some software to insert comments. These can be much like responses in the double-entry journal.

*Focusing Question:* How has cosmetic dentistry changed the way we think of the smile, and what are the repercussions?

*Source:* Walker, Rob. "Consumed; Unstained Masses." New York Times. New York Times, 2 May 2004. Web. 10 Apr. 2009.

*Rapid Summary (one minute):*
What I understand this article to be saying is that the American public is getting more and more vain, as evidenced by the fact that tooth whitening is growing in popularity. While only celebrities used to modify the appearance of their teeth, now average people are doing it. Because of the value of appearance in our society, once we realize we can modify the way we look to our advantage, we seem to flock to it quickly. That's what's happening with the whole trend of smile care — we're using whiteners to change the way our teeth look so maybe we will be judged more profitably. And when a large percentage of society decides to buy something, there will always be corporations and retailers standing alongside to reap a profit.

*Narrative of Thought (six minutes):*
Before I started reading this article I thought that it was the capitalistic profit motive that had introduced whitening products and created a consumer demand for them. Now I understand that all of us as consumers have an equal responsibility with the companies that make and market such products, because we're the ones that buy them and change our standards of beauty. That makes me think that this is a complicated issue. While it's frustrating to feel like I can never be attractive enough, because the standard of attractiveness to which I'm held keeps getting harder and harder to meet, I'm the one that is interested in meeting it in the first place. While it would be easy to denigrate that as vanity, however, I can also see that being judged by others as attractive does have actual benefits, be it a higher salary or better treatment from strangers. In that case I'm put in a tough spot — I can work against the culture that tells me I don't look the right way, and feel negatively judged, or I can conform to it, and feel disappointed that I folded to social pressure. This isn't just an issue about people whitening their teeth for fun, it's about how society changes its standards and how quickly we assimilate to them — and why.

---

**FIGURE 3.7   Amanda's Narrative Notes**

The problem is that most of the software that can annotate PDF files isn't free. For example, while anyone can download Adobe Reader to read PDF documents, you might need to buy Adobe Acrobat to annotate them. There is, however, some free software that can help you organize your digital research files and attach documents to them. That way, you can attach your notes for each source to the digital original. The downside, of course, is that these notes aren't keyed to particular passages in the source, but the software is still useful for researchers. Here's a list of a few you might try:

1. *Zotero* (http://zotero.org). This is a favorite software for research because it not only organizes digital documents in project

folders but also organizes citation information for each source. Zotero is an add-in that only works on the Firefox browser.

2. *Evernote* (http://evernote.com). You can organize your research sources and associated notes and then upload them so they're accessible everywhere you have an Internet connection. The program also runs on all kinds of devices—iPads, iPhones, PCs, Androids, and so on. In addition, Evernote has a function that allows you to search your notes by tags or titles.

3. *Google Docs* (http://google.com). Google Docs is the standard for many users who want to organize (and share) documents, and it's even more useful now that it allows documents like PDFs and Word files to remain in their native formats. As with Evernote, you can access your Google Docs wherever you have an Internet connection.

# When You're Coming Up Short: More Advanced Searching Techniques

During week three of a research project, students often hit a wall. This is the week when students announce, "I can't find anything on my topic! I need to find another one." Their frustration is real, and it often has to do with that moment in a creative process when motivation sinks as the difficulties arise. For student researchers, these difficulties include a lot of things, like trying to remember citation details, worrying about plagiarism, wondering if there's enough time to wait for those interlibrary loan books to come in, and confronting problems with the project's focus or research question. But the problem is rarely that there is not enough information on the topic.

I take that back. Sometimes it *is* a problem, but it's usually one of the easiest to solve: You just need to exploit the many techniques that help researchers to dig more deeply. Here's where advanced searching techniques pay off (see Figure 3.8). We'll look briefly at each of these.

## Advanced Library Searching Techniques

These advanced library searching techniques are listed in the order you might try them.

1. *Vary search terms.* Try using some search terms suggested by your research so far. You might, for instance, try searching using the names of people who have published on your topic.

| **Library** | **Internet** | **Alternative Sources** |
|---|---|---|
| • Vary search terms | • Vary search terms | • Search blogs |
| • Search other databases | • Use advanced search features | • Search images |
| • Check bibliographies | • Use multiple search engines | • Listen to archived radio and podcasts |
| • Use interlibrary loan | • Watch videocasts | • Search iTunes U |
| • Troll government documents | | • Visit local organizations or libraries |
| • Ask a librarian | | |

**FIGURE 3.8**   **More Advanced Searching Techniques**

2. *Search other databases.* Okay, so you've tried a general subject database like Academic OneFile and even a specialized database like PsycINFO. But have you tried another general database like Academic Search Premier or another specialized database like InfoTrac Psychology? Broaden your coverage.

3. *Check bibliographies.* Academic books and articles always include a list of references at the end. These can be gold mines. Look at all the sources that you've collected so far and scan the titles in the bibliographies that seem promising. Find these by searching the library databases.

4. *Consider using interlibrary loan services.* Your campus library will get you that article or book it doesn't have by borrowing the materials from another library. This is an incredibly useful service, often available online. These days, delivery of requested materials can take as little as a few days!

5. *Troll government documents.* The U.S. government is the largest publisher in the world. If your research question is related to some issue of public policy, then there's a decent chance you'll find some government documents on the subject. Try the site USA.gov (see Figure 3.9), a useful index to the gazillions of government publications and reports.

6. *Ask a reference librarian for help.* If you do, you won't be sorry.

## Advanced Internet Searching Techniques

It's more likely that you've tapped out relevant sources on the Internet before you've tapped out those in the library—most of us like to begin with the Internet. But make sure that you've tried some of the following search strategies on the Web.

**FIGURE 3.9** USA.gov is a useful starting point for a search of government documents on your topic.

1. *Vary search terms.* By now, you've gathered enough information on your topic to have some new ideas about terms or phrases that might yield good results. Say you're researching the origins of American blues music, and you discover that among its many traditions is something called the Piedmont style. Try searching using that phrase in quotation marks. Also consider doing Web searches on the names of experts who have contributed significantly to the conversation on your topic.

2. *Use advanced search features.* Few of us use the advanced search page on Google and other search engines. By habit, we just type in a few terms in the simple search window. But advanced searching will allow you to exploit methods that will give you better results—things like phrase searching in conjunction with Boolean operators like AND and OR.

3. *Use multiple search engines.* Don't call for retreat until you've gone beyond Google. Try Yahoo!, Ask.com, and similar search engines. Also try specialized search engines that are relevant to your subject (see Chapter 2).

## Thinking Outside the Box: Alternative Sources

Sometimes you need to be creative. Try searching for sources on your research question in places you hadn't thought to look.

1. *Search blogs.* It's easy to dismiss blogs as merely self-indulgent musings of people with nothing better to do, but some blogs are written by people who really know what they're talking about. Bloggers can be vigilant observers of new developments, breaking news stories, and cutting-edge opinion. There are a number of specialized search engines to scour the blogosphere. Perhaps the best is http://technorati.com.

2. *Search images.* Another source of material you may not have thought of is images available on the Internet. A photograph of a collapsed school building following the 2008 earthquake in central China will do much to dramatize your essay on the vulnerability of buildings to such a disaster. Or a historical essay on lynching in the South might be more powerful with a picture of a murder from the Library of Congress archives (especially see http://memory .loc.gov/). Your campus library may also have a collection of digital images relevant to your project. Remember that if you use them in your essay, images need to be cited like any other source.

3. *Archived radio or podcasts.* Suppose your research question focuses on Martin Luther King Jr. Why not listen to an interview of Taylor Branch, the man who wrote a three-volume biography of the civil rights leader? You can find it on NPR.org. National Public Radio is a particularly good source for material for academic projects. There are also a variety of search engines that will help you find podcasts on nearly any subject.

4. *Check out YouTube.* It isn't just about laughing babies anymore. YouTube is a rich archive of video that can provide material on many topics. For the project on Martin Luther King Jr., for example, you might watch a video of his last speech. There are, of course, other sites that archive video, too. Truveo (http://www .truveo.com/) will help you search them all.

5. *Search iTunes U.* Across the United States, colleges and universities are going online through Apple's iTunes U, putting up video and audio speeches, lectures, and other academic content. You can find iTunes U on iTunes, of course, and you can do a

keyword search on multiple sites using "power search." The term "global warming" produced 90 hits, including lectures, opinions, and reports from some of America's top universities.

6. *Local organizations.* The reference librarians on our campus routinely refer students to the state historical society or state law library when relevant to their projects. Local organizations can be rich sources of not only published information but also interviews and artifacts.

## EXERCISE 3.4

### Building an Annotated Bibliography

Reading to write starts with a very practical motive: *Can I use this source to develop my ideas and argument or to explore my topic?* With this in mind, the most skillful readers intuitively know that there are three kinds of readings they need to do (see Figure 3.10): First, they need to understand what the source is saying (yes, even if they disagree with it); second, they need to try to place what they've read in the context of what they already know about the topic; and finally, they need to imagine how

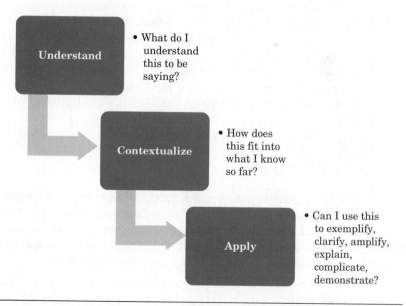

**FIGURE 3.10** **Reading Strategy for Building an Annotated Bibliography**

some of the reading might be *used* in their own writing. This is the kind of reading that will help you develop a certain kind of *annotated bibliography*—in this case, a preliminary list of relevant sources, each of which has a brief summary and evaluation attached to it.

Imagine, for instance, that you were researching these questions: What is the relationship between gender and reactions to facial expressions? Do men and women react differently to expressions of facial emotion? The literature—and conventional wisdom—seem to confirm the view that women are more intuitive than men, and that they have a higher "emotional intelligence." Might a partial explanation for this be that women are better at recognizing facial expressions, including subtle ones that communicate feeling? You find an article[1] in an academic database in which the researchers show 133 students in an undergrad course a series of pictures like this see page 139 one, which includes a variety of facial expressions related to anger, contempt, disgust, fear, happiness, sadness, and surprise. Are both men and women equally competent in recognizing the emotions behind these facial expressions, including the more subtle emotions? Here are some of the results:

1. **Understand.** It's clear that, up to a point, women are better than men at recognizing the feeling behind a facial expression, particularly more subtle feelings. But the study also qualifies this finding by suggesting that when it comes to "highly expressive" expressions, there is no difference between women and men.

2. **Contextualize.** If you had been doing research on this topic, you'd recognize that this study looks at only a small aspect of what psychologists call "emotional competence." It doesn't fully explain whether women have an advantage over men in this ability. It does seem to confirm, however, your own experience that men can be emotional blockheads until things get really out of hand emotionally.

3. **Apply.** The graph is pretty clear. Why not use it to emphasize the idea that women seem to be better than men at recognizing more subtle emotions?

These three readings give you a good start on building a short paragraph annotation of the article that includes all three elements: your summary of what the source says, your comments about how the article fits into a larger understanding of your topic, and a guess about how you might use the article in your essay. For example:

[1]Hoffman, Holger, Henrik Kessler, Tobias Eppel, Stefanie Rukavina, and Harold C. Traue. "Expression Intensity, Gender, and Facial Emotion Recognition: Women Recognize Only Subtle Facial Emotions Better than Men." *Acta Psychologica* 135 (2010): 278–83.

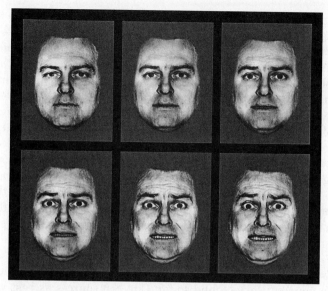

*Note.* The image on the upper left is the neutral face (0% intensity); the image on the lower right is the full-blown emotional face (100% intensity).

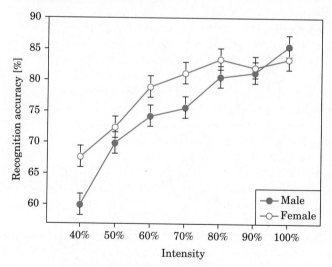

*Note.* Error bars depict standard errors

## Sample Evaluative Annotation

1. Hoffman, Holger, Henrik Kessler, Tobias Eppel, Stefanie Rukavina, and Harold C. Traue. "Expression Intensity, Gender, and Facial Emotion Recognition: Women Recognize Only Subtle Facial Emotions Better than Men." *Acta Psychologica* 135 (2010): 278–83.

This article investigates whether there is a "female advantage" over men when it comes to the ability to recognize facial expressions that imply emotion. This question is a part of larger investigations about "emotional competence" and whether it's related to gender. Conventional wisdom and the popular press suggest women are better at feelings than at reason. My research poses the question of whether, if true, this emotional "advantage" might be related to women's sensitivity to emotional facial expressions. This article, which reports on two studies of college students, seems to confirm it: Women who were quickly shown images of actors with a range of six different emotions, from subtle to "full-blown," were much better than men at detecting the less intense expressions. At higher intensities there was no difference between men and women. A graph in the article might be particularly dramatic evidence of this in my essay.

End the week by writing annotations like this for a handful of the best sources you've found so far. Cite the sources as best you can (refer to Chapter 5 and the Appendices for help with this), but focus especially on your annotations.

# CHAPTER 4

# The Fourth Week

**IN THIS CHAPTER, YOU'LL LEARN TO...**

- Understand the differences between exploratory and argumentative research essays, and how each implies a different way of organizing your draft.

- Refine and revise your inquiry question so that it leads to a judgment rather than simply a report.

- Consider types of "leads" for your draft and apply some of these to determine which best frame your purpose.

- Learn methods of writing for reader interest, and apply these to the draft.

- Understand how to manage your presence in your essay by weaving in your own ideas and controlling quotations, and use these techniques in the draft.

## Getting to the Draft

It is *not* 2 A.M. Your paper is *not* due in 12 hours but in one or two weeks. For some students, beginning to write a research paper this early—weeks before it's due—will be a totally new experience. An early start may also, for the first time, make the experience a positive one. I know that starting early will help ensure writing a better paper.

Still, there are those students who say they thrive on a looming deadline, who love working in its shadow, flirting with failure. "I work best that way," they say, and they wait until the last minute and race to the deadline in a burst of writing, often sustained by energy drinks or strong doses of caffeine. It works for some students. Panic is a pretty strong motivator. But I think most who defend this habit confuse their relief at successfully pulling off the assignment once again with a belief that the paper itself is successful.

Papers done under such pressure often aren't successful, and that is particularly true of the last-minute research paper, where procrastination is especially deadly. Research writing is recursive. You often have to circle back to where you've already been, discovering holes in your research or looking at your subject from new angles. It's hard to fit in a trip back to the library the night before the paper is due, when you've just started the draft and need to check some information. This book is designed to defeat procrastination, and if, in the past few weeks, you've done the exercises, taken thoughtful notes, and attempted a thorough search for information, you probably have the urge to begin writing.

On the other hand, you may feel as though you don't know enough yet about your topic to have anything to say. Or you may be swamped with information, and your head may be spinning. What do you do with it all?

## Exploration or Argument?

What you do with it all depends on what kind of essay you're going to write. Working from an inquiry question, your draft can head in two directions:

1. *Argument.* Your discoveries in the past few weeks may have convinced you that a certain answer to your research question is particularly persuasive. Now you want to prove it. Another way to think about this is to ask yourself whether you want your readers to *think* or possibly even *do* something about your research topic.
2. *Exploratory essay.* On the other hand, maybe you're still not ready to make a judgment about the best answer to your research question and you want to use your essay to continue exploring it. You are less concerned with trying to get readers to think or do something than you are with helping them to appreciate what you find interesting or complicated about your topic.

Sometimes your research question will lead you toward one kind of essay or the other. Compare these two questions:

- *What should be done about the problem of smoking on campus?* (Argument)
- *How do smoking bans on college campuses influence social relationships between smokers?* (Exploration)

While both questions involve open-ended inquiry into the topic of campus smoking, one more naturally leads ultimately to a claim that is supported by reasons and evidence, and the other to an exploration of possible effects.

Your instructor may also give you guidance about whether your draft should be exploratory or argumentative. Depending on which it is, your focus this week might be a bit different. But first, gather your thoughts on everything you've learned about your topic so far.

## EXERCISE 4.1

### Dialogue with Dave

**STEP 1:** Dave is the reader you imagine when you picture the reader of your essay. He's a pretty nice guy, and smart, too. But first off, like any reader, he wants to know why he should care about the subject you're writing about. Then, once you've got Dave's interest, he has questions about what you're telling him about your topic. Like any conversation, what he asks about depends on the details of what you tell him. This conversation can't be scripted. Just let it develop as you write.

When you imagine Dave's persona in this exercise, consider some of the stuff Dave might want to know, like

- Why? Where? Who? When? What?
- What do you mean by _____?
- How do most people see this? How do you see it differently?
- Are you kidding? I didn't know that. What else did you find out?
- Can you give me an example?
- Did that surprise you?
- What other questions does this raise?
- Who does this affect, mostly?
- What should we do about this?
- I'm not sure I believe this. Why do you?
- What do you think we should do about it?

Use the Table feature to format a document on your computer, creating two columns—one for Dave's questions and the other for your answers (see below). Start the conversation with Dave's first question—"What's the big deal about this, anyway?"—and take it from there. *If this is going to be useful, try to keep this conversation going for at least a half hour.*

In Figure 4.1, you can see part of what Mandy did with this exercise. She was exploring how ideas about beauty communicated through the American mass media influence how girls feel about themselves.

**STEP 2:** Many conversations like this one move toward some kind of conclusion. Reread what you wrote, and finish the exercise by crafting an answer to Dave's final question: *Okay, this is all very interesting. But based on everything you've learned so far, what's your point?*

## S.O.F.T.

Many years ago, I was lucky enough to go to graduate school where a wonderful writer and teacher named Donald Murray taught, and he became both a friend and mentor. One of Don's endearing

| DAVE | MANDY |
|------|-------|
| What's the big deal about this anyway? Why should I care? | In society today, girls at young ages are being influenced by the media and society that they should be culturally beautiful in order to live a happy life and gain social acceptance. Many girls compete in beauty pageants at young ages and grow up to have psychological and mental disorders from this pressure to be beautiful. |
| What do you mean by culturally beautiful? | Cultural beauty is where the woman appeals to what is considered attractive to the society at the specific time she is being judged. Cultural beauty is basically meeting society's standards; however, biological beauty for a woman means to be healthy and able to reproduce. |
| Can you give me an example of this cultural beauty affecting girls at a young age? | Beauty, whether it be male or female, will never disappear in society. It is a primitive goal to be considered socially attractive in society, and many people will do anything to gain this social acceptance. Plastic surgery and liposuction are two methods women use to keep their beauty. Also, this pressure on women can lead to eating disorders at a young age. The age group that has the highest rates of anorexia or bulimia is the female age group of 17 years old to 19 years old. A lot of this can be related back to their childhoods and the influences they had. |

**FIGURE 4.1  Mandy's Dialogue with Dave**

habits was to take a saying about which he was particularly fond and print it out on cardboard, which he would then distribute to his students. "Nulla dies sine linea"—never a day without a line—was one of these. Another was "S.O.F.T." This was an acronym for Say One Fricking Thing. Don believed that every piece of writing should say one fricking thing—it may deal with many ideas, but the writer's job is to find the *one* thing he or she wants most to say about an essay topic.

More formally, we often understand this to mean that writing—especially academic writing—should have a thesis, a point, a theme, and a main idea. Too often, I'm afraid, writers arrive at this too early in their research—ending the inquiry process prematurely—or they don't arrive at it at all, and the essay or paper seems pointless.

In Exercise 4.1 you moved toward finding your S.O.F.T., and when you did, several things might have happened:

1. You discovered a point, and maybe it was one you didn't expect. Hallelujah! This one might need some fine-tuning but it seems to reflect your understanding of the topic at this point.
2. You arrived at a point, but it doesn't seem quite right. You feel like you're still groping toward a thesis—an answer to your research question—and this one seems forced or too general.
3. You have no clue what might be the S.O.F.T. All you have is more questions. Or perhaps you realize that you simply don't know enough yet to have any idea what you want to say.

If you find yourself in the first situation—you discovered a thesis that seems right—then maybe your draft should be an argumentative essay in which you attempt to prove your point. The second situation might invite you to continue your investigation by writing an exploratory research essay, and the third probably means that you haven't done nearly enough research yet. Actually, you probably need to do more research in every case—and you will as you continue the process.

## Organizing the Draft

How you approach writing your first draft this week depends on what you decide about which kind of research essay you think you want to write: an argument or an exploratory essay. Let's look at how the two might differ.

But first, the five-paragraph theme. Like a lot of schoolkids, I learned to write something called the "five-paragraph theme": introduction with thesis; three body paragraphs, each with a topic sentence and supporting details; and conclusion. This was the container into which I poured all of my writing back then. Though it didn't produce particularly interesting writing, the five-paragraph structure was a reliable way to organize things. It was very well suited to outlines. I vaguely remember this one from sixth grade:

I.  China is a really big country.
   A. The population of China is really big.
   B. The geographic size of China is really big.
   C. The economic dreams of China are really big.

What's useful about thinking of structure this way is the notion of hierarchy: Some ideas are subordinated to others, and each idea has some information subordinated under it. A problem with it, however, is the assumption that hierarchy is *always* the best way to organize information. For instance, essays can often make relevant digressions, or they might play with one way of seeing the topic and then another.

Perhaps a more basic problem with forms like the five-paragraph theme is the idea that structure is this kind of inert container that stands apart from the things you put into it and from your particular motives in writing about something.

Yet structure is important. And it's even more important when writers begin a draft with an abundance of information. John McPhee has written popular nonfiction essays on such topics as a guy who still makes birch bark canoes, people who study animal road kill, and his own exploration of Atlantic City using the game Monopoly as a guide. He is a careful and meticulous researcher, accumulating material in multiple binders from his interviews, observations, and reading. By the time he sits down to write, he's looking at pages and pages of notes. McPhee's solution to this problem is to use notecards to organize his information on bulletin boards, moving the cards around until he gets a satisfying arrangement. "The piece of writing has a structure inside it," he says, and before he begins drafting, he seeks to find it.

If you don't have much information to begin with, structure is less of a problem. You simply end up using everything you have, and the result is usually a boring, unfocused essay.

I'd like to encourage you, as you start drafting this week, to avoid thinking about the structure of your essay as something set in concrete before you begin. Instead, think of form rhetorically: Who is your audience and what does the assignment say and what is your purpose in writing about your topic? For example, here are two structures to consider depending on whether your research paper is exploratory or argumentative:

- *Delayed thesis structure*—characteristic of the exploratory essay
- *Question–claim structure*—characteristic of the argumentative paper

However you choose to organize it, your research essay will have certain characteristics. For example, nearly any academic research paper includes the following items:

1. A S.O.F.T.—a point, a claim, a thesis—one main thing you are trying to say about the research question
2. A review of what has already been said by others about your topic
3. Specific information—the evidence or data on which your interpretations, conclusions, assertions, and speculations are based
4. A method of reasoning through the question, some pattern of thought—narrative, argument, essaying—that writer and reader find a convincing way to try to get at the truth of things

## Delayed Thesis Structure

In an inquiry-based class, you typically choose a topic because you want to learn what you think. As you work through the research process, as I pointed out earlier, either you arrive at what you think is a persuasive answer to your research question and decide you will argue for it or you believe that you have more to learn and decide you will explore further. This second possibility was my motive for writing "Theories of Intelligence," the essay that opened this book. I didn't want to write an argument. I wanted to write an exploratory essay.

Quite naturally, then, I didn't begin my draft with a thesis—an answer to my questions about why I often felt stupid, despite evidence to the contrary—but sought to use my essay to try to sort this out. If you go with the "delayed thesis" structure in writing your essay, you use the information from your research to think through your research question.

In one version of using the delayed thesis structure, you essentially tell the story of your thinking so that your paper is a kind of "narrative of thought." The plot is something like, "This seems to be the problem and this is the question it raises for me. And here's what this person and that person have said about it, and this is what I think of what they said." The story ends with some kind of

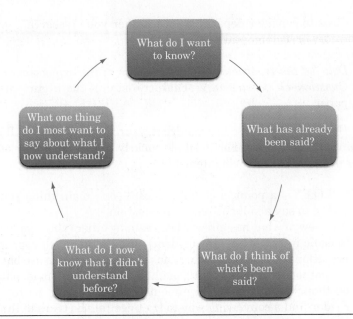

**FIGURE 4.2   The Delayed Thesis Structure.** This method of thinking through a research question might tell the story of your thinking and of how what you've read and heard has helped you to understand what you didn't understand before about your topic.

statement that addresses this question: "What do I understand now about the question I initially asked that I didn't understand when I first asked it, and what in this new understanding is particularly important?" (See Figure 4.2.) This last statement is your delayed thesis. You might also include discussion of questions you would like to further explore. As the arrows in Figure 4.2 show, arriving at a thesis doesn't necessarily mean the end of inquiry. A delayed thesis may end up opening doors rather than closing them.

Figure 4.3 is a more detailed look at a delayed thesis structure. It highlights five parts that a research essay *might* include and lists some specific options for developing each. Figure 4.3 might help you think about how to organize your draft this week.

## Question–Claim Structure

If your initial research question leads you toward an idea about what should be done or what your readers should believe—that is, toward argument—then you'll likely organize your essay differently. Instead of a delayed thesis structure, you might want to use the question–claim structure.

I. **Introduce the research problem or question and then your motive for exploring it. For example:**
   - Tell a story that dramatizes the problem.
   - Describe your own experiences with it.
   - What did you read, observe, or experience that made you curious about it?

II. **Establish the significance of the problem or question and why readers should care about it. For example:**
   - How many other people are affected?
   - What difference will it make in people's lives?
   - Why is this *particular* question significant?

III. **Describe and analyze what has already been written or said by others about the problem or question and how this advances your understanding. For example:**
   - Who has made a significant contribution to the conversation about this?
   - What have they said and how does that relate to your research question?
   - What important questions do these other voices raise for you?

IV. **Explain what you find to be the most persuasive or significant answer to the research question. This is your thesis. For example:**
   - In the end, which voices were most convincing? Why?
   - What might you add to the conversation?
   - What do you want to say?

V. **Describe what you've come to understand about the topic that you didn't fully appreciate when you began the project. What is left to explore? For example:**
   - What difference will the discoveries you made about your question make in your life? In your readers' lives?
   - What do you remain curious about?
   - What questions are unresolved and what directions might more inquiry take if you were to continue?

**FIGURE 4.3** **A Structure for Exploring**

The question–claim structure has some similarities to the delayed thesis structure of an essay—for one thing, it arises from a question—but this method for organizing your draft puts your answer to that question toward the beginning and then proceeds, using your research, to make the most convincing case you can for that answer (see Figure 4.4). It's a

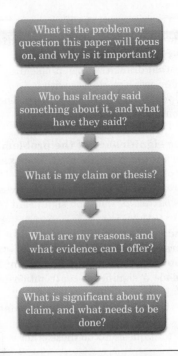

**FIGURE 4.4    The Question–Claim Structure.** This structure, which is characteristic of the argumentative research paper, signals the writer's purpose and point early on and then sets out to prove it.

little like the automobile dealer who, after wandering the lot, decides to put the models he or she most wants to sell in the showroom window. You focus your readers' gaze not on the process of discovery but, rather, on the product of that process: the point you want to make.

The question–claim structure may be the form of the research paper with which you're most familiar. Here's one way to think about organizing your draft using this approach. This structure has five parts (see Figure 4.5), each with various options and considerations. It is a structure that you can adapt to your needs.

## Exploring or Arguing: An Example

Susan was writing an exploratory research essay on the relationship between attendance at preschool and academic success in elementary school. She decided to introduce her topic by describing her own dilemma with her son, Sam. She wanted to send him to preschool, but as a working college student, she wasn't sure she could afford it. Her personal anecdote highlighted the problem many parents face and the question behind her research: Will children who don't attend preschool

I. **Introduce the research question or problem that is the focus of the paper. For example:**
   - Provide factual background.
   - Dramatize with an anecdote.
   - Establish the significance of the problem by citing experts or other observers.

II. **What will be your argument or claim in the paper? This is your thesis.**
   - What do you think your readers should *believe* or what do you think they should *do*? State this thesis clearly.

III. **Review the literature. What have others already said about the question or problem? For example:**
   - Cite published studies, interviews, commentaries, experiments, and so on that are relevant to the question or problem.
   - Which ideas or voices seem most important? Are there identifiable camps in the debate, or certain patterns of argument?
   - Address popular assumptions. What do most people believe to be true?

IV. **What are your reasons for believing what you believe and, for each reason, what specific evidence did you find that you thought was convincing? For example:**
   - What kinds of evidence will your readers find most persuasive?
   - Are there various kinds of evidence that can be brought to bear?
   - How do your reasons square with those who might disagree with you?

V. **What is the significance of your claim? What's at stake for your audience? What might be other avenues for research? For example:**
   - What should we do? What might happen if we don't act?
   - How does the thesis or claim that you propose resolve some part of the problem? What part remains unresolved?
   - What questions remain?

**FIGURE 4.5　A Structure for Argument**

be at a disadvantage in primary school or not? In the middle section of her essay, Susan reported on several studies that looked at a range of skills that were affected by preschool experience and discussed which of these she found most significant, particularly in the context of her personal interviews with several local teachers. In the second-to-last section of her draft, Susan concluded that preschool does indeed make a difference, particularly in the areas of reading and reasoning.

Imagine that Susan wanted instead to write an argumentative research paper, a more conventional form for academic research. Would it be organized differently? While she still might begin with a personal anecdote as a way to dramatize the problem, Susan might choose instead to begin with information, highlighting the statistics and arguments that establish the importance of the problem. How many children in the United States attend preschool? How many don't? What are the trends? Are more parents struggling to find affordable preschools? Are fewer preschools available in disadvantaged areas? Is there a shortage of teachers? A significant difference would be where in the paper Susan puts her thesis. In the argumentative paper, the thesis usually appears toward the beginning (see Figure 4.3) and is stated explicitly: "I will argue in this essay that the growing number of children in the United States who are being denied a preschool experience will be at a serious disadvantage in reading and reasoning skills when they enter elementary school." Her essay would then go on to methodically establish the truth of this claim using her research. Susan might end her essay by suggesting how elementary teachers could address the learning deficits these children bring into their classrooms or how more children could be given access to preschool.

# Preparing to Write the Draft

If research is a little like soup making, then you want to make something hearty, not thin; that's nearly impossible to do unless you have a lot of information. If you slacked on developing focused knowledge last week and didn't do enough research on your question, then you'll find that you have to use almost everything you *do* have to write the first draft. If that happens, your essay will be unfocused and uninformative. Scanty research is one of the most common problems I see in student work at this stage in the process. Your first decision before beginning the draft is whether you've got what it takes to make at least decent soup.

## Refining the Question

But you can't really judge the quality of your information until you feel comfortable with your research question. Are you asking the right question? Is it the question that you find most interesting? Is it focused enough? Did you refine it as you learned more about your topic? Does it incorporate the language or terms you may have learned in your reading? Typically, research questions evolve, especially if you are tackling a topic that you initially didn't know much about.

For these kinds of topics, the research questions we often ask initially are broadly informative or questions of definition:

- *What are the theories of dog training?*

As we learn more about our research topic, the questions frequently become more specific—which is far more helpful in guiding research—and reflect our new understandings of the topic. The next generation of questions often moves beyond questions of fact or definition and reflects a *particular* interest in the topic: Is it any good? What does it mean? What should be done? What might be true? What are important causes? (See Figure 4.6.)

For example, this rewrite of the original research question is a little more specific and also implies value:

- *What are the best theories of dog training?*

The following question is more specific still and incorporates some of the language in the literature:

- *Is there evidence that "dog-centric" approaches to training that reward behavior work better than approaches that emphasize the trainer's dominance over the dog?*

And the following question is even more specific:

- *What is the relationship between the use of shock collars and dog aggression or submission?*

Revisit your research question before you begin your draft. In light of what you've learned about your topic so far, can you rewrite the question so that it provides you with stronger guidance about your purpose in the draft? When you've rewritten your research question, write it on a notecard or sticky note, and put it somewhere on your computer monitor where you can see it as you're writing the draft. Your research question (or thesis) is the sea anchor that will keep you from going adrift.

## Refining the Thesis

If you're writing an argumentative essay, then you need to settle on a tentative thesis. It may change as you continue doing the writing and research, but for now you should have a pretty specific statement

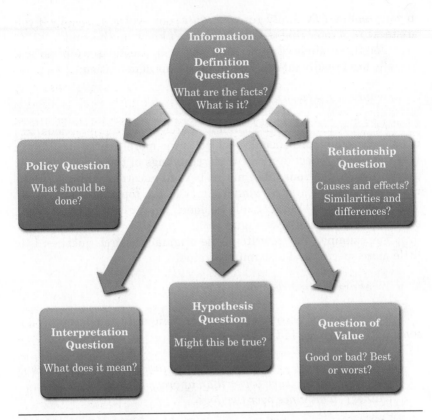

**FIGURE 4.6    Categories of Questions.** Usually our initial research questions are questions of fact or definition: What is known about this topic? What is it? But a strong research essay needs *to do* something with the facts. One way to think about what a question is trying to do is to place it in one of these additional categories: questions of policy, interpretation, hypothesis, value, or relationship. Before you begin your draft, rethink your question. Can it be more specific? Can you rewrite your question so that it gives you a stronger sense of what you're trying to do with your research?

of what you think. Exercise 4.1 might have helped nudge you in this direction. Now work with your thesis a bit more.

There is considerable talk about thesis statements. Sometimes it seems like a thesis (or S.O.F.T., main point, central claim, organizing idea, etc.) is a kind of club required to beat an essay into submission, forcing every part of the work into obedience. In this view, there is no room for digression, contrary evidence, opposing views, or uncertainty. Much writing—like the world that writers attempt to explore in that writing—is much messier than that, and that complexity is what makes inquiry interesting.

And yet, when writers discover what they want to say—the answer to the question, the realization about what should be done, or the interpretation that makes the most sense—it's essential that they say it clearly, first for themselves and then for their readers. At this stage in the research process, your thesis is very tentative, but if you spend some time refining it, it will reward you later. A well-stated thesis gives you a sense of direction and can help you to organize both your research and your essay. Just don't be slavish about it. A thesis isn't a club. It isn't even a tool. A thesis is a way of seeing that is made of sand, not stone, and it is continually reshaped by what you learn.

What do we know about the qualities of a good thesis? For one thing, we know that they are not overly broad or obvious. Take this statement, for example:

> *There are many theories about how to train dogs.*

Yep, there sure are. This is not a thesis; it's just an observation and a statement of the obvious. What's missing here is a judgment. The kind of judgment you make in your thesis is related to the kind of question you're asking about your topic (see Figure 4.6). The observation that there are many theories of dog training is a statement of fact in response to a question of fact. But a thesis is a tentative answer to another kind of question—a question of policy, interpretation, hypothesis, value, or relationship. So if my research question were "What is the *best* method of dog training?" (a question of value), then my thesis might be something like this:

> *The evidence suggests that "human-centric" approaches to dog training—those that work from the premise that the trainer should be dominant over the dog—are less effective than "dog-centric" approaches, which use positive reinforcement.*

Can you see how your thesis is directly related to your research question?

## EXERCISE 4.2

### Sharpening Your Point

Even if you're writing an exploratory essay, it's helpful to think about what your thesis might be at this stage in the inquiry process. This is a kind of reality check: What do I think *right now* based on what I've learned? You are invited to change your mind later. If your essay is argumentative, then it's even more important to establish a tentative thesis. The following templates, each based on the kind of question you're asking, might help:

### Thesis from a Question of Value

*Based on _____, the evidence strongly suggests that _____ is (better / worse, more effective / less effective) than _____.*

**Example:** Based on recent studies comparing how well disciplines teach critical thinking to college students, the evidence suggests that business programs are failing to do a good job of teaching reasoning skills to their undergraduates.

### Thesis from a Question of Policy

*In the debate over _____, I'm persuaded that the most important thing to do is _____.*

**Example:** In the debate over what to do with the overpopulation of wild horses in western rangelands, it's clear that the only effective solution is for the federal agencies to cull the herds.

### Thesis from a Question of Interpretation

*The pattern in _____ that is most (significant / interesting / obvious) is _____.*

**Example**: Throughout Ken Kesey's *One Flew Over the Cuckoo's Nest*, the character of Nurse Ratched represents everything that sexist men fear: the threat of emasculation by a woman.

### Thesis from a Hypothesis Question

*Based on my research, the assumption that _____ appears to be (true / false, qualified / unqualified, accurate / inaccurate, difficult to determine / impossible to determine).*

**Example:** My research on Facebook and social intimacy appears to confirm my impression that "friending" can promote connection but can also be used to manipulate and divide.

### Thesis from a Relationship Question

*There is a (strong / weak) relationship between _____ and _____.*

**Example:** There is a strong relationship between dog owners' views about the need for dominance over their pet and their choice of either "human-centric" or "dog-centric" training methods.

These templates are a bit crude, but try to use them as a starting point to craft a one- or two-sentence thesis that *reflects your current understanding of your topic.* Write this on a sticky note or notecard and, along with your research question, put it on your computer monitor as a reminder when you write the draft.

## Deciding Whether to Say *I*

In addition to refining your research question and thesis, there's something else you should wrestle with before you get started: Will you write your essay in first person? You may think that this isn't even a choice. Academic writing is supposed to be faceless, impersonal, and objective, and the best way to maintain this pretense is to religiously avoid ever using the first person in an academic essay.

The ban on the slender "I" from academic prose by teachers and textbooks is based, in part, on the assumption that this is simply the only way to write scholarship, a myth that studies of academic writing prove wrong again and again. Scholarly writing is diverse and discipline specific, and in a number of fields—for example, business, philosophy, English, and linguistics—articles sometimes use the first person and may even include autobiographical material. Another reason that first person is exiled is that it encourages students to write with needless self-references like "I believe that…" or "In my opinion…." As is so often the case with writing, there aren't really "rules" about how things are supposed to be written; these are rhetorical decisions based on your reasons for composing something, to whom you're writing, and what you're writing about.

There are actually good reasons to consider writing this essay in the first person. The most important is this: When a writer stops pretending that the *text* talks instead of the *author* (e.g., "This paper will argue that…") and actually enters into her text, she is much more likely to initiate a genuine conversation with her readers *and* with her sources. This dialogue might very well lead to some new ways of seeing her topic—which is, after all, the purpose of inquiry.

### Getting Personal Without Being Personal

Conversation takes place among people, and in writing that embodies conversation, readers sense what Gordon Harvey* called *presence*—an awareness that a writer is making sense of things in his own particular ways, that he has a personal stake in what he is

*Harvey, Gordon. "Presence in the Essay." *College English* 56 (1994): 642–54. Print.

## Making Your Presence Felt

Here are some ways to establish your presence in your research essay without necessarily using the first person.

- *Control quotation.* Carefully consider how you use the voices of others—where in your essay and for what purpose—as well as what you choose to emphasize in what those voices say.
- *Find your own way of saying things.* Even when talking about what someone else has said, say it in a way that only you can.
- *Find your own way of seeing things.* How do others usually see your topic, and how do you see it differently?
- *Seize opportunities to comment.* More than anything else, what you *do* with information—evaluate it, relate it, define it, interpret it, establish its significance—gives the essay your signature.

saying. This is most easily achieved when the writer *gets* personal by using the first person and sharing personal experiences and perspectives. I hope that you sense my presence in *The Curious Researcher* through my willingness to do such things.

But I also want you to see, as Harvey observes, that presence in writing can be registered in ways other than simply talking about yourself. That is, you can write a research essay this week that *doesn't* use the first person or isn't autobiographical and still provides your readers with a strong sense of your presence as an individual writer and thinker. (See the box "Making Your Presence Felt" for some specific suggestions.) This presence may be much more subtle when it's not carried on the first-person singular's sturdy back. But it still makes writing come to life.

# Starting to Write the Draft: Beginning at the Beginning

John McPhee, whom I mentioned earlier as one of the masters of the research-based essay, gave a talk some years back about beginnings, which vex many writers.

The first part—the lead, the beginning—is the hardest part of all to write. I've often heard writers say that if you have written your lead you have written 90 percent of the story. You have tens of thousands of words to choose from, after all, and only one can start the story, then one after that, and so forth. And your material, at this point, is all fresh and unused, so you don't have the advantage of being in the middle of things. You could start in any of many places. What will you choose? Leads must be sound. They should never promise what does not follow.

As McPhee said in his talk, "Leads, like titles, are flashlights that shine down into the story."*

## Flashlights or Floodlights?

I love this: *"Leads...are flashlights that shine down into the story."* An introduction, at least the kind I was taught to write in high school, is more like a sodium vapor lamp that lights up the whole neighborhood. I remember writing introductions to research papers that sounded like this:

```
There are many critical problems that face
society today. One of these critical problems
is environmental protection, and especially the
conservation of marine resources. This paper will
explore one of these resources—the whale—and the
myriad ways in which the whale-watching industry
now poses a new threat to this species' survival.
It will look at what is happening today and what
some people concerned with the problem hope will
happen tomorrow. It will argue that new regula-
tions need to be put into effect to reduce boat
traffic around our remaining whales, a national
treasure that needs protection.
```

*McPhee, John. University of New Hampshire, 1977.

This introduction isn't that bad. It does offer a statement of purpose, and it explains the thesis. But the window it opens on the paper is so broad—listing everything the paper will try to do—that readers see a bland, general landscape. What's to discover? The old writing formula for structuring some papers—"Say what you're going to say, say it, and then say what you said"—breeds this kind of introduction. It also gets the writer started on a paper that often turns out as bland as the beginning.

Consider this alternative opening for the same paper:

Scott Mercer, owner of the whale-watching vessel *Cetecea*, tells the story of a man and his son who decide that watching the whales from inside their small motorboat isn't close enough. They want to swim with them. As Mercer and his passengers watch, the man sends his son overboard with snorkel and fins, and the boy promptly swims toward a "bubble cloud," a mass of air exhaled by a feeding humpback whale below the surface. What the swimmer doesn't know is that, directly below that bubble cloud, the creature is on its way up, mouth gaping. They are both in for a surprise. "I got on the P.A. system and told my passengers, just loud enough for the guy in the boat to hear me, that either that swimmer was going to end up as whale food or he was going to get slapped with a $10,000 fine. He got out of the water pretty fast."

I think this lead accomplishes nearly as much as the bland version but in a more compelling way. It suggests the purpose of the paper—to explore conflicts between whale lovers and whales—and even implies the thesis—that human activity around whales needs more regulation, a point that might follow the anecdote. This lead is more like McPhee's "flashlight," pointing out the direction of the paper without attempting to illuminate the entire subject in a paragraph. An interesting beginning will also help launch the writer into a more interesting paper, for both reader and writer.

It's probably obvious that your opening is your first chance to capture your reader's attention. But how you begin your research paper will also have a subtle yet significant impact on the rest of it. The lead starts the paper going in a particular direction; it also establishes the *tone,* or writing voice, and the writer's relationships to the subject and the reader. Most writers at least intuitively know this, which is why beginnings are so hard to write.

## Writing Multiple Leads

One thing that will make it easier to get started is to write three leads to your paper, instead of agonizing over one that must be perfect. Each different opening you write should point the "flashlight" in a different direction, suggesting different trails the draft might follow. After composing several leads, you can choose the one that you—and ultimately, your readers—find most promising.

Writing multiple openings to your paper might sound hard, but consider all the ways to begin:

■ *Anecdote.* Think of a little story that nicely frames what your paper is about, as does the lead about the man and his son who almost became whale food.

■ *Scene.* Begin by giving your readers a look at some revealing aspect of your topic. A paper on the destruction of tropical rain forests might begin with a description of what the land looks like after loggers have left it.

■ *Profile.* Try a lead that introduces someone who is important to your topic. Amanda's essay on the relationship between the popularity of tooth whitening and our changing notions of beauty might begin, for example, by describing Dr. Levine, the man who determined with mathematical precision the dimensions of the "perfect smile."

■ *Background.* Maybe you could begin by providing important and possibly surprising background information on your topic. A paper on steroid use might start by citing the explosive growth in use by high school athletes in the last 10 years. A paper on a novel or an author might begin with a review of what critics have had to say.

■ *Quotation.* Sometimes, you encounter a great quote that beautifully captures the question your paper will explore or the direction it will take. Heidi's paper on whether *Sesame Street* provides children with a good education began by quoting a tribute from *U.S. News and World Report* to Jim Henson after his sudden death.

■ *Dialogue.* Open with dialogue between people involved in your topic. Dan's paper on the connection between spouse abuse and alcoholism began with a conversation between himself and a woman who had been abused by her husband.

■ *Question.* Pointedly ask your readers the questions you asked that launched your research or the questions your readers might raise about your topic. Here's how Kim began her paper on adoption: "Can you imagine going through life not knowing your true identity?"

■ *Contrast.* Try a lead comparing two apparently unlike things that highlight the problem or dilemma the paper will explore. Dusty's paper "Myth of the Superwoman" began with a comparison between her friend Susan, who grew up believing in Snow White and Cinderella and married at 21, and herself, who never believed in princes on white horses and was advised by her mother that it was risky to depend on a man.

■ *Announcement.* Sometimes the most appropriate beginning *is* one like the first lead on whales and whale watchers mentioned earlier, which announces what the paper is about. Though such openings are sometimes not particularly compelling, they are direct. A paper with a complex topic or focus may be well served by simply stating in the beginning the main idea you'll explore and what plan you'll follow.

## EXERCISE 4.3

### Three Ways In

**STEP 1:** Compose three different beginnings, or leads, to your research paper. Each should be one or two paragraphs (or perhaps more, depending on what type of lead you've chosen and on the length of your paper). Think about the many different ways to begin, as mentioned earlier, and experiment. Your instructor may ask you to write the three leads in your research notebook or print them out and bring them to class. (For an example, see Figure 4.7.)

**STEP 2:** Get some help deciding which opening is strongest. Circulate your leads in class, or show them to friends. Ask each person to check the one lead he likes best and that most makes him want to read on.

Here are three openings that Amanda crafted for her draft on our cultural obsession with the "perfect smile." Which do you think is strongest?

1. I haven't felt much like smiling recently. It isn't
   that I've been particularly melancholy or deprived of
   necessary joy. I've actually been hesitant to smile because lately I've felt insecure about my teeth. I brush
   and floss every day and see my dentist twice a year,
   just like any responsible hygiene patient does—but that
   doesn't seem to be enough anymore. My teeth need to be
   white. Now when I feel the corners of my mouth pucker
   upwards and I start to grin at someone, I can't stop
   thinking about my teeth. What once was a simple visual
   expression of happiness has become a symptom of my
   overall doubts about my appearance.

2. Julie Beatty wants people to look at her as a more confident, strong person, so she's doing the only logical
   thing. She's shelling out over $12,500 for an overhaul
   on her teeth. While it sounds completely ridiculous to
   change a person's oral structure to create a different
   persona, Julie is a member of a booming group of people
   who are looking to change their smiles to change their
   lives. Whether or not Julie's straightening, whitening, and tooth reshaping will change her success as an
   executive is still unknown, but the popularity of cosmetic dentistry and smile care is an undeniable new
   phenomenon.

3. I can feel individual molecules of air battering at
   my teeth. It's the middle of the night, but I can't
   sleep because of the constant pain in my mouth. Even
   the weight of my lips pressing down on my teeth is
   agonizing, like I've spent the day being hit in the
   mouth with a hammer and have exposed nerves protrud-
   ing throughout. I haven't been beaten up, though. The
   cause of all my agony is a 10 percent peroxide gel
   I've been smearing into trays and putting on my teeth
   for the past week to whiten them. All this pain is due
   to my vanity and desire for a bit more pearliness in
   my pearly whites. As I watch the numbers of the clock
   roll from 2:00 to 4:00, I wonder why I'm putting up
   with such dental distress just for a more gleaming
   smile.

**FIGURE 4.7   Amanda's Three Leads***

*These excerpts are reprinted with permission of Amanda Stewart.

**STEP 3:** Choose the lead you like (even if no one else does). To determine how well it prepares your readers for what follows, ask a friend or classmate to answer these questions: Based on reading only the opening of the paper: (a) What do you predict this paper is about? What might be its focus? (b) Can you guess what central question I'm trying to answer? (c) Can you predict what my thesis might be? (d) How would you characterize the tone of the paper?

It's easy to choose an opening that's catchy. But the beginning of your paper must also help establish your purpose in writing it, frame your focus, and perhaps even suggest your main point or thesis. The lead will also establish the voice, or tone, the paper will adopt.

That's a big order for one or two paragraphs, and you may find that more than a couple of paragraphs are needed to do it. If you did Exercise 4.3, tentatively select the one opening (or a combination of several) you composed that does those things best. I think you'll find that none of the leads you composed will be wasted; there will be a place for the ones you don't use somewhere else in the paper. Keep them handy.

# Writing for Reader Interest

You've tentatively chosen a lead for your paper. You've selected it based on how well you think it frames your tentative purpose, establishes an appropriate tone or voice, and captures your readers' attention. Once you've gotten your readers' attention, you want to keep it. Consider the following:

1. Give your readers a sense of purpose *throughout* the essay, not just at the beginning.
2. Find ways that your topic intersects with readers' own knowledge of the topic. Build your essay from there.
3. Put a face on your topic—not just how it affects people but *How did it affect a person?*
4. Write an ending that *adds* something rather than tells readers what they already know.
5. Emphasize what's less known about a topic, what may be surprising.

## Who's Steering and Where To?

Imagine that reading is like pedaling a bike up a hill, only the writer is steering the thing while you do all the work. You will not keep pedaling if you think the writer isn't taking you somewhere, and you have to be confident of this within the first few paragraphs of an essay. That's why a strong lead is so important: It gives your readers a sense of direction, a sense of *purpose*. They read an introduction about the rise of the Tea Party in American politics and know that what interests the writer is the Tea Party's constitutional arguments about national health care. Or they read the beginning of an essay on the disgusting habits of ticks, and within a couple paragraphs readers know why the writer is sharing this—to make the argument that climate change is affecting tick-borne illnesses in moose. In each case, if readers know that the bike is headed in a particular direction, they might keep pedaling.

But readers must sense this not just at the beginning but throughout the essay. One way to help readers continue to sense this direction is to keep returning to the question (or thesis) that is driving the essay. This might look something like this:

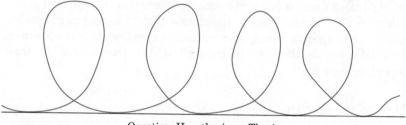

Question, Hypothesis, or Thesis

**FIGURE 4.8**   Keep looping back to your opening question, hypothesis, or thesis.

In other words, look for opportunities to return again and again *throughout your essay* to the question (or thesis) that opened it, and then arc away by examining the relevance of each source before arcing back to how the source advances your thinking or supports (and maybe complicates) your thesis.

## Working the Common Ground

You're writing about the dangers of genetically modified food, and you also know that everyone eats. You're writing about the hemorrhaging economy of Detroit, and you also know that many of us drive cars that were made there. You're writing about the influence of Mississippi delta blues, and you also know that there are traces of that music in Elvis' "Blue Suede Shoes." There are what you know about your topic and what your readers know about your topic, and one way to engage them in what you have to say is to begin with the common ground. Ask yourself this:

- *What are my readers' own experiences with my topic?*
- *Is there some way in my paper that I can help them see that it's relevant to them?*
- *How can I help them see what they may already know?*

## Putting People on the Page

Essayist E. B. White once advised that when you want to write about humankind, you should write about a human. The advice to look at the *small* to understand the *large* applies to most writing, not just the research paper.

Ideas come alive when we see how they operate in the world we live in. Beware, then, of long paragraphs with sentences that begin with phrases such as *in today's society,* where you wax on with generalization after generalization about your topic. Unless your ideas are anchored to specific cases, observations, experiences, statistics, and, especially, people, they will be reduced to abstractions and lose their power for your reader.

### Using Case Studies

Strangely, research papers are often peopleless landscapes, which is one of the things that can make them so lifeless to read. Lisa wrote about theories of child development, citing studies and schools of thought about the topic yet never applying that information to a real child, her own daughter, two-year-old Rebecca. In his paper decrying the deforestation of the Amazon rain forest, Marty never gave his readers the chance to hear the voices of the Indians whose way of life is threatened. *Ultimately, what makes almost any topic matter to the writer or the reader is what difference it makes to people.*

Candy's paper on child abuse and its effect on language development, for example, opened with the tragic story of Genie, who, for nearly 13 years, was bound in her room by her father and beaten whenever she made a sound. When Genie was finally rescued, she could not speak at all. This sad story about a real girl makes the idea that child abuse affects how one speaks (the paper's thesis) anything but abstract. By personalizing the problem, Candy gave her readers reason to care about what she learned about it.

Sometimes, the best personal experience to share is your own. Have you been touched by the topic? Kim's paper about the special problems of women alcoholics included anecdotes about several women gleaned from her reading, but the paper was most compelling when she talked about her own experiences with her mother's alcoholism.

## Using Interviews

Interviews are another way to bring people to the page. Heidi's paper on *Sesame Street* featured the voice of a school principal, a woman who echoed the point the paper made about the value of the program. Such research essays are filled not just with information about the topic but also with people who are touched by it in some way.

As you write your paper, look for opportunities to bring people to the page. Hunt for case studies, anecdotes, and good quotes that will help your readers see how your topic affects how people think and live their lives.

## Writing a Strong Ending

Readers remember beginnings and endings. We already explored what makes a strong beginning: It engages the reader's interest, it's more often specific than general, and it frames the purpose of the paper, defining for the reader where it is headed. A beginning for a research paper should also state its thesis (as in an argumentative essay) or state the question (as in an exploratory essay).

We haven't said anything yet about endings, or "conclusions" as they are traditionally labeled. What's a strong ending? That depends. If you're writing a formal research paper in some disciplines, the basic elements of your conclusion might be prescribed. For example, you might need to summarize major findings and suggest directions for further research. But often, especially if you're writing a less formal research essay, you'll be able select from a wide range of options. For example, in an argumentative research essay, you might end as Figure 4.5 suggests, emphasizing what readers should do about the problem and why it matters. Exploratory essays might end with an anecdote, one that illuminates the understandings the writer has discovered. An ending for either kind of essay might suggest new questions, other avenues for research, or a reconsideration of an initial thesis.

## Endings to Avoid

The ending of your research paper could be a lot of things, and in a way, it's easier to say what it should *not* be:

- Avoid conclusions that simply restate what you've already said. This is the "kick the dead horse" conclusion some of us were taught to write in school on the assumption that our readers probably aren't smart enough to get our point, so we'd better repeat it. This approach annoys most readers, who *are* smart enough to know the horse is dead.

■ Avoid endings that begin with *in conclusion* or *thus.* Words such as these also signal to your reader what she already knows: that your essay is ending. And they often lead into a very general summary, which gets you into a conclusion such as the one mentioned above: dead.

■ Avoid endings that don't feel like endings—that trail off onto other topics, are abrupt, or don't seem connected to what came before them. Prompting your readers to think is one thing; leaving them hanging is quite another.

In some ways, the conclusion of your research paper is the last stop on your journey; the reader has traveled far with you to get there. The most important quality of a good ending is that it adds something to the paper. If it doesn't, cut it and write a new one.

What can the ending add? It can add a further elaboration of your thesis that grows from the evidence you've presented, a discussion of solutions to a problem that has arisen from the information you've uncovered, or perhaps a final illustration or piece of evidence that drives home your point.

Christina Kerby's research essay on method acting explores the controversy over whether this approach is selfish, subverting the playwright's intentions about a character's identity and replacing it with the actor's focus on her own feelings and identity. Christina's ending, however, first transcends the debate by putting method acting in context: It is one of several tools an actor can use to tap her emotions for a role. But then Christina humorously raises the nagging question about selfishness once more: Can we accept that Juliet is not thinking about the fallen Romeo as she weeps by his side but about her dead cat Fluffy? Here's Christina's ending:

```
Acting is no longer about poise, voice qual-
ity, and diction only. It is also about feel-
ing the part, about understanding the emotions
that go into playing the part, and about possess-
ing the skill necessary to bring those emotions
```

to life within the character. . . . Whether an actor
uses Stanislavski's method of physical actions to
unlock the door to her subconscious or whether she
attempts to stir up emotions from deep within herself using Strasberg's method, the actor's goal
is to create a portrayal that is truthful. It is
possible to pick out a bad actor from a mile away,
one who does not understand the role because she
does not understand the emotions necessary to create it. Or perhaps she simply lacks the means of
tapping into them.

If genuine emotion is what the masses
want, method acting may be just what every star-
struck actress needs. Real tears? No problem.
The audience will never know that Juliet was not
lamenting the loss of her true love Romeo but
invoking the memory of her favorite cat Fluffy,
who died tragically in her arms.*

One of the easiest ways to solve the problem of finding a strong
ending is to have the snake bite its tail. In other words, find some
way in the end of your essay to return to where the piece began.
For example, if your research essay began with an anecdote that
dramatized a problem—say, the destruction of old-growth forests
in Washington State—you might return to that opening anecdote,
suggesting how the solutions you explored in your essay might have
changed the outcome. If you pose a question in the first few paragraphs, return to the question in the last few. If you begin with a
profile of someone relevant to your topic, return to him or her in the
end, perhaps amplifying on some part of your picture of the person.
Although this approach is formulaic, it often works well because it
gives a piece of writing a sense of unity.

*Reprinted with permission of Christina B. Kerby.

## Using Surprise

The research process—like the writing process—can be filled with discovery for the writer if he approaches the topic with curiosity and openness. When I began researching lobsters, I was constantly surprised by things I didn't know: Lobsters are bugs; it takes eight years for a lobster in Maine to grow to the familiar one-pound size; the largest lobster ever caught weighed about 40 pounds and lived in a tank at a restaurant for a year, developing a fondness for the owner's wife. I could go on and on. And I did, in the book, sharing unusual information with my readers on the assumption that if it surprised me, it would surprise them, too.

As you write your draft, reflect on the surprising things you discovered about your topic during your research and look for ways to weave that information into the rewrite. Later, after you have written your draft, share it with a reader and ask for his ideas about what is particularly interesting and should be further developed. For now, think about unusual specifics you may have left out.

However, don't include information, no matter how surprising or interesting, that doesn't serve your purpose. For example, Christine's survey on the dreams of college freshmen had some fascinating findings, including some accounts of recurring dreams that really surprised her. She reluctantly decided not to say much about them, however, because they didn't really further the purpose of her paper, which was to discover what function dreams serve. On the other hand, Bob was surprised to find that some politically conservative politicians and judges actually supported decriminalization of marijuana. He decided to include more information in his revision about who they were and what they said, believing it would surprise his readers and strengthen his argument.

# Writing with Sources

The need for *documentation*—that is, citing sources— distinguishes the research paper from most other kinds of writing. And let's face it: Worrying about sources can cramp your style. Many students have an understandable paranoia about plagiarism and tend, as mentioned earlier, to let the voices of their sources overwhelm their own. Students are also often distracted by technical details: Am I getting the right page number? Where exactly should this citation go? Do I need to cite this or not?

As you gain control of the material by choosing your own writing voice and clarifying your purpose in the paper, you should feel less constrained by the technical demands of documentation. The following suggestions may also help you weave reference sources into your own writing without the seams showing.

## The Weave of Research Writing

Imagine that a well-made research essay is a woven piece of fabric made of five colors of thread. Four of the five represent key sources of information from your research: reading, interview, observation, and experience. The fifth thread is the most important of all: your own commentary. This fifth thread is largely missing from a research report, of course, but in a research essay it should be woven throughout the piece, adding color to the beginning and end of the paper, surrounding quotations, wrapping around key arguments and counterarguments, and emerging emphatically as you return again and again to the questions that interest you.

What does this mean, practically speaking? Think of it this way: You have your research question (or thesis), and you have your research. It is the collision of the two that sparks your commentary, whether that's explanation, clarification, analysis, interpretation, argument, or speculation. And where do those two things collide? Wherever one of those other significant threads that you've pulled into your essay appears—a quotation, a table, an interesting fact or report, an anecdote, a case study, field observations, and so on. In other words, whenever you present significant evidence or the voices of others, you should be ready to do your own weaving, braiding your comments into those of outside sources.

Here's an example of what I mean from Ashley Carvalho's research essay in the back of this book (Appendix B, page 231). In this project, Ashley explores how Ireland's so-called "Troubles"—the conflict in the north between Protestants and Catholics, especially in Belfast—ironically helped to inspire medical advances. I've coded each thread with a color:

Writer's commentary (analysis, interpretation, clarification, claim, question, inference, etc.)

Reading

Interview

Observation

Notice how colorful the excerpt is with the thread of Ashley's comments weaving into information she gathered from her reading, interview, and observations. This is the kind of fabric you should create. Later, in the following chapter, you can try coloring your own draft to see what kind of essay you've woven.

The most catastrophic weapon appeared on the stage of the Troubles at the end of 1971. Worried that the British army would not be able to contain the IRA, and wanting to exercise their newfound strength, the loyalist Ulster Volunteer Force (or UVF) in conjunction with the Ulster Defense Association (or UDA) placed a fifty-pound bomb in a small North Belfast Catholic pub called McGurk's Bar. The explosion killed fifteen people and injured many more (McKittrick and McVea 75). This incident marked the debut of the bomb as a means for paramilitary organizations to influence Belfast's street politics.

Bombings provided a sizeable stimulus to Belfast's healthcare services in two ways: first, to develop a system that could provide comprehensive care to the sheer numbers of those injured in a bombing incident, and second, to create new methods of treatment to address the variety of injuries produced in a bomb blast. For example, the McGurk's Bar bombing resulted in a wide range of injury patterns, the worst of which included crush injuries, burn injuries, cranial injuries, lacerations from projectiles, and carbon monoxide poisoning (Gillespie 37–40). . . .

Bomb injuries presented an entirely new set of challenges to Belfast's hospitals. Colin Russell, who worked in the Royal Victoria that day, recalled that mass casualties on this large a scale were an entirely new experience, one that the hospital and its staff weren't totally ready for. "There were horrific injuries," Russell remembers. Making matters worse, this particular bomb was designed to explode outwards, rather than upwards as most bombs do, and the shockwaves from the blast careened along the Abercorn's wooden floors. Trying to contain my horror, I winced inwardly as Russell showed me some slides containing photographs of the horrific injuries that came in to the Royal that day: a chair leg shot through someone's thigh, pieces of amputated limb placed on green towels in the surgical wards, unable to be reunited with the bodies of their owners, faces charred beyond recognition. But none of this prepared me for the emotional shock that came next from Russell's memories: "I remember the senior anesthetist who was on-call at the time, working on one of the victims of the bombing in the operating room. He was completely unaware of the fact that the two sisters who were carrying the bomb and who were killed in the blast were his daughters" (Russell).

The medical progress made in Northern Ireland's hospitals during the Troubles speaks to the remarkable ability of the medical personnel to rise to the challenges posed by the civil violence. Developments in disaster planning, triage, and organization in Northern Ireland's hospitals went

hand-in-hand with the creation of specific medical
treatments to address the needs of civil violence
victims. Throughout the Troubles, paramilitary
violence generated casualties that varied greatly
in the type and pattern of injury as well as in
the numbers of injured, calling attention to the
need for a comprehensive, all-encompassing system
of treatment. In Northern Ireland's hospitals,
the seamless joining of the methods of disaster
planning and the methods of medical treatment
enabled these hospitals to meet the demands
of mass casualty terrorist incidents head-on
throughout the decades of civil violence.

## Handling Quotes

The seams in a research essay often show most when a writer
is using quotations. Understandably, we love to use quotations.
Sometimes a source just says it better than you can. But just as often,
the quotation is the default choice because it is simply *easier.* You don't
have to paraphrase, and you can dodge the danger of plagiarism.

In the section that follows, we'll look at some of the most common
problems that arise when quoting sources and how to solve them.

### Problem #1: Stop and Plop Quotation

The stop and plop quotation is when you suddenly insert a quotation, especially one that might be paraphrased, into the middle of
your own prose without any attribution. Below is an example of this
kind of passive blending of sources into your writing, followed by a
version that is far more active and takes control of the information.

**Passive Blending:**

It's anyone's guess how many people believe in
alien abduction. "One of the earliest studies of
abductions found 1700 claimants, while contested

surveys argued that 5-6 percent of the general
population might have been abducted" (Wallace 4).

A much stronger version would paraphrase the information (it isn't that quotable anyway) and thread it into your paraphrase.

**Active Blending:**

It's anyone's guess how many people believe in
alien abduction, but initial findings were that
1,700 people claimed to have been abducted. Several
"contested" surveys suggested that the number of
abductees' claims might total more than 5 percent
of the population (Wallace 4).

## *Problem #2: Breadless Sandwich Quotation*

The breadless sandwich quotation is another passive approach to using quotations. In this case, the meat (sorry, vegetarians)—the quoted material—is served up without any surrounding commentary or analysis from the writer. Typically you should introduce a quotation with some statement of intention—*why this voice is relevant*—and follow it with interpretation or analysis—*this is what this seems to be saying* or *here's how it addresses the inquiry question or thesis*. Here's what I mean:

**Passive Blending:**

It's easy to dismiss the widespread belief in
alien abduction as a simple delusion suffered by
people who are not quite right. But here's another
view:

> That the abduction phenomenon is frequently
> discussed in popular culture, but is largely
> ignored by establishment sources[,] is not
> socially healthy. By generally refusing even
> to acknowledge the fact that many people are
> suffering from the abduction phenomenon, much
> less to fund research to reveal its cause,

establishment leaders invite the paranoid
fringe to conclude that the "government" is
not only covering up an alien presence, but
worse still is somehow in league with it. Even
the non-paranoid may ask why this phenomenon
is not examined more closely by those in a position to provide a satisfactory explanation
of it. The present essay is in part an attempt
to answer that question (Zimmerman 235).

Mississippian Calvin Parker Jr. is someone who
reported an alien encounter 40 years ago, and he
regretted reporting it until the day he died. . . .

**Active Blending:**   Sandwich a quoted passage—particularly a longer
one—between a brief discussion of your reason for bringing it in (or
to direct readers' attention toward something) and a follow-up commentary that clarifies, summarizes, analyzes, interprets, or otherwise
uses the quotation to move your essay forward.

It's easy to dismiss the widespread belief in
alien abduction as a simple delusion suffered by
people who are not quite right. But even scholars
in reputable journals think that's too narrow a
view because it feeds people's suspicions that
there actually might be something to the claims.
For instance, Michael Zimmerman in *Philosophy
Today* argues that it's not "socially healthy" to
ignore the abduction experience.

That the abduction phenomenon is frequently
discussed in popular culture, but is largely
ignored by establishment sources[,] is not

socially healthy. By generally refusing even
to acknowledge the fact that many people are
suffering from the abduction phenomenon, much
less to fund research to reveal its cause,
establishment leaders invite the paranoid
fringe to conclude that the "government" is not
only covering up an alien presence, but worse
still is somehow in league with it. Even the
non-paranoid may ask why this phenomenon is not
examined more closely by those in a position to
provide a satisfactory explanation of it (235).

Belief in alien abduction, no matter how
crazy it seems, is a cultural phenomenon, and
it's also a belief that Zimmerman observes is
widely shared. To be dismissive of the claims
not only might reinforce the "paranoid fringe"
that believes in a cover-up but also is a missed
opportunity to study the phenomenon itself—how is
it that so many people can hold beliefs that seem
utterly irrational?

Mississippian Calvin Parker Jr. is someone who
reported an alien encounter 40 years ago, and he
regretted reporting it until the day he died. . . .

## Problem #3: The Kitchen Sink Quotation

The easiest thing to do with a quote you like is to use it all, to
throw it all in your essay, kitchen sink and everything. But it's often
far better to pare off the strongest and most relevant lines and passages and blend them into your own writing. To see how this might
work, contrast the use of quotes in this paragraph and in the re-
worked paragraph that follows. I've underlined the quoted material

so that you can visualize the difference between a passage that selectively uses a quotation and one that does not.

### Passive Blending:

> Black Elk often spoke of the importance of the circle to American Indian culture. "You may have noticed that everything an Indian does is in a circle, and that is because the Power of the World always works in circles, and everything tries to be round. . . . The sky is round, and I have heard that the earth is round like a ball, and so are all the stars." He couldn't understand why white people lived in square houses. "It is a bad way to live, for there is not power in a square."

Here the quotes stand out, separate from the writer's own text, but in the revised paragraph they are worked smoothly into the writer's own prose:

### Active Blending:

> Black Elk believed the "Power of the World always works in circles," noting the roundness of the sun, the earth, and the stars. He couldn't understand why white people live in square houses: "It is a bad way to live, for there is not power in a square."

Although long quotes, especially if unintegrated, should usually be avoided, occasionally it may be useful to include a long quotation from one of your sources. A quotation that is longer than four lines should be *blocked,* or set off from the rest of the text by indenting it an inch from the left margin. Like the rest of the paper, a blocked quotation is typed double-spaced. For example:

According to Robert Karen, shame is a particularly modern phenomenon. He notes that in medieval times people pretty much let loose, and by our modern tastes, it was not a pretty sight:

> Their emotional life appears to have been extraordinarily spontaneous and unrestrained. From Johan Huizinga's *The Waning of the Middle Ages,* we learn that the average European town dweller was wildly erratic and inconsistent, murderously violent when enraged, easily plunged into guilt, tears, and pleas for forgiveness, and bursting with psychological eccentricities. He ate with his hands out of a common bowl, blew his nose on his sleeve, defecated openly by the side of the road, made love, and mourned with great passion, and was relatively unconcerned about such notions as maladjustment or what others might think. . . . In post-medieval centuries, what I've called situational shame spread rapidly. . . . (61)

Note that quotation marks are dropped from a blocked quotation. In this case, only part of a paragraph was borrowed, but if you quote one or more full paragraphs, indent the first line of each a quarter inch in addition to the inch the block is indented from the left margin. Note, too, that the writer has introduced this long quote in a way that effectively ties it to his own paper.

We'll examine *parenthetical references* more fully in the next section, but notice how the citation in the blocked quotation above is placed *after* the final period. That's a unique exception to the usual rule that a parenthetical citation is placed *before* the period of the borrowed material's final sentence.

## Other Quick Tips for Controlling Quotations

From our discussion so far, you've seen the hazards and the benefits of using quotations. Quotations from your sources can definitely be overused, especially when they seem dumped into the draft, untouched and unexamined, or used as a lazy substitute for paraphrase. But when it's appropriate, bringing the voices of others into your own writing can bring the work to life and make readers feel as though there is a genuine conversation going on.

You've also seen some basics on how to handle quotes. Here are some specific tips for doing this effectively.

### Grafting Quotes

Frequently, the best way to use quoted material is to graft it onto your own prose. Sometimes you just use a word or phrase:

```
Some words for hangover, like ours, refer prosai-
cally to the cause: the Egyptians say they are
"still drunk," the Japanese "two days drunk," the
Chinese "drunk overnight."*
```

In other situations, especially when you want to add emphasis to what a source has said, you might give over parts of several sentences to a source, like this:

```
The makers of NoHang, on their Web page, say what
your mother would: "It is recommended that you
drink moderately and responsibly." At the same
time, they tell you that with NoHang "you can
drink the night away."*
```

### Billboarding Quotes

Another way you can control quotations is by adding emphasis to billboard parts of a particular quote. Typically you do this by italicizing the phrase or sentence. Here is an example, taken from the end of a block quotation:

*Acocella, Joan. "A Few Too Many." *New Yorker* 26 May 2008: 32–37. Print.

For the sake of Millennials—and, through them, the
future of America—the most urgent adult task is to
*elevate their expectations.* (Emphasis added) (Howe
and Strauss 365)*

Notice that the parenthetical note signals that the original quote has
been altered to add emphasis.

## Splicing Quotes

Sometimes you want to prune away unnecessary information
from a quotation to place emphasis on the part that matters most to
you or to eliminate unnecessary information. Ellipsis points, those
three dots (...) you sometimes see at the beginning, middle, or end of
a sentence, signal that some information has been omitted.

Take this passage, for example:

During the Gen-X child era, the American family
endured countless new movements and trends—
feminism, sexual freedom, a divorce epidemic,
fewer G-rated movies, child-raising handbooks
telling parents to "consider yourself" ahead of a
child's needs, gay rights, Chappaquiddick, film
nudity, a Zero Population Growth ethic, *Kramer vs.
Kramer,* and *Roe v. Wade.* A prominent academic in
1969 proclaimed in the *Washington Post* that the
family needed a "decent burial."

That's a pretty long list of movements and trends, and the
reader could get a taste without being served up the whole thing.
Ellipsis points can help:

During the Gen-X child era, the American family
endured countless new movements and trends—
feminism, sexual freedom, a divorce epidemic...,

*Howe, Neil, and William Strauss. *Millennials Rising.* New York: Vintage, 2000. Print.

> [and a] prominent academic in 1969 proclaimed
> in the *Washington Post* that the family needed a
> "decent burial."

When you have to slightly reword the original text or alter the punctuation for a smoother splice, put the alteration in brackets. In the example above, for instance, I turned what was a separate sentence in the original into a compound sentence using the conjunction *and*.

## Handling Interview Material

The great quotes you glean from your interviews can be handled like quotations from texts. But there's a dimension to a quote from an interview that's lacking in a quote from a book: Namely, you participated in the quote's creation by asking a question, and in some cases, you were there to observe your subject saying it. This presents some new choices. When you're quoting an interview subject, should you enter your essay as a participant in the conversation, or should you stay out of the way? That is, should you describe yourself asking the question? Should you describe the scene of the interview, your subject's manner of responding, or your immediate reaction to what she said? Or should you merely report what was said and who said it?

Christina's essay, "Crying Real Tears: The History and Psychology of Method Acting," makes good use of interviews. Notice how Christina writes about one of them in the middle of her essay:

> During a phone interview, I asked my act-
> ing teacher, Ed Claudio, who studied under
> Stella Adler, whether or not he agreed with
> the ideas behind method acting. I could almost
> see him wrinkle his nose at the other end of
> the connection. He described method acting as
> "self-indulgent," insisting that it encourages
> "island acting." Because of emotional recall,
> acting has become a far more personal art, and

```
the actor began to move away from the script,
often hiding the author's purpose and intentions
under his own.*
```

Contrast Christina's handling of the Claudio interview with her treatment of material from an interview with Dave Pierini later in her essay:

```
Dave Pierini, a local Sacramento actor, pointed
out, "You can be a good actor without using
method, but you cannot be a good actor without at
least understanding it." Actors are perhaps some
of the greatest scholars of the human psyche be-
cause they devote their lives to the study and
exploration of it. Aspiring artists are told to
"get inside of the character's head." They are
asked, "How would the character feel? How would
the character react?"*
```

Do you think Christina's entry into her report of the first interview (with Ed Claudio) is intrusive? Or do you think it adds useful information or even livens it up? What circumstances might make this a good move? On the other hand, what might be some advantages of the writer staying out of the way and simply letting her subject speak, as Christina chooses to do in her treatment of the interview with Dave Pierini?

## Trusting Your Memory

One of the best ways to weave references seamlessly into your own writing is to avoid the compulsion to stop and study your sources as you're writing the draft. I remember that writing my research papers in college was typically done in stops and starts. I'd write a

*Reprinted with permission of Christina B. Kerby.

paragraph of the draft, then stop and reread a photocopy of an article, then write a few more sentences, and then stop again. Part of the problem was the meager notes I took as I collected information. I hadn't really taken possession of the material before I started writing the draft. But I also didn't trust that I'd remember what was important from my reading.

If, during the course of your research and writing so far, you've found a sense of purpose—for example, you're pretty sure your paper is going to argue for legalization of marijuana or analyze the symbolism on old gravestones on Cape Cod—then you've probably read purposefully, too. You *will* likely know what reference sources you need as you write the draft, without sputtering to a halt to remind yourself of what each says. Consult your notes and sources as you need them; otherwise, push them aside, and immerse yourself in your own writing.

## Citing Sources to Tell a Story

Writers of popular articles often use research, and they don't have to cite their sources; so why do academic writers? The simple answer is that scholarly researchers attempt to *build knowledge,* and this involves establishing who has said what before them on a topic. A more interesting way of looking at it is that through citation, academic writers tell a story, one that enlists some of the relevant actors on a research topic—who they were, what they said, what they found, where they agreed and disagreed—and from this, academic writers add their own narratives, extending the story these others started. In a way, then, citations are like the screen credits in a movie, except, of course, they don't come just at the end.

You'll be citing sources *in* your essay next to material that you borrowed, and these are keyed to references at the end of your essay.

There are three or four major citation systems, but the big two are the APA and the MLA. APA is the system of choice in the social sciences, while MLA is associated with the humanities. The big difference between the two is that APA emphasizes *when* something was published whereas MLA highlights *who* said it.

Before you begin writing your draft, go to Appendix B or C and read the sections under "Citing Sources in Your Essay." These will describe in some detail when and where you should put parenthetical references to borrowed material in the draft of your essay. Don't worry too much about the guidelines for preparing the final manuscript, including how to do the bibliography. You can deal with that next week.

# Driving Through the First Draft

You have an opening, a lot of material in your notes—much of it, written in your own words—and maybe an outline. You've considered some general methods of development, looked at ways to write with sources, and completed a quick course in how to cite them. Finish the week by writing through the first draft.

Writing the draft may be difficult. All writing, but especially research writing, is a recursive process. You may find sometimes that you must circle back to a step you took before, discovering a gap in your information, a new idea for a thesis statement, or a better lead or focus. Circling back may be frustrating at times, but it's natural and even a good sign: It means you're letting go of your preconceived ideas and allowing the discoveries you make *through writing* to change your mind.

It's too early to worry about writing a research paper that's airtight, with no problems to solve. Too often, student writers think they have to write a perfect paper in the first draft. You can worry about plugging holes and tightening things up next week. For now, write a draft, and if you must, put a reminder on a piece of paper and post it on the computer next to your thesis statement or research question. Look at this reminder every time you find yourself agonizing over the imperfections of your paper. The reminder should say, "It Doesn't Count."

Keep a few other things in mind while writing your first draft:

1. *Focus on your tentative thesis or your research question.* In the draft, consider your thesis a theory you're trying to prove but are willing to change. If your paper is more exploratory than argumentative, use your focusing question as a reminder of what you want to know. Remember, your question and thesis can change, too, as you learn more about your subject.
2. *Vary your sources.* Offer a variety of different sources as evidence to support your assertions. Beware of writing a single page that cites only one source.
3. *Remember your audience.* What do your readers want to know about your topic? What do they need to know to understand what you're trying to say?
4. *Write with your notes.* If you took thoughtful notes during the third week—carefully transforming another author's words into your own, flagging good quotes, and developing your own analysis—then you've already written at least some of your paper. You may only need to fine-tune the language in your notes and then plug them into your draft.

5. *Be open to surprises.* The act of writing is often full of surprises. In fact, it should be, because *writing* is *thinking,* and the more you think about something, the more you're likely to see. You might get halfway through your draft and discover the part of your topic that *really* fascinates you. Should that happen, you may have to change your thesis or throw away your outline. You may even have to reresearch your topic, at least somewhat. It's not necessarily too late to shift the purpose or focus of your paper (though you should consult your instructor before totally abandoning your topic at this point). Let your curiosity remain the engine that drives you forward.

CHAPTER **5**

# The Fifth Week

---

**IN THIS CHAPTER, YOU'LL LEARN TO...**

- Identify problems in your draft that involve purpose, thesis, question, or structure and apply revision strategies to address those problems.

- Learn techniques to find quick facts on the Web, and use those facts to fill factual gaps in your essay.

- Understand persona as a rhetorical concept, and analyze the persona in your draft.

- Identify problems with integrating sources, organizing paragraphs, and writing strong sentences, and apply techniques for rewriting and copy-editing that address these problems.

- Analyze the appearance of your essay, and consider approaches to make it have a more reader-friendly design.

---

## Revision Is Re-Seeing (or Breaking Up Is Hard to Do)

My high school girlfriend, Jan, was bright, warmhearted, and fun, and I wasn't at all sure I liked her much—at least at first. Though we had a lot in common—we both loved sunrises over Lake Michigan, bird watching, and Simon and Garfunkel—I found Jan a little intimidating, a little too much in a hurry to anoint us a solid "couple." But we stuck together for three years, and as time passed, I persuaded myself—despite lingering doubts—that I couldn't live without her. There was no way I was going to break my white-knuckled hold on that relationship. After all, I'd invested all that time.

As a writer, I used to have similar relationships with my drafts. I'd work on something very hard, finally finishing the draft. I'd know there were problems, but I'd developed such a tight relationship with my draft that the problems were hard to see. And even when I recognized some problems, the thought of making major changes seemed too risky. Did I dare ruin the things I loved about the draft? These decisions were even harder if the draft had taken a long time to write.

Revision doesn't necessarily mean you have to sever your relationship with your draft. It's probably too late to make a complete break with the draft and abandon your topic. However, revision does demand finding some way to step back from the draft and change your relationship with it, trying to see it more from the reader's perspective than the writer's. Revision requires that you loosen your grip. And when you do, you may decide to shift your focus or rearrange the information. At the very least, you may discover gaps in information or sections of the draft that need more development. You will certainly need to prune sentences.

You've spent more than four weeks researching your topic and the last few days composing your first draft. You may find that you've spent so much time seeing one vision of your topic, the way you chose to see it in your first draft—that doing a major revision is about as appealing as eating canned beets. How do you get the perspective to "re-see" the draft and rebuild it into a stronger paper?

# Global Revision: Revising for Purpose, Thesis, and Structure

Your instinct when you revise may be to take out the microscope rather than the binoculars. But if revision is a process of re-seeing—of not just shutting things down but opening them up—then your rewrite this week should begin with the whole rather than with the details. Rather than trying to "fix" the small things—grammar, citations, diction, and so on—take the large view. Ask yourself these questions: What is my draft trying to do? How well does it do it? And, especially, will it make sense to someone else?

## Writer- to Reader-Based Prose

Writing theorist Linda Flower distinguishes between "writer-based prose" and "reader-based prose." When we first start writing about something in notebooks, journals, and sometimes first drafts, we are our own audience. Sure, we might have a vague sense that someone else will be reading what we write, but often our energies are focused on whether it makes sense to us. "Writer-based prose" like this often works from the tacit assumption that readers and writers share the same understanding and knowledge about a topic. As a result, writers may assume that certain things that should be explained don't need to be. Writers may also assume that the things they find interesting or relevant will also be interesting or relevant to their readers. In "reader-based prose," writers have confronted these assumptions. They have revised their work with their readers in mind.

Reading anything is work. Most of us are willing to do the work if we sense that an author is taking us somewhere interesting. More specifically, readers must trust that writers know what they're doing—the writers have a destination in mind, they are reliable guides, and the journey will likely yield something worth knowing or thinking about.

One way to see if your draft research essay is sufficiently "reader-based" is to determine whether it does three things that all essays must do (see Figure 5.1):

- *Have a clear purpose:* What exactly did you want to find out in this investigation of your topic? What is your research question?
- *Establish why the question (and its answer) are significant:* What stake might readers have in your inquiry?
- *Say one main thing:* Among the possible answers to the question you pose, which one seems most persuasive, most significant, or most revealing?

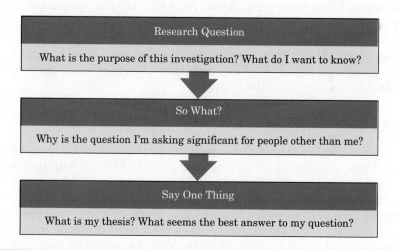

**FIGURE 5.1** **Three Things the Essay Must Do.** As you revise your draft, you can measure your progress by asking whether you've answered these three basic questions: *Is the question I'm asking clear and sufficiently limited? Have I answered the "So what?" question? Is there one most important thing I'm trying to say?* If your draft explicitly answers each of these, then the boat at least will float and have a clear destination.

## Is It Organized Around a Clear Purpose?

Purpose, like a torch, lights the way in the darkness. It illuminates one part of your subject, helping to guide your readers in the direction you want them to go. You should determine whether the purpose of your paper is clear and examine how well the information is organized around that purpose.

Presumably, by now you know the purpose of your essay. You know, for instance, whether you're exploring or arguing. But what exactly are you exploring or arguing? Your ability to state this purpose as clearly as you can is a great foundation for revision this week. Try completing one of the following sentences:

**For an exploratory essay:**   The main purpose of my essay on _____ is to explore _____. In particular, I will consider the questions raised by _____ and _____ as well as _____.

**For an argument essay:**   Because of _____ and _____ as well as _____, in this essay I am arguing _____.

Another way of getting at purpose is to clarify your research question, something that you were working on last week. Is it time to revise it again? For example, Amanda's piece on tooth whitening began with this research question: *How has cosmetic tooth-whitening changed the way Americans feel about their teeth?* After a few clarifications she made as she learned more, Amanda had this question: *How does the tooth-whitening trend reflect our culture's quickly changing definitions of beauty, and what does that mean for people who don't fit that definition?*

Go back to the beginning. What was your initial research question? What is it now? If you're struggling with this, revist "Refining the Question" in Chapter 4, page 152.

Yet another way of checking purpose is to see whether in your draft your sources are all serving your purpose. Writing with research is a wrestling match. You're the 120-pound weakling who may not have written many college research essays before, trying to take on the heavyweight experts on your topic. You're fighting for your life, trying to use what these authorities say or think for your own purpose without getting slammed to the floor for meekly submitting a report rather than an essay. The challenge is to get control of the information, to muscle it to the ground using the strength of your purpose. Establishing this control is one of the hardest parts of drafting research papers. Two extreme responses to this problem are giving up entirely and turning your paper over to your sources (letting them do all the talking) and pretending that you're not really wrestling with anyone and writing a paper that includes only your own opinions. Neither option is what you want.

Who won the wrestling match in your draft? To what extent did you have a coherent purpose and succeed in using other people's ideas and information in the service of your purpose? One way to see who is getting the upper hand in the draft is to mark it up, noting where you've given control to your sources and where you've taken it back. Exercise 5.1 can graphically illustrate who is winning the wrestling match. To what extent is your purpose in the essay enabling you to *use* the information you've gathered to explore your research question or prove your point? The exercise will also reveal how well you've managed to surround your research with your own analysis, interpretations, arguments, and questions.

## EXERCISE 5.1

### Wrestling with the Draft*

For this exercise you'll use two highlighters, each a different color.

1. Choose a random page or two of your draft, somewhere in the middle.
2. First mark the parts in which you're a less active author. As you read the page, highlight every sentence that reports facts, quotes sources, or otherwise presents information or ideas that belong to someone else.
3. Now, using the other highlighter, mark the parts in which you're a more active author. Read the same page or pages again, but this time highlight every sentence or paragraph that represents *your* ideas, analysis, commentary, interpretation, definition, synthesis, or claims.
4. Repeat the previous steps with two more pages of your draft.

Which color dominates? Are you turning over too much of the text to your sources? Are you ignoring them and rattling on too much about what you think? Or does your source use seem appropriate to support your purpose?

In addition, look at the pattern of color. What do you notice about this pattern? Are you taking turns paragraph by paragraph

---

*This exercise is adapted from one I borrowed from my colleague Dr. Mike Mattison, who borrowed it from his former colleagues at the University of Massachusetts–Amherst. Thanks to all.

with your sources, or is your own analysis and commentary nicely blended *within* paragraphs so that the information is always anchored to your own thoughts? Do you surround quoted passages with your own voice and analysis? Who wins the wrestling match? See Figure 5.2 for an example of this exercise.

Our tooth whiteners are safer, and a study by James W. Curtis, DMD, discovered that bleaching through carbamide peroxide actually decreases the amount of plaque on teeth, but we're still doing it for beauty reasons rather than health ones (Nuss 28).

In her article "Bright On," Molly Prior notes that Procter & Gamble and Colgate-Palmolive revolutionized the whitening industry by bringing over-the-counter whiteners to drugstores everywhere at the turn of the twenty-first century (39). No longer did people have to pay high prices for professional whitening—they could do it themselves, at home, for a reasonable cost. In the past, a patient had to eat a bill of $1,000 for a laser whitening treatment, or $10,000 for a full set of veneers; now a package of Crest Whitestrips retails for only $29.99 (Gideonse). Suddenly, whiter teeth were available to everyone. While a shining smile once indicated wealth and the ability to splurge on cosmetic dentistry, it became affordable to the dentally discolored masses eager to emulate the lifestyles of the people they saw in magazines and on television.

Companies didn't create whitening products to fill a demand created by the public for whiter teeth. While Hollywood glitterati did pay high prices

**FIGURE 5.2   Amanda Wins the Wrestling Match.** The sections of text highlighted in gray are passages from Amanda's sources, and the sections highlighted in blue are passages in which she is commenting, clarifying, asserting, or interpreting. Notice the balance between gray and blue. Clearly Amanda has a strong authorial presence. Also notice how quotations are surrounded by her commentary. By controlling quotations like this, she is also using rather than being used by her sources.

*for iconic smiles, most people seemed happy with functional teeth. However, companies saw money to be made in creating a whiter norm for teeth, so they barraged the airwaves with advertisements featuring people complaining about the dullness and imperfection of their teeth. Natural teeth were denigrated as ugly. Crest and Colgate-Palmolive wanted to make money, so they appealed to the American obsession with beauty to secure a financial reason to smile. As Jonathan Levine, DDS, notes, "It's lately seeming much harder to go broke by overestimating the vanity of the American public" (Walker). The companies succeeded in making mouthfuls of money, netting $450 million and getting 45 percent of Americans to try some form of whitening (Prior 42). In effect, they appealed to our egos to get to our pocket books.*

---

**FIGURE 5.2**   (Continued)

## Does It Establish Significance?

So what? That's the blunt question here. Any reader will need a *reason* to care about what you have to say. So what reasons might there be for someone to care about a research essay on theories of intelligence, or an investigation of video game addiction, or an argument about what should be done about dog poop in city parks? In other words, what stake might readers have in the question you are exploring? Your mother will think nearly anything you write is significant. But what might make someone else consider that you have important things to say? Here are five possible reasons. Do any apply to your draft and, if so, do you emphasize the significance of your inquiry enough?

Readers may find your discussion of a topic significant if:

1. *It raises questions they want to know the answers to.* As a pet owner, I'm interested in theories of dog training because Fred digs in the garden.
2. *It helps them to see what they've seen before in a way they haven't seen it.* Is the destruction of jack pines in Yellowstone National Park really being caused by global warming and not the drought, as I had assumed?

3. *It amplifies what they may already know and care about, leading to new learning.* I play video games and know they're habit forming, but I didn't know the effects on my brain of my playing them.
4. *It moves them emotionally.* The story of the failure of Haitian relief efforts in protecting the health and welfare of children is heartbreaking. Something should be done about it. But what?
5. *It takes a surprising point of view.* The research leads you to believe that decriminalizing marijuana will actually reduce its use.

You should be able to read your draft and see exactly where you establish the significance of your project to your readers, perhaps touching on one or more of the five reasons above. Is this content sufficient or is there more you might say?

## Does It Say One Thing?

When I write an exploratory essay, I'm essentially in pursuit of a point and, not infrequently, it playfully eludes me. Just when I think I've figured out exactly what I'm trying to say, I have the nagging feeling that it's not quite right—it's too simplistic or obvious, it doesn't quite account for the evidence I've collected, or it just doesn't capture the spirit of the discoveries I've made. A thesis is often a slippery fish—just when I think I've figured out what I think, I start to think something else.

A thesis can present different problems in an argumentative essay. As we saw in the last chapter, it can become a club—rigid and unyielding—that we use to beat a draft into submission. Yet, the very reason to do research is to *test* your ideas about things, and as your draft evolves, so should your thesis.

Now is a good time to consider revising your thesis again. Does it accurately capture what you're trying to say—or *think* you're trying to say? Is it specific enough? Is it interesting? If you need to, return to "Refining the Thesis" on page 153 in the Chapter 4 to rework your main idea.

## Using a Reader

If you wanted to save or improve a relationship, you might ask a friend for advice. Then you'd get the benefit of a third-party opinion, a fresh view that could help you see what you may be too close to see.

A reader can do the same thing for your research paper draft. She will come to the draft without the entanglements that encumber the writer and provide a fresh pair of eyes through which you can see the work. Your reader can tell you what kind of guide you are in the draft: Is it clear where you're headed, why it's significant, and what your most important discovery is?

Your instructor may be that reader, or you might exchange drafts with someone else in class. You may already have someone whom you share your writing with—a roommate, a friend. Whomever you choose, try to find a reader who will respond honestly *and* make you want to write again.

What will be most helpful from a reader at this stage? Comments about your spelling and mechanics are not critical right now. You'll deal with those factors later. For now, the most useful feedback will focus on whether there's a disconnect between what you *intend* in your draft and how a reader understands those intentions.

## EXERCISE 5.2

### Directing the Reader's Response

Though you could ask your reader for a completely open-ended reaction to your paper, the following questions might help her focus on providing comments that will help you tackle a revision:

1. After reading the draft, what would you say is the main question the paper is trying to answer or focus on?
2. In your own words, what is the main point?
3. What did you learn about the topic after reading the paper that you didn't fully appreciate *before* you read it? Is this something you find significant or interesting? If so, why?

How your reader responds to the first two questions will tell you a lot about how well you've succeeded in making the purpose and thesis of your paper clear. The answer to the third question will too, but it may also tell you whether you've established the significance of your project.

## Reviewing the Structure

In addition to focusing on your paper in terms of its purpose and thesis, this global revision is also about focusing on structure. If you did Exercise 5.1, about purpose, you've already begun to take a closer look at the structure of your essay. There are various other ways of focusing on structure, including using your thesis.

## Using Your Thesis to Revise

The payoff for crafting a stronger thesis is huge. As you will see in Exercise 5.3, a thesis can help you decide what to put in your essay and what to leave out, and in research-based writing, this is a decision that comes up again and again.

# EXERCISE 5.3

### Cut-and-Paste Revision

Try this cut-and-paste revision exercise (a useful technique inspired by Peter Elbow and his book *Writing with Power**):

1. On a notecard or sticky note, write your focusing question, thesis, or main idea. Make sure that it is plainly stated and fully captures what you think you're trying to say or explore in your research essay. Set it aside.

2. Photocopy or print two copies of your first draft (one-sided pages only). Save the original; you may need it later.

3. Cut apart a copy of your research paper, paragraph by paragraph. (You may cut it into even smaller pieces later.) Once the draft has been completely disassembled, shuffle the paragraphs—get them wildly out of order so the original draft is just a memory.

4. Retrieve the notecard or sticky note with your thesis on it, and set it before you. Now work your way through the stack of paragraphs and make two new stacks: one of paragraphs that are relevant to your thesis or question and one of paragraphs that don't seem relevant, that don't seem to serve a clear purpose in developing your main idea or question. Be as tough as a drill sergeant as you scrutinize each scrap of paper. What you are trying to determine is whether each piece of information, each paragraph, is there for a reason. Ask yourself this question as you examine each paragraph:

> *Does this paragraph (or part of a paragraph) develop my thesis or address my question and further the purpose of my paper, or does it seem an unnecessary tangent that could be part of another paper with a different focus?*

*Elbow, Peter. *Writing with Power.* New York: Oxford University Press, 1981. Print.

For example,

- Does it provide important *evidence* that supports my main point?
- Does it *explain* something that's key to understanding what I'm trying to say?
- Does it *illustrate* a key concept?
- Does it help establish the *importance* of what I'm trying to say?
- Does it raise (or answer) a *question* that I must explore, given what I'm trying to say?

You might find it helpful to write on the back of each relevant paragraph which of these specific purposes it serves. You may also discover that *some* of the information in a paragraph seems to serve your purpose while the rest strikes you as unnecessary. Use your scissors to cut away the irrelevant material, pruning back the paragraph to include only what's essential.

5. You now have two stacks of paper scraps: those that seem to support your thesis or research question and serve your purpose and those that don't. For now, set aside your "reject" pile. Begin to reassemble a very rough draft using what you've saved. Play with order. Try new leads, new ends, new middles. As you spread out the pieces of information before you, see if a new structure suddenly emerges. *But especially, look for gaps—places where you should add information.* On a piece of paper, jot down ideas for material you might add; then cut up this paper as well and insert these in the appropriate places. You may rediscover uses for information in your "reject" pile as well. Mine that pile, if you need to.

6. As a structure begins to emerge, reassemble the draft by taping together the fragments of paper, including the ideas for new information and any rejects you've decided to use after all. Don't worry about transitions; you'll deal with those later. When you're done with the reconstruction, the draft might look totally unlike the version you started with.

**Examining the Wreckage.** If you did Exercise 5.3, as you dealt with the wreckage your scissors wrought on your first draft, you might have discovered that the information in your draft suggested a revision of your thesis or inquiry question, pointed toward another thesis or question, or simply suggested that it was unworkable.

To your horror, you may have found that your "reject" pile of paragraphs is bigger than your "save" pile. If that's the case, you won't have much left to work with. You may need to reresearch the topic (returning to the library or going online this week to collect more information) or shift the focus of your paper. Perhaps both. But even if your cut-and-paste went well, you will likely need to do more research this week to fill the gaps you found. That's perfectly normal.

To your satisfaction, you may have discovered that your reconstructed draft looks familiar. You may have returned to the structure you started with in the first draft. If that's the case, it might mean your first draft worked pretty well; breaking it down and putting it back together confirmed that and showed you where you might need to prune and fine-tune.

When Jeff cut up his essay "The Alcoholic Family," he discovered immediately that much of his paper did not seem clearly related to his point about the role outsiders can play in helping the family of an alcoholic. His "reject" pile had paragraph after paragraph of information about the roles that other family members take on when there's an alcoholic in the house. Jeff asked himself, What does that information have to do with the roles of outsiders? He considered changing his thesis to say something about how each family member plays a role in dealing with the drinker. But Jeff's purpose in writing the paper was to discover what *he,* as an outsider, could do to help.

As Jeff played with the pieces of his draft, he began to see two things. First of all, he realized that some of the ways members behave in an alcoholic family make them resistant to outside help; this insight allowed him to salvage some information from his "reject" pile by more clearly connecting the information to his main point. Second, Jeff knew he had to go back to the well: He needed to return to the library and recheck his sources to find more information on what family friends can do to help.

When you slice up your draft and play with the pieces, you are experimenting with the basic architecture of your essay. If the result is going to hold up, certain fundamentals must be in place. You need to be transforming your draft in a direction that is making it more "reader based," with a clear purpose, significance, and point.

## Other Ways of Reviewing the Structure

Exercise 5.3, "Cut-and-Paste Revision," invited you to experiment with the organization of your draft by disassembling and then rebuilding your essay, imagining different ways to order information. Its starting point was the thesis. There are other starting points for an examination of structure. Here are a few of these alternative starting points:

**Type of Essay.**    The structure of a research essay is partly a function of the type of essay—of whether you are writing an exploratory or an argumentative essay. Depending on the type of essay you're writing, return to Figure 4.2 or 4.4 in the last chapter for an idea about how to organize your paper.

**Lead.**    How you begin your paper has a huge influence on how it develops from there. As we discussed in Chapter 4, a lead or introduction should not only draw readers in but also dramatize or introduce the dilemma, problem, question, or argument that is the focus of your inquiry. You might find a stronger lead buried in the middle of your draft. Try it as an alternative introduction and follow it from there.

**Logical Structure.**    In a very general sense, most writing can be said to be structured by either narrative or logic. Essays that focus on the writer's experience tend to rely on some form of narrative structure, though it may not be chronological. Essays that focus on a subject other than the writer often rely on structures that reflect a pattern of reasoning. (And many research essays might employ both types of structures because they can be experiential *and* focused on a subject other than the writer.) Most of us have more experience with narrative structures; after all, part of being human is telling stories. Logical structures are less familiar. They usually spring from either a question or a thesis (or both) and are designed to methodically explore a question or prove a point. Consider various ways essays might do this:

- Thesis to proof
- Problem to solution
- Question to answer
- Comparison and contrast
- Cause and effect, or effect and cause
- Known to unknown or unknown to known
- Simple to complex

Review your draft with these possible structures in mind. You may see a way to strengthen it by reshaping its structure to better fit one of these structures. Remember that while your research essay might generally use one of the logical structures, often a piece of writing that generally uses one structure uses others as microstructures. For example, an essay that has a comparison-and-contrast structure might have elements of narrative.

# Reresearching

I know. You thought you were done digging. But as I said last week, research is a recursive process. (Remember, the word is *research,* or "look again.") You will often find yourself circling back to the earlier steps as you get a clearer sense of where you want to go. I want to emphasize this. It's actually *unusual,* after you've written a draft, to discover that you're done with research. This means returning to the library databases, trying a different Google Scholar search, going back to interview someone, or returning to the field for more observations. You've got the skills now to do this. Make time for it.

As you stand back from your draft, looking again at how well your research paper addresses your research question or thesis, you'll likely see holes in the information. They may seem more like craters. Jeff discovered he had to reresearch his topic, returning to the library to hunt for new sources to help him develop his point. Because he had enough time, he repeated some of the research steps from the third week. This time, though, he knew exactly what he needed to find.

You may find that you basically have the information you need but that your draft requires more development. Candy's draft on how child abuse affects language included material from some useful studies from the *Journal of Speech and Hearing Disorders,* which showed pretty conclusively that abuse cripples children's abilities to converse. At her reader's suggestion, Candy decided it was important to write more in her revision about what was learned from the studies, because they offered convincing evidence for her thesis. Though she could mine her notes for more information, Candy decided to recheck the journal databases to look for any similar studies she may have missed.

## Finding Quick Facts

If you're lucky, the holes of information in your research paper draft will not be large at all. What's missing may be an important but discrete fact that would really help your readers understand the point you're making. For example, when Janabeth looked over her draft on the impact of divorce on father-daughter relationships, she realized she was missing an important fact: the number of marriages that end in divorce in the United States. This single piece of information could help establish the significance of the problem she was writing about. And Janabeth could obtain it by simply looking online.

One of the Internet's greatest strengths is its usefulness in searching for specific facts. What are the ingredients in a Big Mac? How high is the Great Wall of China? How many high school kids in Illinois go on to college? What does a map of Brazilian deforestation look like? A quick click or two and the Web can yield a rich harvest of facts and information. Google and similar search engines are naturally where we start looking for that kind of information, and because what you want to know is pretty specific, there's a good chance you'll find what you're looking for. But there are some particularly useful statistical references on the Web that you might want to check out as well.

## Facts on the Web

### General

- *American Factfinder* (http://factfinder2.census.gov). A rich site maintained by the U.S. Census Bureau. It includes data on population and economic trends, both national and local.
- *FedStats* (http://www.fedstats.gov). A superstore of statistical resources that allows users to find information from all U.S. government agencies.
- Refdesk.com (http://refdesk.com). Links to the usual references—dictionaries, biographical indexes, encyclopedias, and government information.
- *STATS America* (http://www.statsamerica.org). Search page allows users to find a range of data for states and counties in the United States, including facts on demographics, economics, education, and the workforce.

### Subject Specific

#### Crime

- *National Criminal Justice Reference Service* (http://www.ncjrs.gov). Allows keyword searches to find not just facts but articles on crime, drug abuse, corrections, juvenile justice, and more.

#### Education

- *National Center for Educational Statistics* (http://nces.ed.gov). The U.S. Department of Education site includes statistics on everything related to schooling in the United States and also features an annual report on the state of education.

*(continued)*

### Economics

- *Bureau of Economic Analysis* (http://www.bea.gov/). This U.S. Department of Commerce site includes statistics on key economic indicators, trade, corporate profits, and much more.

### Energy

- *U.S. Energy Information Administration* (http://www.eia .doe.gov/). Includes use forecasts, environmental impacts, reserves, alternative energy information, and much more.

### Health

- *National Center for Health Statistics* (http://www.cdc.gov/ nchs). Offers information about injuries, diseases, life-styles, death rates, and more provided by the Centers for Disease Control.

### International

- *U.N. Food and Agricultural Organization* (http://www.fao .org/corp/statistics/en/). The FAO site allows users to search not just for statistics on food and hunger but also for information on such topics as world foresty practices and water issues.
- *NationMaster* (http://www.nationmaster.com). Drawing in part from the *CIA Factbook* and UN information, Nation-Master will also generate interesting maps and graphics on a wide range of subjects.

In addition to these Web resources, the standard print texts for researchers hunting down facts and statistics are still quite useful. They include the *Statistical Abstracts of the United States,* the *Information Please Almanac, Facts on File,* and the *World Almanac Book of Facts*—all published annually. A number of these are now available on the Web.

Like the online sources mentioned, these fact books can be especially valuable resources when you need to plug small holes in your draft. But even if you're not sure whether you can glean a useful statistic from one of these sources, they might be worth checking anyway. There's a good chance you'll find something useful.

# Local Revision: Revising for Language

Most of my students have the impression that revision begins and ends with concerns about language—that it's about *how* they say it rather than *what* they say. Revising for language is really a tertiary concern (though an important one) to be addressed after the writer has dealt with global revision: clear purpose, significance, and thesis as well as structure.

Once you're satisfied that your paper's purpose is clear, that it provides readers with the information they need to understand what you're trying to say, and that it is organized in a logical, interesting way, *then* focus your attention on the fine points of *how* it is written. Begin with voice.

## Who Are You in Your Draft?

Yesterday was Halloween here in Boise, Idaho, and I made numerous costume sightings on campus: a yellow dog, a Red Sox player, and a weird guy with a sword. This is a holiday that celebrates alternate personas, masking our usual identities and trying out others. To some extent we do this when we write, too. We imagine the kind of person we're supposed to be in a piece of writing, assumptions that may arise from our understanding of what's expected in the genre we're writing in or the audience we're writing for. But just as often, we adopt personas in writing purely out of habit: "This is how I write for school." Of all the writing assignments in college, the research paper might be the most plagued by unexamined assumptions about how it's "supposed to" sound.

However, persona in writing is a rhetorical choice, just like deciding to write a letter instead of a memo to a close friend. How do you decide on the persona that's appropriate for this essay?

1. Ask your instructor.
2. Consider your purpose. What are you trying *to do* and *to whom* are you trying to speak?
3. How much does your intended audience know about your topic? Typically, more expert audiences expect a more formal tone and treatment than do less knowledgeable audiences.
4. Consider the genre. Are there established conventions on persona that you might need to follow?

## Managing Persona Through Diction and Style

If you have a Facebook account, you already know how to manage a persona. In school writing, it's not all that different—you may not be able to post a new profile pic, but you can control your diction and your point of view. We've already talked about point of view in the last chapter (see page 141): Will you write your essay in the first-person singular? The decision to write, "I'm convinced that professional cycling is a corrupt sport" is different from the decision to write, "This paper argues that it's corrupt" or "One believes that it's corrupt." The latter two variations create a more distanced, "objective" persona. But there are also somewhat more subtle ways of managing persona in your writing. Consider, for example, the following different ways the same sentence might be written by controllng word choice and style:

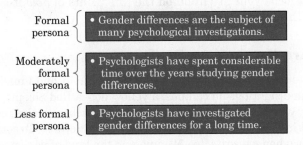

Formal persona
- Gender differences are the subject of many psychological investigations.

Moderately formal persona
- Psychologists have spent considerable time over the years studying gender differences.

Less formal persona
- Psychologists have investigated gender differences for a long time.

You might notice the following differences in each version:

1. ***Passive or active voice:*** "Gender differences are the subject of investigations" vs. "***Psychologists*** have investigated gender differences." Passive voice is more formal. (See page 207 for more discussion of active voice in writing.)
2. ***Level of style:*** The phrase "have spent considerable time" is more formal than the phrase "for a long time."
3. ***Verb choice:*** "Investigated" is a slightly livelier (and less formal) verb than "studied."

Beware, though, of a voice that calls more attention to itself than to the substance of what you're saying.

Sometimes, in an attempt to sound natural, a writer will take on a folksy or overly colloquial voice, which is much worse than sounding dry and flat. What impression does the following passage have on you?

```
The thing that really blew my mind was that
marijuana use among college students had actually
declined in the past ten years! I was psyched to
learn that.
```

## Tightening the Seams Between What You Say and What They Say

One of the basic challenges of writing with sources is integrating them seamlessly. In the past, you may have practiced the "data dump" strategy, or simply dropped factual information into your papers in little or big clumps. Of course, this won't do. Not only does it make the writing horribly dull, but it means that you're not *making use* of the information you worked so hard to find. Surrounding your sources with your own prose and according to your own purposes is an important skill you need to learn, and it's something we discussed at length in Chapter 4 (see "The Weave of Research Writing" on page 171) and looked at Exercise 5.1 earlier in this chapter.

In particular, think about the following points:

■ *Find your own way of saying things.* This is one of the best ways to take possession of information.

■ *Surround factual information with your own analysis.* Provide a context for any quotation you use. Comment on the significance of a fact or statistic. Look for ways to connect any information to your research question or thesis.

■ *Make analogies or comparisons.* Is something like something else? Advocates for addressing climate change, for example, have used an extended analogy of a bathtub to illustrate how easy it is to ignore a problem until it's too late. You start the water running, get involved in, say, a computer game, and then have to decide when to check whether the tub is full. How long do you wait? What goes into this calculation?

### Verbal Gestures

Remember Burke's metaphor for the knowledge-making process (see page 116–117)? He imagined a parlor full of people having an ongoing conversation about what might be true—arguing, agreeing, raising questions, suggesting new ideas, critiquing old ideas, everyone trying to push the conversation along. Any roomful of people in a conversation about things that cause disagreement is also a roomful of gestures. People wave off a point. They nod in assent. They raise a single finger to raise a new question or make a new point. They invite someone to step forward to speak and ask another to step aside.

Similarly, an essay that is a writer's conversation with others about a question that matters to all of them also includes words and phrases that serve as verbal gestures. Some are gestures that invite some people in the room to provide *background* on the question so that everyone understands what has already been said. Other gestures signal *analysis,* or a closer examination and critique of something someone said. Sometimes these verbal gestures signify *speculation*; the writer isn't quite sure what to think for sure, but maybe....Or they might indicate *agreement* or *disagreement*—the writer is taking sides with a particular idea, position, or way of seeing.

Consider whether verbal gestures like these will help you manage the conversation about your topic. Go through your draft, and identify those moments in which you seem to be providing background, analyzing something, agreeing or disagreeing, or speculating. Might some of the following language help you signpost that material?

### BACKGROUND

Among the most important voices on _____, the most relevant to this inquiry are _____.

Most people _____.

The major sources of controversy are _____.

One idea emerges again and again, and it's _____.

Like most people, I believed that _____.

The unanswered questions are _____.

This much is clear: _____.

_____'s most important contribution is _____.

Most relevant is _____.

### ANALYSIS

The most relevant point is _____.

In comparison,...

In contrast,...

What is most convincing is _____.

What is least convincing is _____.

What's most interesting is _____.

The surprising connection is _____.

Paradoxically,...

Actually,...

What isn't clear is _____.

### SPECULATION

Perhaps...

Maybe...

It's possible that _____.

**AGREEMENT AND DISAGREEMENT**

Indeed,...

Obviously,...

Alternatively,...

While others have argued that _____, I think _____.

On balance, the most convincing idea is _____.

What _____ has failed to consider is _____.

The more important question is _____.

Based on my research, _____.

A better explanation is _____.

It's hard to argue with _____.

What I understand now that I didn't understand before is _____.

## Scrutinizing Paragraphs

### Is Each Paragraph Unified?

Each paragraph should be about one idea and organized around that idea. You probably know that already. But applying this notion is a particular problem in a research paper, where information abounds and paragraphs sometimes approach marathon length.

If any of your paragraphs seem too long (say, over a page or even verging on a page), look for ways to break them up into shorter paragraphs. Is more than one idea embedded in the long version? Are you explaining or examining more than one thing?

Even short paragraphs can lack unity, so look at those, too. Do any present minor or tangential ideas that belong somewhere else? Are any of the ideas irrelevant? In other words, should the information in the paragraph be moved into another paragraph of your paper, or should the paragraph just be cut? The cut-and-paste exercise (Exercise 5.3) may have helped you with this already.

## Scrutinizing Sentences

### Using Active Voice

Which of these two sentences seems more passive, more lifeless?

```
Steroids are used by many high school athletes.
```

*or*

```
Many high school athletes use steroids.
```

The first version, written in the passive voice, is clearly the more limp of the two. It's not grammatically incorrect; in fact, you may have found texts written in the passive voice to be pervasive in the reading you've done for your research paper. Research writing is plagued by passive voice, and that's one of the reasons it can be so mind-numbing to read.

*Passive voice* construction is easy to understand: The subject of the sentence is not the thing *doing the action* of the verb but, rather, the thing *acted upon* by the verb. For instance, in the following pair, the *active voice* sentence has as its subject Clarence, who does the action of kicking, but the passive sentence has the dog as the subject, which was kicked:

```
Clarence kicked the dog.
```

*versus*

```
The dog was kicked by Clarence.
```

Sometimes in passive sentences, the subject of the corresponding active sentence may be missing altogether, as in:

```
The study was released.
```

*Who* or *what* released it?

If you have passive sentences, you can remedy the problem by using *active voice* to place the doer of the action up front in the sentence or adding a doer if one is missing. For example:

```
Many high school athletes use steroids.
```

A telltale sign of passive voice is that it usually requires a form of the verb *to be* (*is, was, are, were, am, be, being, been*). For example:

```
Alcoholism among women has been extensively
studied.
```

Search your draft for *be's,* and see if any sentences are written in the passive voice. (Some word processing programs will search for you.) Unless this is a sentence that is more appropriate in passive voice, make the passive sentence active. To make a sentence active, move its doer from after the verb into the subject position or supply the appropriate doer if the sentence doesn't have one.

## Using Strong Verbs

Though this may seem like nitpicking, you'd be amazed how much writing in the active voice can revitalize research writing. The use of strong verbs can have the same effect.

As you know, verbs make things happen. Some verbs can create the difference between a sentence that crackles and one that merely hums. Instead of this:

> The study *suggested* that the widespread assumption
> that oral sex is common among American teenagers
> might be wrong.

write this:

> The study *shattered* the common belief that
> American teens increasingly indulge in oral sex.

Just because you're writing about other people's ideas doesn't mean you can't use strong verbs. See the box "Verbs for Discussing Ideas" on the following page, which was compiled by a colleague of mine, Cinthia Gannett. If you're desperate for an alternative to *says* or *argues,* check out the 135 alternatives this box offers.

## Varying Sentence Length

Here's part of a research essay on the promise of wind energy. When you read it, I think you'll find the writing choppy. What's going on? One way to understand the problem is to count the number of syllables in each sentence. That's the number in the parentheses.

> The idea of alternative energy is sweeping the country and numerous other developed nations. (29) People are beginning to recycle more plastic and metals. (16) They are also more interested in energy efficiency. (16) Wind energy is among the renewable resources sprouting up around the United States. (25) Wind energy affects the environment, wildlife, society, humans, and politics. (23)

It's not hard to see that the sentence length, measured by syllables, doesn't vary much. There are three sentences in the passage that run between 23 and 29 syllables, and the others both have 16. In addition, the structure of these sentences doesn't vary much.

## Verbs for Discussing Ideas

| | | | |
|---|---|---|---|
| accepts | critiques | implies | refutes |
| acknowledges | declares | infers | regards |
| adds | defends | informs | rejects |
| admires | defies | initiates | relinquishes |
| affirms | demands | insinuates | reminds |
| allows | denies | insists | repudiates |
| analyzes | describes | interprets | resolves |
| announces | determines | intimates | responds |
| answers | diminishes | judges | retorts |
| argues | disagrees | lists | reveals |
| assaults | disconfirms | maintains | reviews |
| assembles | discusses | marshalls | seeks |
| asserts | disputes | narrates | sees |
| assists | disregards | negates | shares |
| believes | distinguishes | observes | shifts |
| buttresses | emphasizes | outlines | shows |
| categorizes | endorses | parses | simplifies |
| cautions | enumerates | perceives | states |
| challenges | exaggerates | persists | stresses |
| claims | experiences | persuades | substitutes |
| clarifies | experiments | pleads | suggests |
| compares | explains | points out | summarizes |
| complicates | exposes | postulates | supplements |
| concludes | facilitates | praises | supplies |
| condemns | formulates | proposes | supports |
| confirms | grants | protects | synthesizes |
| conflates | guides | provides | tests |
| confronts | handles | qualifies | toys with |
| confuses | hesitates | quotes | treats |
| considers | highlights | ratifies | uncovers |
| contradicts | hints | rationalizes | urges |
| contrasts | hypothesizes | reads | verifies |
| convinces | identifies | reconciles | warns |
| criticizes | illuminates | reconsiders | |

*Source:* Reproduced with permission of Cinthia Gannett.

Each has just one main clause. Prose that doesn't vary much in sentence length or structure is invariably boring to read. So what can you do about it?

- *Vary sentence length.* Do a syllable count on a paragraph in your draft that seems clunky, and you'll probably find that you need to vary sentence length. Develop the instinct to follow a long sentence, for example, with a short, punchy one from time to time.
- *Combine sentences.* This often works wonders. Can you use punctuation or conjunctions like *or, but,* and *and* to join separate sentences together? For example, you might take this sequence of sentences in the passage on wind energy:

    *People are beginning to recycle more plastic and metals. (16)*
    *They are also more interested in energy efficiency. (16)*

    and revise it through sentence combining to read like this:

    *People are beginning to recycle more plastic and metals, and they're also more interested in energy efficiency. (32)*

    Notice that you now have a compound sentence. In varying length, you'll often also be varying structure.

## Editing for Simplicity

Somewhere, many of us got the idea that simplicity in writing is a vice—that the long word is better than the short word, that the complex phrase is superior to the simple one. The misconception is that to write simply is to be simpleminded. Research papers, especially, suffer from this mistaken notion. They are often filled with what writer William Zinsser calls *clutter.*

## EXERCISE 5.4

### Cutting Clutter

The following passage is an example of cluttered writing at its best (worst?). It contains phrases and words that often appear in college research papers. Read the passage once. Then take a few minutes and rewrite it, cutting as many words as you can without sacrificing the meaning. Look for ways to substitute a shorter word for a longer one and to say in fewer words what is currently said in many. Try to cut the word count by half.

> The implementation of the revised alcohol policy in the university community is regrettable at the present time due to the fact that the administration has not facilitated sufficient student input, in spite of the fact that there have been attempts by the people affected by this policy to make their objections known in many instances. *(55 words)*

## Avoiding Stock Phrases

A place to begin cutting unnecessary clutter in your essay is to hack away at stock phrases. Like many types of writing, the language of the college research paper is littered with words and phrases that find their way to the page as inevitably as drinking root beer prompted my 12-year-old daughter and her friends to hold burping contests. In each case, the one just seems to inspire the other. Following is a list of stock phrases that I often find in research papers. There is nothing grammatically wrong with these. It's simply that they are old, tired phrases, and you can say the same thing more freshly and with fewer words. Look for them in your draft and then edit them out.

| TIRED PHRASES | BETTER ALTERNATIVES |
|---|---|
| *Due to the fact that…* | *Because…* |
| *At this point in time,…* | *Now…* |
| *In my opinion,….* | *(Unnecessary. We know it's your opinion.)* |
| *A number of…* | *Many…/ Some…* |
| *A number of studies point to the fact that…* | *Many / Some researchers conclude (or argue)…* |
| *In the event of…* | *If…* |
| *In today's society…* | *Today we…* |
| *In conclusion,….* | *(Omit. If you're at the end of the paper, you're probably concluding.)* |

| TIRED PHRASES | BETTER ALTERNATIVES |
|---|---|
| *Until such time as...* | *Until...* |
| *Referred to as...* | *Called...* |
| *It should be pointed out that...* | *(Omit. You are pointing it out.)* |
| *Is in a position to...* | *Can* |
| *It is a fact that...* | *(Omit. Just state the fact, ma'am.)* |
| *It may be said that...* | *(Omit. Just say it.)* |
| *There can be little doubt that...* | *It's likely...* |
| *It is possible that...* | *Perhaps...* |

# Preparing the Final Manuscript

I wanted to title this section "Preparing the Final Draft," but it occurred to me that *draft* doesn't suggest anything final. I always call my work a draft because until it's out of my hands, it never feels finished. You may feel that way, too. You've spent five weeks on this paper—and the last few days, disassembled it and put it back together again. How do you know when you're finally done?

For many students, the deadline dictates that: The paper is due, say, tomorrow. But you may find that your paper really seems to be coming together in a satisfying way. You may even like it, and you're ready to prepare the final manuscript.

## Considering a "Reader-Friendly" Design

As consumers of texts these days—especially online—we are constantly influenced by visual rhetoric even if we aren't aware of it. "Eye-tracking" studies, for example, suggest that there is a sequence in how we look at a Web page: Most readers typically read a Web page in an upside-down "L" pattern, reading across the top of the page and then down the left side. Print advertisers are also acutely aware of visual rhetoric for obvious reasons—text works better with images if they are designed to work together.

A research essay like the one you're working on right now would seem to have little to do with visual rhetoric. The form of an academic paper, particularly if the emphasis is on the text—and it usually is—seems largely prescribed by the Modern Language Association or the American Psychological Association. Some papers in the social sciences, for example, require certain sections (abstract, introduction, discussion of method, presentation of results, and discussion of results), and these sections need to be clearly defined with subheadings, making it easy for readers to examine the parts they're most interested in. You probably discovered that in your own reading of formal research. You'll likely learn the formats research papers should conform to in various disciplines as you take upper-level courses in those fields.

While you should document your paper properly, you may have some freedom to develop a format that best serves your purpose. As you consider format in revising, keep readers in mind. How can you make your paper more readable? How can you signal your plan for developing the topic and what's important? Some visual devices might help, including:

- Subheadings
- Bulleted lists (like the one you're reading now)
- Graphs, illustrations, tables
- Block quotes
- Underlining and paragraphing for emphasis
- White space

Long, unbroken pages of text can appear to be a gray, uninviting mass to the reader. All of the devices listed above help break up the text, making it more "reader friendly." Subheadings, if not overused, can also cue your reader to significant sections of your paper and how they relate to the whole. Long quotes, those over four lines, should be blocked, or indented one inch from the left margin, so that they're distinct from the rest of the text. (See "Writing with Sources" in Chapter 4, for more on blocking quotes.) Bullets—dots or asterisks preceding brief lines of text—can be used to highlight a list of important information. Graphs, tables, and illustrations also break up the text but, more importantly, they can also help clarify and explain information. (See Section 2.1.5, "Placement of Tables, Charts, and Illustrations," in Appendix B or Section 2.1.8, "Tables and Figures," in Appendix C.)

## Using Images

Thanks to digital imaging, it's easier than ever to find pictures and use them in papers. (For an example of this, see Ashley Carvalho's essay, "Patching Up Belfast," in Appendix B.) As you probably know, Google allows users to do keyword searching specifically for images. You're writing an essay on the nutritional problems with fast food? You won't have any trouble finding a picture of a Big Mac that you can drop into your essay. Even better, perhaps you're writing your essay on a historical event, a local controversy, or perhaps a profile. With a few clicks you may find a less generic and more relevant image: a photograph of your profile subject or of the Civil War battle that you're analyzing.

You can do this. But should you?

That's up to your instructor, of course. But if she allows it, any visual addition to your essay—and especially an image—needs to do much more than take up space or break up gray text. It must do some work. What kind of work can an image do?

■ *Pictures can dramatize a moment, situation, or outcome that you emphasize in your text:* a photograph of the space shuttle's missing insulation in a paper arguing for an end to funding space exploration programs; a picture of the shootings of students on the Kent State campus in 1970 in a paper exploring campus violence.

■ *Pictures can help clarify difficult explanations:* Like a well-crafted analogy, an image can help readers to see more clearly what you're trying to explain. To explain quantitative data, you typically turn to tables and charts. But how can you use pictures? Use images that don't simply reinforce what you say in words but that also amplify what you say. An obvious example: If you're writing about a painting, then surrounding an image of the work with your textual explanations will bring your words to life. Readers will simply have more to work with to understand what you want them to see.

■ *A sequence of pictures can tell a story or illustrate a process:* A disturbing example of this is a series of photos of a meth addict—usually police booking shots—that tell the story of addiction to the drug in the steady deterioration of the user's face. Pictures of Brazilian rain forests before and after logging can help make an argument about loss of biodiversity.

## Following MLA Conventions

I've already mentioned that formal research papers in various disciplines may have prescribed formats. If your instructor expects a certain format, he has probably detailed exactly what that format should be. But in all likelihood, your essay for this class doesn't need to follow a rigid form. It will, however, probably adhere to the basic Modern Language Association (MLA) guidelines, described in detail in Appendix B. There, you'll find methods for formatting your paper and instructions for citing sources on your "Works Cited" page. You'll also find a sample paper in MLA style by Ashley Carvalho, "Patching Up Belfast." The American Psychological Association (APA) guidelines for research papers, the primary alternative to MLA guidelines, are described in Appendix C. You'll find a sample paper in APA style by Laura Burns, titled "Looking for Utopia."

## Proofreading Your Paper

You've spent weeks researching, writing, and revising your paper. You want to stop now. That's understandable, no matter how much you were driven by your curiosity. But before you sign off on your research paper, placing it in someone else's hands, take the time to proofread it.

I was often so glad to be done with a piece of writing that I was careless about proofreading it. That changed about 10 years ago, after I submitted a portfolio of writing to complete my master's degree. I was pretty proud of it, especially an essay about dealing with my father's alcoholism. Unfortunately, I misspelled that word—*alcoholism*—every time I used it. Bummer.

### Proofreading on a Computer

Proofreading used to necessitate gobbing on correction fluid to cover up mistakes and then trying to line up the paper and type in the changes. Writing on a computer, you're spared from that ordeal. The text can be easily manipulated.

Software programs can, of course, also help with the actual job of proofreading. Most word processing programs, for example, come with spelling and grammar checkers. These programs will count the number of words in your sentences, alerting you to particularly long ones, and will even point out uses of passive voice. While these style-checkers may not be all that helpful because of their dubious assumptions about what constitutes "good" style, spell-checkers are an invaluable feature. You probably already know that.

Some writers proofread on-screen. Others find they need to print out their paper and proofread the hard copy. They argue that they catch more mistakes if they proofread on paper than if they proofread on-screen. It makes sense, especially if you've been staring at the screen for days. A printed copy of your paper *looks* different, and I think you see it differently—maybe with fresher eyes and a more energetic attitude. You might notice things you didn't notice before. Decide for yourself how you want to proofread.

## *Looking Closely*

You've already edited the manuscript, pruning sentences and tightening things up. Now proofread for the little errors in grammar and mechanics that you missed. Aside from misspellings (usually typos), some pretty common mistakes appear in the papers I see. For practice, see if you can catch some of them in the following exercise.

## EXERCISE 5.5

### Picking Off the Lint

I have a colleague who compares proofreading to picking the lint off an outfit, which is often your final step before heading out the door. Examine the following excerpt from a student paper. Proofread it, catching as many mechanical errors as possible. Note punctuation mistakes, agreement problems, misspellings, and anything else that seems off.

In an important essay, Melody Graulich notes how "rigid dichotomizing of sex roles" in most frontier myths have "often handicapped and confused male as well as female writers (187)," she wonders if a "universel mythology" (198) might emerge that is less confining for both of them. In Bruce Mason, Wallace Stegner seems to experiment with this idea; acknowledging the power of Bo's male fantasies *and* Elsa's ability to teach her son to feel. It is his strenth. On the other hand, Bruces brother chet, who dies young, lost and broken, seems doomed because he lacked sufficient measure of both the feminine and masculine. He observes that Chet had "enough of the old man to spoil him, ebnough of his mother to soften him, not enough of either to save him (*Big Rock*, 521)."

If you did this exercise in class, compare your proofreading of this passage with that of a partner. What did each of you find?

## Ten Common Things to Avoid in Research Papers

The following is a list of the ten most common errors (besides misspelled words) made in research papers that should be caught in careful proofreading. A number of these errors occurred in the previous exercise.

1. Commonly confused words, such as *your* instead of *you're*. Here's a list of others:

| | |
|---|---|
| their/there/they're | advice/advise |
| know/now | lay/lie |
| accept/except | its/it's |
| all ready/already | passed/past |

2. Possessives. Instead of *my fathers alcoholism,* the correct form is *my father's alcoholism.* Remember that if a singular noun ends in *s,* still add *'s: Tess's laughter.* If a noun is plural, just add the apostrophe: *the scientists' studies.*

3. Vague pronoun references. The excerpt in Exercise 5.5 ends with the sentence *He observes that Chet....*Who's *he?* The sentence should read, *Bruce observes that Chet....*Whenever you use the pronouns *he, she, it, they,* and *their,* make sure each clearly refers to someone or something.

4. Subject and verb agreement. If the subject is singular, its verb must be, too:

```
The perils of climate change are many.
```

What confuses writers sometimes is the appearance before the verb of a noun that is not really the subject. Exercise 5.5 begins, for example, with this sentence:

```
In an important essay, Melody Graulich notes how
"rigid dichotomizing of sex roles" in most fron-
tier myths have "often handicapped and confused
male as well as female writers."
```

The subject here is not *frontier myths* but *rigid dichotomizing,* a singular subject. The sentence should read:

> In an important essay, Melody Graulich notes how "rigid dichotomizing of sex roles" in most frontier myths has "often handicapped and confused male as well as female writers."

The verb *has* may sound funny, but it's correct.

5. Punctuation of quotations. Note that commas belong inside quotation marks, not outside. Periods belong inside, too. Colons and semicolons are exceptions—they belong *outside* quotation marks. Blocked quotes don't need quotation marks at all unless there is a quote within the quote.

6. Commas. Could you substitute periods or semicolons? If so, you may be looking at *comma splices* or *run-on sentences.* Here's an example:

> Since 1980, the use of marijuana by college students has steadily declined, this was something of a surprise to me and my friends.

The portion after the comma, *this was...,* is another sentence. The comma should be a period, and *this* should be capitalized.

7. Parenthetical citations. In MLA style, there is no comma between the author's name and page number: (*Marks 99*).

8. Dashes. Though they can be overused, dashes are a great way to break the flow of a sentence with a related bit of information. You've probably noticed that I like them. In a manuscript, type dashes as *two* hyphens (--), not one. Most word processing programs will automatically turn the hyphens into a solid dash, which is what you want.

9. Names. After mentioning the full name of someone in your paper, you should normally use her *last name* in subsequent references. For example, this is incorrect:

> Denise Grady argues that people are genetically predisposed to obesity. Denise also believes that some people are "programmed to convert calories to fat."

Unless you know Denise or for some reason want to conceal her last name, change the second sentence to this:

```
Grady also believes that some people are "pro-
grammed to convert calories to fat."
```

One exception to this is when writing about literature. It is often appropriate to refer to characters by their first names, particularly if characters share last names (as in Exercise 5.5).

10. Colons and semicolons. A colon is usually used to call attention to what follows it: a list, quotation, or appositive. A colon should also follow an independent clause. For example, this won't do:

```
The  most  troubling  things  about  child  abuse
are:  the  effects  on  self-esteem  and  language
development.
```

In this case, eliminate the colon. A semicolon should be used as a period, separating two independent clauses. It simply implies that the clauses are closely related. Semicolons should *not* be used as if they were colons or commas.

## Using the "Find" or "Search" Function

Use the "Find" or "Search" function in your word processing program to help you track down consistent problems. You simply tell the computer what word or punctuation to look for, and it will locate all occurrences in the text. For example, if you want to check for comma splices, search for commas. The cursor will stop on every comma, and you can verify if you have used it correctly. You can also search for pronouns to locate vague references or for words (like those listed in item 1) that you commonly confuse.

## Avoiding Sexist Language

One last proofreading task is to do a *man* and *he* check. Until recently, sexism wasn't an issue in language. Use of words such as *mankind* and *chairman* was acceptable; the implication was that the terms applied to both genders. At least, that's how use of the terms was defended when challenged. Critics argued that words such as *mailman* and *businessman* reinforced the idea that only men could fill these roles. Bias in language is subtle but powerful. And it's often unintentional. To avoid sending the wrong message, it's worth making the effort to avoid sexist language.

If you need to use a word with a *man* suffix, check to see if there is an alternative. *Congressperson* sounds pretty clunky, but *representative* works fine. Instead of *mankind,* why not humanity? Substitute *camera operator* for *cameraman.*

Also check your use of pronouns. Do you use *he* or *his* in places where you mean both genders? For example:

```
The writer who cares about his topic will bring

it to life for his readers.
```

Because a lot of writers are women, this doesn't seem right. How do you solve this problem? You can ask your instructor what she prefers, but here are some guidelines:

1. Use *his or her, he or she,* or the mutation *s/he.* For example:

```
The writer who cares about his or her topic will

bring it to life for his or her readers.
```

This is an acceptable solution, but using *his or her* repeatedly can be awkward.

2. Change the singular subject to plural. For example:

```
Writers who care about their topics will bring

them to life for their readers.
```

This version, which also avoids discriminatory language, sounds much better.

3. Alternate *he* and *she, his* and *hers* whenever you encounter an indefinite person. If you have referred to writers as *he* in one discussion, refer to them as *she* in the next. Alternate throughout.


# Looking Back and Moving On

This book began with your writing, and it also will end with it. More than a month ago, you began your inquiry project, and even if you're still not happy with your essay, you probably learned some things that influenced the way you think about yourself as a writer, about the nature of research in a university, and how to solve typical problems that arise when you're writing research-based papers.

In this final exercise, you'll do some thinking about all of this in your journal, or perhaps on a class blog or discussion board.

## EXERCISE 5.6

### Another Dialogue with Dave

You may remember Dave from Chapter 4 (see Exercise 4.1, "Dialogue with Dave"). He's back, and has some things to ask you about your experience with this project. Draw a line down the middle of a blank page in your journal, or create two columns in a Word document. Ask each of Dave's questions by writing them in the left column, and then fastwrite your response in the right column. Spend *at least* 3 minutes with each question.

**DAVE**                                              **YOU**

1. "Hey, you, I think you can't really say that one opinion is better than another one. Don't you agree?"
2. "There's all this stuff in the book about research as a process of discovery. What did you discover?"
3. "What do you figure was the most challenging problem you had to solve while working on this research project? How did you solve it?"
4. "After all this work, what do you take away from this experience? What have you learned that you can *use*?"

# APPENDIX A

# Understanding Research Assignments

About 15 years ago, on the dark, dimly lit basement floor of the University of New Hampshire library, I discovered the textbook that may have had the very first research paper assignment for undergraduates. Charles Baldwin's 1906 *A College Manual of Rhetoric* encouraged students to write essays based on reading that emphasized "originally" compiling facts so that the writer gives "already known" information his "own grouping and interpretation." In an article that year, Baldwin noted that "from the beginning a student should learn that his use of the library will be a very practical measure of his culture."

In the century since Baldwin's book, the college research paper has become probably the most common genre of student writing in the university. It is a fixture in composition classes and many other courses that require a "term paper." Naturally, this is why there are books like *The Curious Researcher*—to help students understand these assignments and give them guidance in the process of writing them. As you know, this book emphasizes the research *essay* rather than the formal research paper. My argument is that this more exploratory, possibly less formal researched piece is the best way to introduce you to the spirit of inquiry that drives most academic research. The habits of mind that come from essaying, along with the research and writing skills that essaying develops, should help you whenever you're asked to write a paper that involves research. Put another way, exploration *seeds* argument, and while the argumentative research paper is more common than the exploratory essay, exploration is fundamental to all academic inquiry. Why not take the opportunity to experience what exploration is like?

There's another skill that's invaluable when you encounter a research paper assignment in another class: knowing how to interpret exactly what you're being asked to do. This involves reading your writing assignment rhetorically. In other words, analyze the *situation* for each assignment: How does it fit with other writing projects in the course? What particular purpose does this assignment have? What do you know about the instructor's particular attitudes about research and about writing? How do you figure out the best approaches to the research project? Apparently, this analysis can pose a huge problem for students. In one study, for example, 92 percent of students said that the most frustrating part of doing research is figuring out what their professor wants.*

Instructors aren't trying to be obtuse. They want you to understand the assignment, and most have made an effort to be clear. While there's not much you can do about *how* the assignment is conceived or described, you can be savvy at analyzing the assignment's purpose and guidelines.

I've recently conducted a review of research paper assignments from courses across the disciplines, and actually there are striking similarities among them. I tried to read them as a student would, actively looking for guidance about how to approach the assignment and also alert to subtleties that students might miss. In the following sections, I break this rhetorical analysis into parts, drawing on what I learned.

## Analyzing the Purpose of the Assignment

One of the things I hear most often from my students who have research assignments in other classes is that the instructor "doesn't want my opinion in the paper." Frankly, I'm often skeptical of this. College writing assignments typically are about what or how you think. But because research papers involve considerable time collecting and considering the ideas of others, it's easy to assume that you're supposed to be a bystander.

Actually, even some instructors seem to equate the term "research paper" with merely reporting information. "This is not a

---

*Head, Alison. "Beyond Google: How Do Students Conduct Academic Research?" *First Monday* 12.8 (6 Aug. 2007): n. pag. Web. 30 Mar. 2008.

research paper," said one assignment. "The idea here is not to pack in as much information as you can, but instead to present a thoughtful and clearly written analysis." Another noted that "although this is a research paper, the focus is fundamentally on your own analysis and interpretation...."

What these instructors are at pains to point out is that, contrary to what you might think, they are actively interested in what you think. They want students to *do* something with the information they collect. But merely having an opinion isn't enough. As one assignment put it, "You are not being graded on your opinion, but your ability to communicate and support a point of view (your thesis)."

Writing a convincing, well-supported paper is straightforward enough. But why do the project in the first place? What is the purpose of writing a research paper? The assignments I reviewed sometimes talked about encouraging "critical thinking" or helping students enter "a scholarly conversation." A few talked about "advancing your knowledge" about a topic or learning the conventions of research writing in a particular discipline. But many, unfortunately, just focused on a requirement that your paper make an argument.

# Argumentative Research: Open or Closed?

The language that research assignments use to emphasize argument is quite often very explicit: "You are to write a research paper in which you make an argument related to some aspect of life in Southeast Asia." Not much ambiguity there. Similarly, some assignments ask that you "take a position" on a topic. Argumentative research papers are most often organized around a thesis, and some assignment descriptions go to great lengths to explain what makes a strong thesis (usually, sufficiently narrow, addressing a significant question, and explicitly stated).

What may not be obvious, however, is how much latitude you have in letting your research revise your thesis or even dramatically change your initial point of view. Most often, instructors *expect* the research to change your thinking, and they often use the term "working thesis" to describe your initial position. These are the more open-ended assignments that might specify that the crafting of a final thesis can occur late rather than early in the research process. These are also assignments that emphasize a focus on a *research question*, much like we've discussed in this book.

More rarely, an assignment will imply a closed approach: First identify a thesis, and then seek evidence from your research that will support it. This is the conventional thesis-support model in which the expectation is that you will use your thesis, and not your research question, to dictate not just the structure of your paper but also the goal of your research. These kinds of assignments tend not to mention that a thesis might be revised and are silent on how it arises from a research question or problem. Always ask your instructor whether your reading of the assignment as more closed-ended is accurate. The key questions are these:

### Questions to Ask Your Instructor About the Thesis

- Where should the thesis in this assignment come from?
- What process do you suggest for arriving at it?
- Finally, might it be revised—even substantially—later in the process?

In a more open-ended research paper, the inquiry-based methods of *The Curious Researcher* directly apply. For example, crafting a researchable question is an important route to coming up with a strong working thesis, and the dialogue or double-entry journal can help you think through how your research might develop or revise that thesis. The strict thesis-support paper seems to have little opportunity for inquiry. Indeed, the emphasis in these assignments is frequently on the formal qualities of the paper—how well it's organized around and supports a thesis, the proper use of citations, and mechanical correctness. Developing an outline at the front end of the project is usually helpful. However, there's no reason that after developing working knowledge of your topic, you can't use exercises like "Dialogue with Dave" or "Sharpening Your Point" (Exercises 4.1 and 4.2) in Chapter 4, or "Using Your Thesis to Revise" in Chapter 5 on page 196. All of these elements will help you come up with a strong thesis that is based on what you've discovered in your research.

# Audience

For whom are you writing? So much hinges on the answer to this question: the tone of the paper, how specialized its language might be, the emphasis you give on providing background information on the research question, and the degree to which you stress reader interest. Despite the importance of audience, research paper assignments frequently fail to mention it at all. This omission can often mean that you are writing for your instructor. But it actually might surprise you how often this isn't intended to be the case. Particularly if your assignment includes peer review of drafts or class presentations, you may be writing for a more general audience. Sometimes this is explicit: "Your paper should be able to be understood by a broader audience than scholars in your field. You will have to explain concepts and not expect your audience to understand in-house jargon." If the audience for your paper isn't clear, ask your instructor this simple question:

### Question to Ask Your Instructor About the Audience

- Who is the audience for this assignment—readers like the instructor who are knowledgeable about the topic and/or readers who are not?

# Extent of Emphasis on Formal Qualities

An essay like "Theories of Intelligence" in the Introduction of this book is relatively informal: It's casual in tone, has a strong individual voice, and is structured to explore a question—*to find out* rather than *to prove*. It certainly has a thesis, but it is a delayed thesis, appearing not in the beginning but toward the end of the essay. The essay is organized around the writer's questions, not around making a point and logically providing evidence to support it. It does, however, have some formal qualities, including careful citation and attribution, the marshalling of appropriate evidence to explore the topic, and a sensible organization that moves from question to answers.

Research paper assignments in other classes are likely to put considerably more emphasis on a structure based on logic and reasoning. Put another way, these papers differ from an exploratory essay like "Theories of Intelligence" in that they report the *products* of the process of thinking about and researching the question, rather than describe the *process* of thinking and researching the question. The chief product, of course, is your thesis—the thing you are trying to say—and typically you're expected to place this in the introduction of your paper. Fairly often, research paper assignments instruct you to state your thesis or position explicitly in a sentence. Along with a thesis, however, many assignments, in keeping with the approach of this book, ask that you develop a research question from which the thesis then emerges. These are the open assignments we discussed earlier. As one put it, "[The] introduction should make three points: It should briefly introduce your question and its significance, state your answer, and orient the reader regarding your way of proceeding. This is the place to say, 'I'm going to argue....'" The APA-style essay "Looking for Utopia" in Appendix C is a great example of a thesis-driven essay like this.

Also pay close attention to what context the assignment asks you to establish for your research question—course discussion, literature review, or both. Some instructors are keen on having you write a paper that in some way extends the course's readings or discussion points. Others want you to become familiar with the scholarly conversation that might extend beyond the class. Here's a question to ask about this:

## Question to Ask Your Instructor About the Context

- What is the more important context for establishing the significance of my research question or thesis—what we talked about in class or what I discover when I review the relevant literature?

The logical structure of an argumentative research paper doesn't vary much (see the discussion about this in Chapter 4), although in some disciplines you will be instructed to use the organizational conventions of the field; for example, scientific papers might require an abstract, introduction, methods, results, discussion, and conclusion, in that order. Generally, the body of your paper must draw on evidence from your research to support your thesis, though frequently your assignment requires that you also consider opposing points of view. How are they misguided? In what ways do they fail to address your research question? Also pay attention to whether your assignment asks you to tightly tether each paragraph to the thesis using topic sentences that address how that paragraph supports the thesis.* If so, you might find it useful to outline the topic sentences before you draft your essay.

Because one of the aims of teaching research writing is to help students understand its conventions, assignments almost always discuss the need for proper citation, correct format, the required number of scholarly sources, and so on, as well as attending to grammar and mechanics. You need to determine the relative importance of these conventions. Some research paper assignments, for example, devote

---

*Some instructors heavily stress the use of topic sentences in paragraph writing, though there is considerable evidence that much writing, including academic prose, doesn't consistently feature topic sentences.

much more ink to describing the required format—location of page numbers, font, margins—and the need for "perfect" grammar than they do to discussing the research process, formulating a thesis, or the larger goals of the assignment. In this case, you might give these conventions more attention. If you're not sure how to weigh them, ask this question:

### Question to Ask Your Instructor About the Importance of Formal Qualities

- When you evaluate the paper, what is the relative importance of my getting the format right? Do you give that concern as much weight as the quality of my thesis or the soundness of my thinking?

As you know, *The Curious Researcher* encourages essays in which writers have a strong presence. The easiest way to do this is to enter the text directly by using the first person, though in Chapter 4 we explored other ways to do this. Research paper assignments rarely mention whether you can use "I." Silence on this issue usually means that you should not. One of the conventions of much academic writing is a more formal register, which gives the impression that the paper speaks rather than the writer. Yet a considerable number of the assignments I reviewed encouraged students to write with "voice" and lively, vigorous prose. The most effective way to inject voice into your research writing is to find your own way of saying things, something that "writing in the middle"—the notetaking strategies encouraged in this book—should help you with. Assignments that say nothing about voice or style probably expect what one assignment described as writing that is "formal in tone, working to establish an authoritative, critical, and analytical voice." If you're unsure about this, consider asking your instructor the following question:

### Question to Ask Your Instructor About Tone

- Should the voice in my paper mimic the scholarly sources I'm reading, or can it be somewhat less formal, perhaps sounding a bit more like me?

# Types of Evidence: Primary or Secondary

As you move from a general audience (people who may know little about your topic) to a more specialized audience (people who know more), the tone and structure of your paper will change. So will the types of evidence that will make your argument persuasive. In popular writing—say, articles in *Wired* or *Discover* or op-ed pieces in the newspaper—the types of evidence that writers use to convince readers are quite varied. Personal experience and observation, for instance, are often excellent ways to support a point. But as you begin writing research papers in academic disciplines, you need to pay attention to what your instructor considers *appropriate* evidence in that field and for that particular assignment. Scientific papers, for example, often rely on experimental data. Literature papers lean most heavily on evidence culled from the literary text you're writing about. Papers in anthropology might rely on field observations.

Sometimes assignments explicitly talk about appropriate evidence for your paper. More often they do not. Generally speaking, research papers that are assigned in lower-division courses won't require you to conduct experiments or generate field notes. They will likely ask you to draw evidence from already published, or secondary, sources on your topic. But this isn't always the case. A history paper, for example, might require that you study primary texts, perhaps letters by historical figures, political documents, or archived newspapers. This is something you need to know. If the types of evidence you should use in your paper aren't clear, ask this question:

### Question to Ask Your Instructor About Evidence

- What types of evidence should I rely on for this paper? Primary or secondary sources? And is personal experience and observation, if relevant, appropriate to use?

In the spirit of writing a conventional conclusion, let me restate what might be apparent by now: The most important thing you must do when you get a research assignment is read the handout carefully, considering what you've already learned in the class about writing in that discipline. I read a lot of research paper assignments, and they usually provide very good guidance. But if they don't, that's never an excuse for floundering. Ask, ask, ask. Your instructor wants you to.

# Guide to MLA Style

Appendix B contains guidelines for preparing your essay in the format recommended by the Modern Language Association, or MLA, a body that, among other things, decides documentation conventions for papers in the humanities. The information here reflects the most recent changes by the MLA, as described in the group's definitive reference for students, the *MLA Handbook for Writers of Research Papers,* 7th edition. By the way, the American Psychological Association (APA) is a similar body for the social sciences, with its own documentation conventions. You will find it fairly easy to switch from one system to the other once you've

## Checklist Before Handing in a Paper in MLA Style

- My paper has a title but no separate title page (unless my instructor has said otherwise).
- My name, the instructor's name, the course, and the date are in the upper left-hand corner of the first page (see page 245).
- All my pages are numbered in the upper right-hand corner, using my last name next to the page number (see page 244).
- My Works Cited list begins on a new page.
- Everything, including my Works Cited page(s), is double-spaced.
- Every page of the paper's text is readable.
- There are no commas in my parenthetical citations between the author's name and the page number (see page 234).
- All my parenthetical citations are *before* the periods at the ends of sentences, unless the citation appears at the end of a blocked quote (see pages 237 and 247–248).
- The entries in my Works Cited page(s) are listed alphabetically, and every line after the first one in an entry is indented a half inch.

learned both (Table 1, on page 232, summarizes the important differences). Appendix B covers MLA conventions, and Appendix C explains APA conventions.

Part One of this appendix, "Citing Sources in Your Essay," will be particularly useful as you write your draft; it provides guidance on how to parenthetically cite the sources you use in the text of your essay. Part Two, "Formatting Your Essay," will help you with formatting the manuscript, something you will likely focus on after revising; it includes guidelines for margins, pagination, and tables, charts, and illustrations. Part Three, "Preparing the Works Cited Page," offers detailed instructions on how to prepare your bibliography at the end of your essay; this is usually one of the last steps in preparing the final manuscript. Finally, Part Four presents a sample research essay in MLA style, which will show you how it all comes together.

## Directory of MLA Style

# Part One: Citing Sources in Your Essay

## 1.1 When to Cite

Before examining the details of how to use parenthetical citations, remember when you must cite sources in your paper:

1. Whenever you quote from an original source
2. Whenever you borrow ideas from an original source, even when you express them in your own words by paraphrasing or summarizing

3. Whenever you borrow from a source factual information that is *not common knowledge*

## The Common Knowledge Exception

The business about *common knowledge* causes much confusion. Just what does this term mean? Basically, *common knowledge* means facts that are widely known and about which there is no controversy.

Sometimes, it's really obvious whether something is common knowledge. The fact that the Super Bowl occurs in late January or early February and pits the winning teams from the American Football Conference and the National Football Conference is common knowledge. The fact that President Ronald Reagan was once an actor and starred in a movie with a chimpanzee is common knowledge, too. But what about Carolyn's assertion that most dreaming occurs during rapid eye movement (REM) sleep? This is an idea about which all of her sources seem to agree. If you find that four or more sources cite the same information, then you can probably assume that it's common knowledge. But if you have any doubt, cite it!

## 1.2 The MLA Author/Page System

The Modern Language Association (MLA) uses the author/page parenthetical citation system. As you can see in Appendix C, the American Psychological Association (APA) uses the author/date system.

### The Basics of Using Parenthetical Citation

The MLA method of in-text parenthetical citation is fairly simple: As close as possible to the borrowed material, you indicate in parentheses the original source (usually, the author's name) and the page number in the work that the borrowed material came from. For example, here's how you'd cite a book or article with a single author using the author/page system:

```
From the very beginning of Sesame Street in
1969, kindergarten teachers discovered that
incoming students who had watched the program
already knew their ABCs (Chira 13).
```

The parenthetical citation here tells readers two things: (1) This information about the success of *Sesame Street* does not originate with the writer but with someone named *Chira,* and (2) readers can consult the original source for further information by looking on page 13 of Chira's book or article, which is cited fully at the back of the paper in the Works Cited. Here is what readers would find there:

```
              Works Cited
   Chira, Susan. "Sesame Street at 20: Taking

      Stock." New York Times 15 Nov. 1989: 13.

      Print.
```

Here's another example of a parenthetical author/page citation, from another research paper. Note the differences from the previous example:

```
   "One thing is clear," writes Thomas Mallon,

   "plagiarism didn't become a truly sore point

   with writers until they thought of writing as

   their trade. . . . Suddenly his capital and iden-

   tity were at stake" (3-4).
```

The first thing you may have noticed is that the author's last name—Mallon—was omitted from the parenthetical citation. It didn't need to be included because it had already been mentioned in the text. *If you mention the author's name in the text of your paper, then you need to parenthetically cite only the relevant page number(s).* This citation also tells us that the quoted passage comes from two pages rather than one.

**Placement of Citations.**     Place the citation as close as you can to the borrowed material, trying to avoid breaking the flow of the sentences, if possible. To avoid confusion about what's borrowed and what's not—particularly if the material you're borrowing spans more than a sentence—when possible mention the name of the original author *in your paper* in a way that clarifies what you've borrowed. Note that in the next example, the writer simply cites the source at the end of the paragraph, not naming the source in the text. As a result, it is hard for the reader to figure out

## Citations That Go with the Flow

There's no getting around it: Parenthetical citations can be like stones on the sidewalk. Readers stride through a sentence in your essay and then have to step around the citation at the end before they resume their walk. Yet citations are important in academic writing because they help readers know who you read or heard that shaped your thinking. And you can write your citations in such a way that they won't trip up readers. As a result, your essay will be more readable. Try these techniques:

- Avoid lengthy parenthetical citations by mentioning the name of the author in your essay. That way, you usually have to include only a page number in the citation.
- Try to place citations where readers are likely to pause anyway—for example, at the end of the sentence or right before a comma.
- Remember you *don't* need a citation when you're citing common knowledge or referring to an entire work by an author.
- If you're borrowing from only one source in a paragraph of your essay and all of the borrowed material comes from a single page of that source, don't repeat the citation over and over again with each new bit of information. Just put the citation at the end of the paragraph.

whether Blager is the source of the information in the entire paragraph or just in part of it:

Though children who have been sexually abused
seem to be disadvantaged in many areas,
including the inability to forge lasting
relationships, low self-esteem, and crippling
shame, they seem advantaged in other areas.
Sexually abused children seem to be more socially mature than other children of their

```
same age group. It's a distinctly mixed bless-
ing (Blager 994).
```

In the following example, notice how the ambiguity about what's borrowed and what's not is resolved by careful placement of the author's name and parenthetical citation in the text:

```
Though children who have been sexually abused
seem to be disadvantaged in many areas, includ-
ing the inability to forge lasting relation-
ships, low self-esteem, and crippling shame,
they seem advantaged in other areas. According
to Blager, sexually abused children seem to be
more socially mature than other children of
their same age group (994). It's a distinctly
mixed blessing.
```

In this latter version, it's clear that Blager is the source for one sentence in the paragraph and that the writer is responsible for the rest. When you first mention authors, use their full names, and when you mention them again, use only their last names. Also note that the citation is placed *before* the period of the sentence (or last sentence) that it documents. That's always the case, except at the end of a blocked quotation, where the parenthetical reference is placed *after* the period of the last sentence. The citation can also be placed near the author's name, rather than at the end of the sentence, if it doesn't unnecessarily break the flow of the sentence. For example:

```
Blager (994) observes that sexually abused chil-
dren tend to be more socially mature than other
children of their same age group.
```

### 1.2.1 WHEN YOU MENTION ONE AUTHOR

It's generally good practice in research writing to identify who said what. The familiar convention of using attribution tags such as "According to Fletcher,..." or "Fletcher argues..." and so on helps readers attach a name with a voice or an individual with certain claims or findings. As just discussed, when you mention the author of a source in your sentence, the parenthetical citation includes only the page number. For example,

```
Robert Harris believes that there is "widespread
uncertainty" among students about what consti-
tutes plagiarism (2).
```

As was also discussed, the page number could come directly after the author's name.

```
Robert Harris (2) believes that there is "wide-
spread uncertainty" among students about what
constitutes plagiarism.
```

### 1.2.2 WHEN YOU MENTION MORE THAN ONE AUTHOR

Often your sources will have more than one author. If the book or article has two or three authors, list all their last names in the parenthetical citation, with *and* before the final author; for example:

```
(Oscar and Leibowitz 29)
```

If your source has more than three authors, you can either list them all or use the first author and *et al.* Just make sure that you identify the authors the same way in the Works Cited entry.:

```
(Kemp et al. 199)
```

### 1.2.3 WHEN THERE IS NO AUTHOR

Occasionally, you may encounter a source whose author is anonymous—that is, who isn't identified. This isn't unusual with pamphlets, editorials, government documents, some newspaper articles, online sources, and short filler articles in magazines. If you can't parenthetically name the author, what do you cite?

Most often, cite the title (or an abbreviated version, if the title is long) and the page number. If you abbreviate the title, begin with the word under which it is alphabetized in the Works Cited list. For example:

```
Simply put, public relations is "doing good and
getting credit" for it (Getting Yours 3).
```

Here is how the publication cited above would be listed at the back of the paper:

Works Cited

*Getting Yours: A Publicity and Funding Primer*

*for Nonprofit and Voluntary Organizations.*

Lincoln: Contact Center, 2008. Print.

As with other sources, for clarity, it's often helpful to mention the original source of the borrowed material in the text of your paper. Refer to the publication or institution (e.g., the American Cancer Society or Department of Defense) you're citing or make a more general reference to the source. For example:

An article in *Cuisine* magazine argues that the

best way to kill a lobster is to plunge a knife

between its eyes ("How to Kill" 56).

*or*

According to one government report, with the

current minimum size limit, most lobsters end up

on dinner plates before they've had a chance to

reproduce ("Size" 3-4).

Note the abbreviations of the article titles; for example, the full title for "How to Kill," listed in the Works Cited, is "How to Kill a Lobster." Note also that article titles are in quotation marks and book titles are italicized.

### 1.2.4 WORKS BY THE SAME AUTHOR

Suppose you end up using several books or articles by the same author. Obviously, a parenthetical citation that merely lists the author's name and page number won't do because it won't be clear *which* of several works the citation refers to. In this case, include the author's name, an abbreviated title (if the original is too long), and the page number. For example:

The thing that distinguishes the amateur from

the experienced writer is focus; one "rides off

in all directions at once," and the other finds
one meaning around which everything revolves
(Murray, *Write to Learn* 92).

The Works Cited list would show multiple works by one author
as follows:

Works Cited

Murray, Donald M. *Write to Learn*. 8th ed.

Boston: Heinle, 2004. Print.

---. *A Writer Teaches Writing*. Boston: Heinle,

2004. Print.

It's obvious from the parenthetical citation which of the two
Murray books is the source of the information. Note that in the parenthetical reference, no punctuation separates the title and the page
number, but a comma follows the author's name. If Murray had been
mentioned in the text of the paper, his name could have been dropped
from the citation.

How to handle the Works Cited list is explained more fully later
in this appendix, but for now, notice that the three hyphens used in
the second entry signal that the author's name in this source is the
same as in the preceding entry.

### 1.2.5 WORKS BY DIFFERENT AUTHORS WITH THE SAME NAME

How do you distinguish between different authors who
have the same last name? Say you're citing a piece by someone
named Lars Anderson as well as a piece by someone named Kelli
Anderson. The usual in-text citation, which uses the last name only
(Anderson 2), wouldn't help the reader much. In this situation,
add the author's first initial to the citation: (L. Anderson 2) or
(K. Anderson 12).

### 1.2.6 INDIRECT SOURCES

Whenever you can, cite the original source for material you use.
For example, if an article on television violence quotes the author of a
book and you want to use the quote, try to hunt down the book. That
way, you'll be certain of the accuracy of the quote and you may find
some additional usable information.

Sometimes, however, finding the original source is not possible.
In those cases, use the term *qtd. in* to signal that you've quoted or

paraphrased material that was quoted in your source and initially appeared elsewhere. In the following example, the citation signals that the quote from Bacon was in fact culled from an article by Guibroy, rather than from Bacon's original work:

> Francis Bacon also weighed in on the dangers of imitation, observing that "it is hardly possible at once to admire an author and to go beyond him" (qtd. in Guibroy 113).

### 1.2.7 PERSONAL INTERVIEWS

If you mention the name of your interview subject in your text, no parenthetical citation is necessary. If you don't mention the subject's name, cite it in parentheses after the quote:

> The key thing when writing for radio, says one journalist, is to "write to the sound if you've got great sound, and read your stuff aloud" (Tan).

Regardless of whether you mention your subject's name in your text, you should include a reference to the interview in the Works Cited. In this case, the reference would look like this:

> Works Cited
>
> Tan, Than. Personal interview. 28 Jan. 2011.

### 1.2.8 SEVERAL SOURCES IN A SINGLE CITATION

Suppose two sources both contributed the same information in a paragraph of your essay. Or, even more likely, suppose you're summarizing the findings of several authors on a certain topic—a fairly common move when you're trying to establish a context for your own research question. How do you cite multiple authors in a single citation? Use author names and page numbers as usual, and separate them with a semicolon. For example,

> A whole range of studies have looked closely at the intellectual development of college students, finding that they generally assume

```
"stages" or "perspectives" that differ from
subject to subject (Perry 122; Belenky
et al. 12).
```

## Sample Parenthetical References for Other Sources

MLA format is pretty simple, and we've already covered some of the basic variations. You should also know the following four additional variations:

### 1.2.9  AN ENTIRE WORK

If you mention an author's name and his or her work in the text but don't refer to specific details, no citation is necessary. The work should, however, be listed in the Works Cited. For the following example, Edel's book would be listed in the Works Cited.

```
Leon Edel's Henry James is considered by many to
be a model biography.
```

### 1.2.10  A VOLUME OF A MULTIVOLUME WORK

If you're working with one volume of a multivolume work, it's a good idea to mention which volume in the parenthetical reference. The citation below attributes the passage to the second volume, page 3, of a work by Baym and other authors. The volume number is always followed by a colon, which is followed by the page number:

```
By the turn of the century, three authors
dominated American literature: Mark Twain,
Henry James, and William Dean Howells (Baym
et al. 2: 3).
```

### 1.2.11  A LITERARY WORK

Because so many literary works, particularly classics, have been reprinted in so many editions, and readers are likely using different editions, it's useful to give readers information about where a passage can be found regardless of edition. You can do this by listing not only the page number but also the chapter number—and any other relevant information, such as the section or volume—separated from the page number by a semicolon. Use arabic rather than roman numerals.

> ```
> Izaak Walton warns that "no direction can be
> given to make a man of a dull capacity able to
> make a Flie well" (130; ch. 5).
> ```

When citing poems or plays, instead of page numbers, cite line numbers for poems and act, scene, and line numbers, separated with periods, for plays. For example, (*Othello* 2.3.286) indicates act 2, scene 3, line 286 of that play.

### 1.2.12 AN ONLINE SOURCE

If you're using material from a book on your Kindle or iPad, you'll notice that there are "location numbers" or percentages rather than page numbers. (Other e-text devices may have page numbers.) And you've probably already noticed that many online documents don't have page numbers or don't have permanent ones. What should you do when you want to cite sources that don't have page numbers?

When a document or Web page lacks permanent page numbers, you can cite just the author, but you may be able to alert readers to a more general location: "In the first chapter, Payne argues that...." If the source is authorless, the citation would include just a title, as in this citation of an article from the Web:

> ```
> Many women who wait to begin a family may
> wonder if prior birth control choices
> negatively affect their fertility. It's not
> uncommon, for instance, for a woman to take
> oral contraceptives for 10 years or longer.
> However, the birth control pill itself doesn't
> affect long-term fertility ("Infertility: Key
> Q and A").
> ```

On the other hand, PDF files frequently have permanent pagination, particularly if the document is a copy of the original article. In that case, the page numbers should be used in your citation.

# Part Two: Formatting Your Essay

## 2.1 The Layout

There is, well, a certain fussiness associated with the look of academic papers. The reason for it is quite simple—academic disciplines generally aim for consistency in format so that readers of scholarship know exactly where to look to find what they want to know. It's a matter of efficiency. How closely you must follow the MLA's requirements for the layout of your essay is up to your instructor, but it's really not that complicated. A lot of what you need to know is featured in Figure B1.

### 2.1.1 PRINTING

Print your paper on white, 8½ × 11-inch paper. Make sure the printer has sufficient ink or toner.

### 2.1.2 MARGINS AND SPACING

The old high school trick is to have big margins so you can get the length without the information. Don't try that trick with this

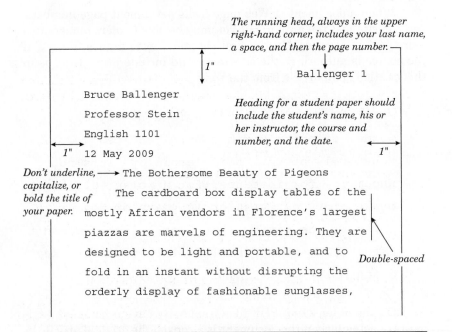

**FIGURE B1    The Basic Look of an MLA-Style Paper**

paper. Leave one-inch margins at the top, bottom, and sides of your pages. Indent the first line of each paragraph a half inch, and indent blocked quotes an inch. Double-space all of the text, including blocked quotes and Works Cited.

### 2.1.3 TITLE

Your paper doesn't need a separate title page; the title will go on your first page of text. On that page, one inch from the top on the upper left-hand side, type your name, your instructor's name, the course name and number, and the date. Below that, type the title, centered on the page. Begin the text of the paper below the title. For example:

```
Karoline Ann Fox

Professor Dethier

English 401

15 December 2008
              Metamorphosis, the Exorcist,
                    and Oedipus
        Ernst Pawel has said that Franz Kafka's The
Metamorphosis...
```

Note that everything is double-spaced. The title is not italicized (although italics would be used for the name of a book or other work that should be italicized), underlined, or boldfaced.

### 2.1.4 HEADER WITH PAGINATION

Make sure that every page is numbered. That's especially important with long papers. Type your last name and the page number in the upper right-hand corner, a half inch from the top and flush with the right margin: Ballenger 3. Don't use the abbreviation *p.* or a hyphen between your name and the number.

### 2.1.5 PLACEMENT OF TABLES, CHARTS, AND ILLUSTRATIONS

With MLA format, papers do not have appendixes. Tables, charts, and illustrations are placed in the body of the paper, close to the text that refers to them. Number tables and charts consecutively (Table 1, Table 2, and so on; Fig. 1, Fig. 2, and so on; notice

```
Table 1
Percentage of Students Who Self-Report Acts of Plagiarism
```

| Acts of Plagiarism | Never/ Rarely | Some- times | Often/ Very Freq. |
|---|---|---|---|
| Copy text without citation | 71 | 19 | 10 |
| Copy paper without citation | 91 | 5 | 3 |
| Request paper to hand in | 90 | 5 | 2 |
| Purchase paper to hand in | 91 | 6 | 3 |

```
Source: Scanlon, Patrick M., and David R. Neumann; "Internet
   Plagiarism among College Students"; Journal of College Student
   Development 43.3 (2002): 379; Print.
```

**FIGURE B2   Example of Format for a Table**

the abbreviation of "Figure"). Place the title of a table above it, flush left. Place the caption for a chart or illustration below it. For tables, charts, and illustrations that are borrowed, give full citations. This information goes at the bottom of a table or at the end of a caption for a chart or illustration. See Figure B2 for an example of a table formatted according to MLA guidelines.

## 2.2 Some Style Considerations

### 2.2.1 HANDLING TITLES

The general MLA rule for capitalization of titles is that the writer should capitalize the first letters of all principal words in a title, including any that follow hyphens. Words not capitalized include articles (*a, an,* and *the*), prepositions (*for, of, in, to,* and so on), coordinating conjunctions (*and, or, but, for*), and *to* in infinitives. However, these words are capitalized if they appear at the beginning or end of the title.

In May 2008, the MLA updated its citation style, and among the changes is a no-brainer in this era of word processing: a shift to *italicizing* titles of works rather than <u>underlining</u> them. The APA figured this out about a decade ago.

The new rules for deciding whether to italicize a title or place it in quotation marks (the usual alternative) make this distinction:

1. If the work is "published independently," italicize it. These works are typically books, Web sites, online databases, TV broadcasts, plays, periodicals, and so on.

2. If the title is part of a larger work—say, an article in a periodical or an episode of a TV program—then place it in quotation marks.

Here are examples:

*The Curious Researcher* (book)

*A Streetcar Named Desire* (play)

"Once More to the Lake" (essay in a collection)

*New York Times* (newspaper)

"Psychotherapy" (encyclopedia article)

"Funny Talking Animals" (YouTube clip)

### 2.2.2 STYLE RELATED TO SOURCES AND QUOTATIONS

**Names.**   Though it may seem by the end of your research project as if you're on familiar terms with some of the authors you cite, it's not a good idea to call them by their first names. Give the full names of people you cite when you first mention them, and then give only their last names if you mention them again.

**Ellipsis Points.**   Those are the three dots (or four, if the omitted material comes at the end of a sentence where they join a period) that indicate you've left out a word, phrase, or even whole section of a quoted passage. It's wise to use ellipsis points and omit material when you want to emphasize part of a quotation and don't want to burden your reader with unnecessary information, but be careful to preserve the basic intention and idea of the author's original statement. Ellipsis points can come at the beginning of a quotation, in the middle, or at the end, depending where it is you've omitted material. For example,

> "After the publication of a controversial picture that shows, for example, either dead or grieving victims..., readers in telephone calls and in letters to the editor, often attack the photographer for being tasteless..." (Lesser 56).

**Quotations.**   Quotations that run more than four lines long should be blocked, or indented one inch from the left margin. If your quote is longer than a single paragraph, indent the first sentence of each additional paragraph an additional quarter inch.

The quotation should be double-spaced. Quotation marks should not be used. The parenthetical citation is placed *after* the period at the end of the quotation. A colon is a customary way to introduce a blocked quotation. For example,

> Chris Sherman and Gary Price, in *The Invisible Web*, contend that much of the Internet, possibly most, is beyond the reach of researchers who use conventional search engines:
>
>> The problem is that vast expanses of the Web are completely invisible to general-purpose search engines like AltaVista, HotBot, and Google. Even worse, this "Invisible Web" is in all likelihood growing significantly faster than the visible Web that you're familiar with. It's not that search engines and Web directories are "stupid" or even badly engineered. Rather, they simply can't "see" millions of high-quality resources that are available exclusively on the Invisible Web. So what is this Invisible Web and why aren't search engines doing anything about it to make it visible? (xxi)

# Part Three: Preparing the Works Cited Page

The Works Cited page ends the paper. (This may also be called the "References Cited" or "Sources Cited" page, depending on the preference of your instructor.) Occasionally, instructors may want another kind of source list along with or instead of a Works Cited list: An "Annotated List of Works Cited" includes a brief description of each source; a "Works Consulted" list includes not only the sources you cited but also others that shaped your thinking; a "Content Notes" page, keyed to superscript numbers in the text of the paper, lists short asides that are not central enough to the discussion to be included in the text itself.

The Works Cited page is the workhorse of most college papers. Works Cited is essentially an alphabetical listing of all the sources you quoted, paraphrased, or summarized in your paper. If you have used MLA format for citing sources, your paper has numerous parenthetical references to authors and page numbers. The Works Cited page provides complete information on each source cited in the text for the reader who wants to know. (In APA format, this page is called "References" and is slightly different in how items are listed. See Appendix C for APA guidelines.)

## 3.1 Format

### Alphabetizing the List

Works Cited follows the text of your paper on a separate page. After you've assembled complete information about each source you've cited, put the sources in alphabetical order by the last name of the author. If the work has multiple authors, alphabetize by the last name of the first author listed. If the source has no author, then alphabetize it by the first key word of the title. If you're citing more than one source by a single author, you don't need to repeat the name for each source; simply place three hyphens followed by a period (- - - .) for the author's name in subsequent listings.

### Indenting and Spacing

Type the first line of each entry flush left, and indent subsequent lines of that entry (if any) a half inch. Double-space between each line and each entry. For example:

```
                                          Hall 10
                    Works Cited
      Biernacki, Patrick. Pathways from Heroin
          Addiction. Philadelphia: Temple UP, 1986.
          Print.
```

Brill, Leon. *The De-Addiction Process.*
    Springfield: Thomas, 1972. Print.

Epstein, Joan F., and Joseph C. Gfroerer.
    "Heroin Abuse in the United States."
    *National Clearinghouse for Alcohol and*
    *Drug Information.* US Dept. of Health and
    Human Services, Aug. 1997. Web. 24 Nov.
    2008.

Hall, Lonny. Personal interview. 1 Mar. 2009.

Kaplan, John. *The Hardest Drug: Heroin and*
    *Public Policy.* Chicago: U of Chicago P,
    1983. Print.

"Methadone." *Encyclopaedia Britannica.* 1999 ed.
    CD-ROM.

Shaffner, Nicholas. *Saucerful of Secrets: The*
    *Pink Floyd Odyssey.* New York: Dell, 1992.
    Print.

Strang, John, and Michael Gossop. *Heroin*
    *Addiction and Drug Policy: The British*
    *System.* New York: Oxford UP, 1994. Print.

Swift, Wendy, et al. "Transitions between Routes
    of Heroin Administration: A Study of
    Caucasian and Indochinese Users in South-
    Western Sydney, Australia." *Addiction*
    (1999): 71-82. Print.

## 3.2 Citing Books, in Print and Online

You usually need three pieces of information to cite a book: the name of the author or authors, the title, and the publication information. Information you need to cite for an online text depends on whether the book is also available in print. The following chart shows the basics for citing in-print and electronic books.

| CITING A BOOK IN PRINT | CITING AN E-BOOK |
| --- | --- |
| 1. Author(s) | 1. Author(s) |
| 2. *Title* | 2. *Title* |
| 3. Edition and/or volume (if relevant) | 3. Edition and/or volume (if relevant) |
| 4. Where published, by whom, and date | 4. If also in print, where published, by whom, and date; in any case, sponsoring organization, date of electronic publication |
| 5. Medium: Print | 5. Medium: Web |
| | 6. Date of access |

| SAMPLE CITATION: BOOK IN PRINT | SAMPLE CITATION: E-BOOK (WEB ONLY) |
| --- | --- |
| Donald, David H. *Lincoln.* New York: Simon, 1995. Print. | Lincoln, Abraham. *The Writings of Abraham Lincoln.* 2009. *B & R Samizdat Express.* Web. 28 Jan. 2011. |

**Author(s).**   Authors' names should appear as they do in the source. List an author's name with initials only if it appears that way on the title page. You don't need to include titles or degrees that sometimes follow an author's name (e.g., Diana Rosenstein PhD).

**Title.**   As a rule, the titles of books are italicized, with capitalization of the first letters of the first word and all principal words, including in any subtitles. Titles that are not italicized are usually those of pieces found within larger works, such as poems and short stories in anthologies. These titles are set off by quotation marks. Titles of religious works (the Bible, the Koran) are neither italicized nor enclosed within quotation marks. (See the guidelines in "Handling Titles," in Part Two.)

**Edition.**   If a book doesn't indicate an edition number, then it's probably a first edition, a fact you don't need to cite. Look on the title page. Signal an edition like this: *2nd ed., 3rd ed.,* and so on. If you're citing a multivolume work, include the total number of volumes in the citation following the book's title, using the abbreviation *vols.* (e.g., 2 vols.).

**Publication Information.**   For any book that has been published in print, this includes place, publisher, and date. Look on the title page to find out who published the book. Publishers' names are usually shortened in the Works Cited list; for example, *St. Martin's Press, Inc.,* is shortened to *St. Martin's.*

What publication place to cite may be unclear when several cities are listed on the title page. Cite the first one.

The date a book is published is usually indicated on the copyright page. If several dates or several printings by the same publisher are listed, cite the original publication date. However, if the book is a revised edition, give the date of that edition. One final variation: If you're citing a book that's a reprint of the original edition, give both dates. For example:

```
Stegner, Wallace. Recapitulation. 1979. Lincoln:

    U of Nebraska P, 1986. Print.
```

This book was first published in 1979 and then republished in 1986 by the University of Nebraska Press.

Online books also often appear in print, and in such cases your citation will include all the usual print publication information. For all online books you must give the date of electronic publication and the organization that is sponsoring the electronic text. These organizations range from commercial sponsors like Amazon to nonprofit groups like Project Gutenberg. You can usually find the name of the sponsor either in the text itself or on the Web page from which you downloaded the book.

**Medium.**    Following the publication information, you indicate the medium—*Print* or *Web*. Capitalize the word and follow it with a period.

**Date of Access.**    For electronic sources, the citation also includes the date you accessed the work. In the example that follows, notice the form for the date, as well as the print publication information and the sponsoring organization:

```
Badke, William. Research Strategies: Finding

    Your Way through the Information Fog.

    Lincoln: Writers Club P, 2000. iUniverse.

    Web. 12 July 2008.
```

**Page Numbers.**    Normally, you don't list page numbers of a book in your Works Cited. The parenthetical reference in your paper specifies the particular page or pages the material you borrowed is from. But if you use only part of a book—an introduction or an essay—list the appropriate page numbers following the publication date. A period should follow the page numbers. Notice in this example that if the author(s) or editor(s) of the entire work also wrote the introduction or essay you're citing, the second mention in that citation uses last name only:

> Lee, L. L., and Merrill Lewis. Preface. *Women,*
>
> *Women Writers, and the West.* By Lee and
>
> Lewis. Troy: Whitston, 1980. v-ix. Print.

## Sample Book Citations

The examples that follow show the form for some common variations on the basic book citation format. Although most of the examples are for printed books, the corresponding online source entries work in much the same way. Remember that for an online source, you would give print publication information if the source has also been published in print and then give the sponsoring organization and date of electronic publication, indicate Web as the medium, and give the date of access.

### 3.2.1 A BOOK WITH ONE AUTHOR

> Armstrong, Karen. *The Spiral Staircase.* New
>
> York: Knopf, 2004. Print.

*In-Text Citation:* (Armstrong 22)

### 3.2.2 A BOOK WITH TWO OR THREE AUTHORS

If a book has two authors, give the second author's names uninverted. Authors' names should be listed in title page order, not alphabetical order.

> Ballenger, Bruce, and Michelle Payne. *The*
>
> *Curious Reader.* New York: Longman, 2006.
>
> Print.

*In-Text Citation:* (Ballenger and Payne 14)

Cite a book with three authors like this:

Bloom, Lynn Z., Donald A. Daiker, and Edward M.
      White, eds. *Composition Studies in the New*
      *Millennium*. Carbondale: Southern Illinois
      UP, 2003.

*In-Text Citation:* (Bloom, Daiker, and White 200)

### 3.2.3 A BOOK WITH MORE THAN THREE AUTHORS

If a book has more than three authors, you may list the first and substitute the term *et al.* for the others.

Jones, Hillary, et al. *The Unmasking of Adam.*
      Highland Park: Pegasus, 1992. Print.

*In-Text Citation:* (Jones et al. 21-30)

### 3.2.4 SEVERAL BOOKS BY THE SAME AUTHOR

Baldwin, James. *Going to Meet the Man.* New York:
      Dell-Doubleday, 1948. Print.
---. *Tell Me How Long the Train's Been Gone.* New
      York: Dell-Doubleday, 1968. Print.

*In-Text Citation:* (Baldwin, *Going* 34) or (Baldwin,
      *Tell Me* 121)

### 3.2.5 AN ENTIRE COLLECTION OR ANTHOLOGY

Crane, R. S., ed. *Critics and Criticism: Ancient*
      *and Modern.* Chicago: U of Chicago P, 1952.
      Print.

*In-Text Citation:* (Crane xx)

### 3.2.6 A WORK IN A COLLECTION OR ANTHOLOGY

The title of a work in a collection should be enclosed in quotation marks. However, if the work was originally published as a book, its title should be italicized.

Jones, Robert F. "Welcome to Muskie Country."

*The Ultimate Fishing Book.* Ed. Lee

Eisenberg and DeCourcy Taylor. Boston:

Houghton, 1981. 122-34. Print.

*In-Text Citation:* (Jones 131)

Bahktin, Mikhail. *Marxism and the Philosophy of*

*Language: The Rhetorical Tradition.* Ed.

Patricia Bizzell and Bruce Herzberg.

New York: St. Martin's, 1990. 928-44.

Print.

*In-Text Citation:* (Bahktin 929-31)

### 3.2.7 AN INTRODUCTION, PREFACE, FOREWORD, OR PROLOGUE

Scott, Jerie Cobb. Foreword. *Writing Groups:*

*History, Theory, and Implications.* By Ann

Ruggles Gere. Carbondale: Southern Illinois

UP, 1987. ix-xi. Print.

*In-Text Citation:* (Scott x-xi)

Rich, Adrienne. Introduction. *On Lies, Secrets,*

*and Silence.* By Rich. New York: Norton,

1979. 9-18. Print.

*In-Text Citation:* (Rich 12)

### 3.2.8  A BOOK WITH NO AUTHOR

*Merriam-Webster Dictionary Online. Encyclopaedia*
   *Britannica*, 2011. Web. 8 Feb. 2011.

*In-Text Citation:* (Merriam-Webster 444)

### 3.2.9  AN ENCYLOPEDIA ARTICLE

"City of Chicago." *Encyclopaedia Britannica.*
   1999 ed. Print.

*In-Text Citation:* ("City of Chicago" 397)

For online encyclopedias, as for other online sources, include the name of the sponsor of the Web site and the date you accessed the site. Notice the in-text citation for this source without page numbers.

"Diarrhea." *Columbia Encyclopedia Online.* 6th
   ed. New York: Columbia UP, 2008. Web. 10
   June 2008.

*In-Text Citation:* ("Diarrhea")

*Wikipedia* raises eyebrows among many academics who don't consider it a particularly authoritative source, but should you need to cite it, include the date of the latest revision of the page you're citing. You can find that date at the bottom of the page.

"Flesh Fly." *Wikipedia.* Wikimedia Foundation,
   27 Jan. 2011. Web. 28 Jan. 2011.

*In-Text Citation:* ("Flesh Fly")

### 3.2.10  A BOOK WITH AN INSTITUTIONAL AUTHOR

Hospital Corporation of America. *Employee*
   *Benefits Handbook.* Nashville: HCA, 2004.
   Print.

*In-Text Citation:* (Hospital Corporation of
   America 5-7)

### 3.2.11 A BOOK WITH MULTIPLE VOLUMES

If you are using material from more than one volume of a multivolume work, include the number of volumes after the title (or edition number if appropriate). In your in-text citations, indicate the relevant volume.

> Baym, Nina, ed. *The Norton Anthology of American Literature*. 6th ed. 2 vols. New York: Norton, 2002. Print.

*In-Text Citation:* (Baym 2: 3)

If you use only one volume of a multivolume work, indicate which one along with the page numbers. The in-text citation then includes only the page number.

> Baym, Nina, ed. *The Norton Anthology of American Literature*. 6th ed. Vol 2. New York: Norton, 2002: 1115. Print.

*In-Text Citation:* (Baym 1115)

### 3.2.12 A BOOK THAT IS NOT A FIRST EDITION

Check the title page to determine whether the book is an edition other than the first (2nd, 3rd, 4th, etc.); if no edition number is mentioned, assume it's the first. Put the edition number right after the title.

> Ballenger, Bruce. *The Curious Researcher*. 8th ed. Boston: Longman, 2015. Print.

*In-Text Citation:* (Ballenger 194)

Citing the edition is necessary only for books that are *not* first editions. This includes revised editions (*Rev. ed.*) and abridged editions (*Abr. ed.*).

### 3.2.13  A BOOK PUBLISHED BEFORE 1900

For a book published before 1900, it's usually unnecessary to list the publisher.

Hitchcock, Edward. *Religion of Geology*. Glasgow,

    1851. Print.

*In-Text Citation:*  (Hitchcock 48)

### 3.2.14  A TRANSLATION

Montaigne, Michel de. *Essays*. Trans. J. M.

    Cohen. Middlesex: Penguin, 1958. Print.

*In-Text Citation:*  (Montaigne 638)

### 3.2.15  GOVERNMENT DOCUMENTS

Because of the enormous variety of government documents, citing them properly can be a challenge. Because most government documents do not name authors, begin an entry for such a source with the level of government (United States, State of Illinois, etc., unless the author is obvious from the title), followed by the sponsoring agency, the title of the work, and the publication information. Look on the title page to determine the publisher. If it's a federal document, then the Government Printing Office (abbreviated *GPO*) is usually the publisher.

United States. Bureau of the Census. *Statistical*

    *Abstract of the United States*. Washington:

    GPO, 1990. Print.

*In-Text Citation:*  (United States, Bureau of the

Census 79-83)

### 3.2.16  A BOOK THAT WAS REPUBLISHED

A fairly common occurrence, particularly in literary study, is to find a book that was republished, sometimes many years after the original publication date. In addition, some books first appear in hardcover and then are republished in paperback. To cite one, put the original date of publication immediately after the book's title, and then include the more current publication date, as usual, at the end of the citation. Do it like so:

> Ballenger, Bruce, and Barry Lane. *Discovering*
>
>     *the Writer Within: 40 Days to More*
>
>     *Imaginative Writing.* 1989. Shoreham:
>
>     Discover Writing P, 2008. Print.

*In-Text Citation:* (Ballenger and Lane 31)

## 3.3 Citing Articles, in Print and Online

Citations for articles from periodicals—magazines, newspapers, journals, and other such publications that appear regularly— are similar to those for books but include somewhat different information. As with books, citations for online articles have their own special requirements. The following chart shows, in the appropriate order, the elements for citations for a print article and an article from the Web or your library's online databases. As the following pages show, the elements actually included vary a bit depending on specifics of the source.

| PRINT ARTICLE | ARTICLE FROM A DATABASE OR THE WEB |
|---|---|
| 1. Author(s) | 1. Author(s) |
| 2. "Article Title" | 2. "Article Title" |
| 3. *Periodical Title* | 3. *Periodical Title* |
| 4. Volume and issue | 4. Volume and issue |
| 5. Date published | 5. Date published |
| 6. Page numbers | 6. Page numbers, if any (usually present in versions also in print) |
| 7. Medium: Print | 7. *Database* or Sponsor |
| | 8. Medium: Web |
| | 9. Date of access |

*(continued)*

| SAMPLE CITATION:<br>PRINT ARTICLE | SAMPLE CITATION:<br>DATABASE ARTICLE |
|---|---|
| Martinello, Marian L. "Learning to Question for Inquiry." *Educational Forum* 62 (1998): 164-71. Print. | Greenebaum, Jessica B. "Training Dogs and Training Humans: Symbolic Interaction and Dog Training." *Anthrozoos: An Interdisciplinary Journal of the Interactions of People & Animals* 23.2 (2010): 129-41. *ArticleFirst*. Web. 28 Jan. 2011. |

**Author(s).**  List the author(s)—one, two, or three or more—as you would for a book citation.

**Article Title.**  Unlike book titles, which are italicized, article titles are usually enclosed in quotation marks. Capitalize same as book citations.

**Periodical Title.**  Italicize periodical names, dropping introductory articles (*Aegis,* not *The Aegis*). Capitalize as for book citations. If you're citing a newspaper your readers may not be familiar with, include in the title—enclosed in brackets but not italicized—the city in which it was published. For example:

> MacDonald, Mary. "Local Hiker Freezes to Death."
>
> *Foster's Daily Democrat* [Dover] 28 Jan.
>
> 1992: 1. Print.

**Volume Number.**  Most academic journals are numbered as volumes (or, occasionally, feature series numbers); the volume number should be included in the citation. Popular periodicals sometimes have volume numbers, too, but these are not included in the citations. Indicate the volume number immediately after the journal's name. Omit the tag *vol.* before the number.

**Issue Number.**  Most scholarly journals have issue numbers as well as volume numbers. Include the issue number in your citation if one is given. Follow the volume number with a period and then the issue number, with no spaces. Volume 12, issue 1, would appear in your citation as "12.1."

**Date(s).**   When citing popular periodicals (newspapers, magazines, and so on), include the day, month, and year of the issue you're citing—in that order—following the periodical name. Academic journals are a little different. Because the issue number indicates when the journal was published within a given year, just indicate that year. Put it in parentheses following the volume number and before the page numbers. For example,

```
Elstein, David. "Training Dogs to Smell Off-
     Flavor in Catfish." Agricultural Research
     52.4 (2004): 10. Print.
```

Electronic-source citations usually include two dates: the date of publication and the date of access (when you visited the site and retrieved the document). There is a good reason for listing both dates: Online documents are changed and updated frequently—when you retrieved the material matters.

**Page Numbers.**   The page numbers of the article follow the volume and issue numbers or date. Just list the pages of the entire article, omitting abbreviations such as *p.* or *pp.* It's common for articles in newspapers and popular magazines *not* to run on consecutive pages. In that case, indicate the page on which the article begins, followed by a "+": (12+).

Newspaper pagination can be peculiar. Some papers wed the section (usually designated by a letter) with the page number (A4); other papers simply begin numbering anew in each section. Most, however, paginate continuously. See the following sample citations for newspapers for how to deal with these peculiarities.

Online sources, which often have no pagination at all, present special problems. If the article you're using from an online source also appeared in print, then you'll often find the same page numbers that are in the print version. But if an article appeared only online and has no page numbers, all you can do is signal that's the case, using the abbreviation *N. pag.* (no page numbers).

**Databases.**   The availability of full-text versions of many articles through the campus library's databases makes it possible for researchers to retrieve materials without hiking to the library. In recent years these databases have evolved to be highly user friendly, not only enabling researchers to easily search multiple databases at once but also offering them nifty features like citation formatting. Earlier in *The Curious Researcher* we explored the wide range of general and subject databases available to you. Citations for an article you've found on such a database should contain the same information as one for the print version, with the addition of the name of the database (in italics). Here's an example:

> Winbush, Raymond A. "Back to the Future:
>
> Campus Racism in the 21st Century." *Black*
>
> *Collegian* Oct. 2001: 102-03. *Expanded*
>
> *Academic ASAP*. Web. 12 Apr. 2002.

*In-Text Citation:*  (Winbush 102)

When citing an abstract from a library database, include the word "abstract" in the citation. For example,

> Erskine, Ruth. "Exposing Racism, Exploring
>
> Race." *Journal of Family Therapy* 24 (2002):
>
> 282-97. Abstract. *EBSCO Online Citations*.
>
> Web. 3 Dec. 2002.

*In-Text Citation:*  (Erskine)

**Medium.**    As with books, indicate the medium of the source (*Print, Web*).

## Sample Periodical Citations

### 3.3.1  A JOURNAL OR MAGAZINE ARTICLE

Cite articles from print magazines like this (notice that for a monthly magazine, only the month and year are given):

> Oppenheimer, Todd. "The Computer Delusion."
>
> *Atlantic Monthly* July 1997: 47-60. Print.

*In-Text Citation:*  (Oppenheimer 48)

```
Zimmer, Marc. "How to Find Students' Inner
    Geek." Chronicle of Higher Education 12
    Aug. 2005: B5. Print.
```

*In-Text Citation:* (Zimmer B5)

Cite print journal articles like this:

```
Allen, Rebecca E., and J. M. Oliver. "The
    Effects of Child Maltreatment on Language
    Development." Child Abuse and Neglect 6.2
    (1982): 299-305. Print.
```

*In-Text Citation:* (Allen and Oliver 299-300)

Online articles usually come from either a library database or a periodical's Web site. The key thing you need to know is whether the article is online only or also appeared in print, as in the latter case you need to include information about the print version as well.

Cite an article that appeared online only like this:

```
Beyea, Suzanne C. "Best Practices of Safe
    Medicine Administration." AORN Journal Apr.
    2005. Web. 26 Aug. 2005.
```

*In-Text Citation:* (Beyea)

For this document without page or paragraph numbers, simply give the author's name. Or avoid parenthetical citation altogether by mentioning the name of the source in your essay (for example: "According to Suzanne Beyea, medications are...").

Cite an online article that also appeared in print like this (this example is from a library database):

```
Liu, Eric Zhi Feng, and Chun Hung Liu.
    "Developing Evaluative Indicators for
    Educational Computer Games." British
```

```
Journal of Educational Technology 40.1

(2009): 174-78. Academic Search Complete.

Web. 5 Feb. 2009.
```

*In-Text Citation:*  (Liu and Liu 174)

### 3.3.2 A NEWSPAPER ARTICLE

Some newspapers have several editions (late edition, national edition), each of which may contain different articles. If an edition is listed on the masthead, include it in the citation.

```
Mendels, Pamela. "Internet Access Spreads to

More Classrooms." New York Times 1 Dec.

1999, late ed.: C1+. Print.
```

*In-Text Citation:*  (Mendels C1)

Some papers begin numbering pages anew in each section. In that case, include the section number if it's not part of pagination.

```
Brooks, James. "Lobsters on the Brink." Portland

Press 29 Nov. 1999, sec. 2: 4. Print.
```

*In-Text Citation:*  (Brooks 4)

Increasingly, full-text newspaper articles are available online using library databases such as Newspaper Source or through the newspapers themselves. As when citing other online articles, you'll need to include the database in italics if you used a database (e.g., *Newspaper Source*) and the date of access.
Cite a newspaper article from a database like this:

```
"Lobsterman Hunts for Perfect Bait." AP Online 7

July 2002. Newspaper Source. Web. 13 July

2008.
```

*In-Text Citation:*  ("Lobsterman")

An entry for an article from a newspaper's Web site would include both the title of the online site (in italics) and the name of the publication, even if they're the same, as in this example:

Wiedeman, Reeves. "A Playwright Whose Time Seems
    to Be Now." *New York Times*. New York Times,
    9 Feb. 2011. Web. 10 Feb. 2011.

*In-Text Citation:* (Wiedeman)

### 3.3.3 AN ARTICLE WITH NO AUTHOR

"The Understanding." *New Yorker* 2 Dec. 1991:
    34-35. Print.

*In-Text Citation:* ("Understanding" 35)

### 3.3.4 AN EDITORIAL

Unsigned editorial entries begin with the title.

"Paid Leave for Parents." Editorial. *New York
    Times* 1 Dec. 1999: 31. Print.

*In-Text Citation:* ("Paid Leave" 31)

To cite an editorial found online, include the date of access.

McGurn, William. "Obama, Religion, and the Public
    Square." Editorial. *WSJ.com*. Wall Street
    Journal, 8 June 2008. Web. 10 June 2008.

*In-Text Citation:* (McGurn)

### 3.3.5 A LETTER TO THE EDITOR

Ault, Gary Owen. "A Suspicious Stench." Letter.
    *Idaho Statesman* 18 Aug. 2005: 14. Print.

*In-Text Citation:* (Ault 14)

```
Wood, Bradford. "Living with a Disability, in a
    Caring Setting." Letter. Washington Post 27
    Jan. 2011. Web. 28 Jan. 2011.
```

*In-Text Citation:* (Wood)

#### 3.3.6 A REVIEW

```
Page, Barbara. Rev. of Allegories of Cinema:
    American Film in the Sixties, by David E.
    James. College English 54 (1992): 945-54.
    Print.
```

*In-Text Citation:* (Page 945–46)

```
O'Connell, Sean. "Beauty Is as Bardam Does." Rev.
    of Biutiful. WashingtonPost.com. Washington
    Post, 28 Jan. 2011. Web. 28 Jan. 2011.
```

*In-Text Citation:* (O'Connell)

#### 3.3.7 AN ABSTRACT

It's usually better to have the full text of an article for research purposes, but sometimes all you can come up with is an abstract, a short summary of the article that highlights its findings or summarizes its argument. Online databases frequently offer abstracts when they don't feature full-text versions of articles.

To cite an abstract, begin with information about the full version, and then include the information about the source from which you got the abstract. Unless the title of the source makes it obvious that what you are citing is an abstract (i.e., as with *Psychological Abstracts*), include the word "Abstract" after the original publication information, but don't italicize it or put it in quotation marks. In this example, the source of the abstract is a periodical database:

```
Edwards, Rob. "Air-raid Warning." New Scientist
    14 Aug. 1999: 48-49. Abstract. MasterFILE
    Premier. Web. 1 May 2009.
```

*In-Text Citation:* (Edwards)

The following citation is from the print version of *Dissertation Abstracts International,* a useful source of abstracts (notice that the word "abstract" isn't needed because this source contains just abstracts):

McDonald, James C. "Imitation of Models in

　　　the History of Rhetoric: Classical,

　　　Belletristic, and Current-Traditional."

　　　Diss. U of Texas, Austin. *DAI* 48 (1988):

　　　item 2613A. Print.

*In-Text Citation:* (McDonald)

## 3.4 Citing Web Pages and Other Online Sources

### 3.4.1 A WEB SITE OR PAGE FROM A WEB SITE

If you're citing a Web site, you're referring to either the entire site or a particular page. A citation for an entire Web site includes the author's name, though it's rare for an entire site to have identifiable authors. Lacking an author or compiler, begin with the Web site's name (in italics), the sponsoring organization and date published, medium of publication, and date of access. For example,

*Son of Citation Machine.* Landmark Project, 2009.

　　　Web. 12 Feb. 2009.

*In-Text Citation:* (*Son*)

More commonly, though, you'll be citing a page on a Web site, and this citation must include, along with all the Web site information mentioned above, the title of the Web page itself (in quotation marks). Begin with the author of the Web page, if there is one, as in this example:

Rogers, Scott. "The Stupid Vote." *The Conser-*

　　　*vative Voice.* Salem Web Network, 7 June

　　　2008. Web. 10 June 2008.

*In-Text Citation:* (Rogers)

268    *Appendix B  /  Guide to MLA Style*

Here's a citation for a page with an institutional sponsor rather than an author:

"ESL Instructors and Students." *The OWL at*
    *Purdue*. Purdue Online Writing Lab, 2011.
    Web. 8 Feb. 2011.

*In-Text Citation:* ("ESL Instructors")

Finally, here is a citation for a Web page with no author or institutional sponsor (notice it begins with the title of the Web site):

*Urban Wildlands*. Center for Biological
    Diversity, n.d. Web. 28 Jan. 2011.

*In-Text Citation:* (Urban Wildlands)

### 3.4.2 AN ONLINE POSTING

An online post can be a contribution to an e-mail discussion group like a listserv, a post to a bulletin board or usenet group, or an entry on a WWW forum. The description "Online posting" is included if there is no title. (The title is usually drawn from the message subject line.) List the author's name, Web site name, the date the material was posted, the medium, and the access date, as you would for other online citations.

Justin, Everett. "Team Teaching in Writing—
    Intensive Courses in a Science Context."
    *Writing Program Administration Listserv*.
    Arizona State U, 29 Jan. 2011. Web. 8 Feb.
    2011.

*In-Text Citation:* (Justin)

### 3.4.3 AN E-MAIL MESSAGE

Kriebel, David. "Environmental Address." Message
    to the author. 8 June 2008. E-mail.

*In-Text Citation:* (Kriebel)

### 3.4.4 A SOUND CLIP OR PODCAST

Cite an audio clip from a Web site like this:

Gonzales, Richard. "Asian American Political
       Strength." *Morning Edition.* Natl. Public
       Radio, 27 May 2008. Web. 12 July 2008.

*In-Text Citation:* (Gonzales)

A citation for a podcast should explicitly say that is the medium.
For example,

Johnson, Roberta. "Climate Changes, People
       Don't." *This American Life.* Natl. Public
       Radio, 14 Jan. 2011. Podcast. 8 Feb. 2011.

*In-Text Citation:* (Johnson)

### 3.4.5 AN ONLINE VIDEO

"Daughter Turns Dad In." Online video clip.
       *CNN.com.* Cable News Network, 4 Apr. 2008.
       Web. 10 Apr. 2008.

*In-Text Citation:* ("Daughter")

Shimabukuro, Jake. "Ukelele Weeps by Jake
       Shimabukuro." Online video clip. *YouTube.*
       YouTube, 4 Apr. 2008. Web. 6 Apr. 2008.

*In-Text Citation:* (Shimabukuro)

### 3.4.6 AN INTERVIEW

Boukreev, Anatoli. Interview. *Outside.* Mariah
       Media, 14 Nov. 2007. Web. 27 May 2008.

*In-Text Citation:* (Boukreev)

### 3.4.7  A BLOG ENTRY OR BLOG COMMENT

For a blog entry, include the author's name (or screen name), title of the entry, the phrase "Weblog entry," name of the blog, sponsoring organization (if any), date of update, the medium, and your date of access.

```
Dent, Shirley. "Written on the Body: Literary

    Tattoos." Weblog entry. The Blog: Books.

    Guardian News and Media, 9 June 2008. Web.

    10 June 2008.
```

*In-Text Citation:*  (Dent)

If you want to cite a comment on a blog—and sometimes they're pretty interesting—then include the author's name (or screen name); a title, if there is one, or the first few words of the post if there isn't one; "Weblog comment"; and the date it was posted. Then include the information on the blog that is the subject of the comment.

```
MargotBlackSheep. "Tattoos Exist in Every

    Culture." Weblog comment. 10 June 2008.

    Dent, Shirley. "Written on the Body:

    Literary Tattoos." The Blog: Books.

    Guardian News and Media, 9 June 2008. Web.

    10 June 2008.
```

*In-Text Citation:*  (MargotBlackSheep)

### 3.4.8  AN ONLINE IMAGE

Online images often don't give you much to go on. If there is a name of the artist and a title of the image, include them. If not, at least describe the image, and include the name of the sponsoring organization or site and when you downloaded it.

```
"China Town Engulfed." Online image. 12 May

    2008. BBC News. BBC, 8 June 2008. Web.

    10 June 2008.
```

# 3.5 Citing Other Sources

### 3.5.1 AN INTERVIEW

If you conducted the interview yourself, list your subject's name first, indicate what kind of interview it was (telephone interview, e-mail interview, or personal interview), and provide the date.

Hall, Lonny. Personal interview. 1 Mar. 2005.

*In-Text Citation:* (Hall)

Or avoid parenthetical reference altogether by mentioning the subject's name in the text: According to Lonny Hall, . . .

If you're citing an interview done by someone else (perhaps from a book or article) and the title does not indicate that it was an interview, you should include "interview" after the subject's name. Always begin the citation with the subject's name.

Stegner, Wallace. Interview. *Conversations with*

*Wallace Stegner.* By Richard Eutlain and

Wallace Stegner. Salt Lake: U of Utah P,

1990. Print.

*In-Text Citation:* (Stegner 22)

### 3.5.2 SURVEYS, QUESTIONNAIRES, AND CASE STUDIES

If you conducted a survey or case study, list it under your name and give it an appropriate title.

Ball, Helen. "Internet Survey." Boise State U,

1999. Print.

*In-Text Citation:* (Ball)

### 3.5.3 RECORDINGS

Generally, list a recording by the name of the performer and italicize the recording's title. Also include the recording company and year of issue. If you don't know the year, use the abbreviation *n.d.* Include the medium (CD, Audiocassette, LP, etc.).

Orff, Carl. *Carmina Burana.* Cond. Seiji Ozawa.

Boston Symphony. RCA, n.d. CD.

*In-Text Citation:* (Orff)

When citing a single song from a recording, put it in quotation marks:

Larkin, Tom. "Emergence." *Oceans*. Enso,

    1997. CD.

*In-Text Citation:* (Larkin)

### 3.5.4 TELEVISION AND RADIO PROGRAMS

List the title of the program (italicized), the station, and the date. If the episode has a title, list that first in quotation marks. You may also want to include the name of the narrator or producer after the title.

*All Things Considered.* Interview with Andre

    Dubus. Natl. Public Radio. WBUR, Boston, 12

    Dec. 1990. Radio.

*In-Text Citation:* (*All Things*)

"U.S. to Limit Sales Related to Amphetamine

    Scourge." *All Things Considered*. Natl.

    Public Radio. WBUR, Boston, 18 Aug. 2005.

    Radio.

*In-Text Citation:* ("U.S. to Limit")

### 3.5.5 FILMS, VIDEOS, AND DVDS

Begin with the title (italicized), followed by the director, the distributor, and the year. You may also include names of writers, performers, or producers. End with the date and any other specifics about the characteristics of the film or video that may be relevant (length and size).

*Saving Private Ryan.* Dir. Steven Spielberg.

    Perf. Tom Hanks, Tom Sizemore, and Matt

    Damon. Paramount, 1998. Film.

*In-Text Citation:* (*Saving*)

You can also list a video or film by the name of a contributor you'd like to emphasize.

```
Capra, Frank, dir. It's a Wonderful Life. Perf.

    James Stewart and Donna Reed. RKO Pictures,

    1946. Film.
```

*In-Text Citation:* (Capra)

### 3.5.6 ARTWORK

List each work by artist. Then cite the title of the work (italicized), the year of its creation, and where it's located (institution and city). If you've reproduced the work from a published source, include that information as well.

```
Homer, Winslow. Casting for a Rise. 1889.

    Hirschl and Adler Galleries, New York.

    Ultimate Fishing Book. Ed. Lee Eisenberg

    and DeCourcy Taylor. Boston: Houghton,

    1981. Print.
```

*In-Text Citation:* (Homer 113)

### 3.5.7 AN ADVERTISEMENT

To cite an advertisement in a periodical, first list the company behind the ad, the word "Advertisement," and then the publication information.

```
Volkswagen. Advertisement. Men's Health August

    2005: 115. Print.
```

*In-Text Citation:* (Volkswagen)

### 3.5.8 LECTURES AND SPEECHES

List the name of the speaker, followed by the title of the address (if any) in quotation marks, the name of the sponsoring organization, the location, and the date. Also indicate what kind of address it was (lecture, speech, etc.).

```
Naynaha, Siskanna. "Emily Dickinson's Last

    Poems." Sigma Tau Delta, Boise, 15 Nov.

    2011. Lecture.
```

*In-Text Citation:*

Avoid the need for parenthetical citation by mentioning the speaker's name in your text.

```
    In her presentation, Naynaha argued that

Dickinson. . . .
```

### 3.5.9 PAMPHLETS

Cite a pamphlet as you would a book.

```
New Challenges for Wilderness Conservationists.

    Washington: Wilderness Society, 1973.

    Print.
```

*In-Text Citation:*  (New Challenges)

# Part Four:
# Student Paper in MLA Style

Ashley Carvalho's essay, "Patching Up Belfast," is a compelling research essay on the innovations in trauma care that emerged from the decades of death during the conflict between Catholics and Protestants in Northern Ireland. During a semester abroad in Ireland, Ashley experienced the legacy of the conflict firsthand—through the colorful murals on public buildings, the lingering tension on the faces of Belfast residents, and, most of all, the words of several of the doctors who cared for victims. She combines firsthand observations, interviews, and other research to tell an amazing story of the courage and inventiveness of Belfast's health care providers, particularly those at Royal Victoria Hospital, which was at the epicenter of the violence. "Patching Up Belfast" is an inspiring example of how a writer can take a personal experience and use research to make it richer and more meaningful for both reader and writer.

Carvalho 1

Ashley Carvalho

Prof. Jill Heney

English 201

10 November 2010

Patching Up Belfast

It was May of 1972, and from his van-
tage point in a pub on the Malone Road,
Colin Russell saw the thick, inky pall of
smoke erupt and curdle blackly over Belfast city center. Mere seconds had gone
by when, right on cue, the pub's telephone trilled. Before the barman could
answer, before his ruddy face could pale
slightly, and even before his eyes could
flash uneasily to Colin and his mouth
could speak the words "Dr. Russell, it's
for you," Colin knew by the sinking feeling in his gut that it was the hospital,
calling him in despite the fact he was
off duty. It wasn't the first time this
scenario had happened, and, disturbingly,
it wouldn't be the last. "Tell them I'm
on my way"—and Colin was out the door,
leaving behind an untouched pint and a
pubful of people expecting the worst.

Take a walk down any major West
Belfast thoroughfare, particularly near
the Catholic Falls and Protestant Shankill
roads, and you'll see Northern Ireland's

*Ashley uses a "scene lead" (see page 172) to dramatize the purpose of her essay—an examination of the medical innovations that came from the tragedy of Northern Ireland's "Troubles."*

Carvalho 2

history splashed vividly onto walls, sides
of houses and buildings, like so many
pages torn from a giant coloring book. The
infamous political murals of West Belfast
illustrate a range of visceral emotions:
vengeance, hatred, sorrow, desperation,
and, above all, ferocious pride. Even before the Troubles, mural-painting had been
a conduit of self-expression for Belfast
natives, but the way these sentiments are
expressed has changed over the years. At
the height of the conflict, the sentiments behind the murals that sprang up
almost overnight were those of aggression
and anger. Nowadays, new murals continue
to appear almost weekly, but most focus on
moving toward a brighter, more peaceful
future, not only for Belfast, but also for
the world (see fig. 1).

Just as art can be inspired by tragedy, the violence and wartime atmosphere
of the Troubles have also resulted in the
creation of some of the most innovative
medical treatments the world has seen, and
it is this violence that provided a stimulus to Northern Ireland's hospitals to
make progress in medicine. Like the mural
painters, Northern Ireland's doctors and

Carvalho 3

Fig. 1.  Graffiti, Peace Wall, Belfast.

surgeons expressed their frustration and despair through their work. From something bad, they created good.

Although the deep-seated divide between Catholics and Protestants frequently put Northern Ireland in national news headlines from 1968 onward, the roots of sectarianism—the opposition between Nationalist Catholics and Unionist Protestants in Northern Ireland—date back to the seventeenth century, to the time of Oliver Cromwell. In 1649, Cromwell led English forces in an invasion of Ireland

*Images can enhance a paper if they add something to the discussion. See page 214 for things to consider about using pictures.*

Carvalho 4

to suppress Catholic power, and, within
three years, Cromwell's forces defeated
the major Irish cities and their armies
(Bardon 140-41). This paved the way for
English and Scottish Protestants to begin settling in the North of Ireland,
alongside the Irish Catholics who already
inhabited the area. With the close proximity of Catholics and Protestants con-
centrated in the North, the stage was set
for the sectarianism that fueled the fire
of the Troubles, and still lingers in today's Belfast.

Throughout the Troubles, Catholics
and Protestants were seemingly at logger-
heads, pitted against one another, which
leads to the common misconception that
the Troubles was primarily a religious
conflict. But the religious identity of
these groups is a secondary association;
the conflict is predominantly political. Republican and Nationalist parties
envision a united Ireland that includes
Northern Ireland and is independent of
British influence, whereas Loyalists
and Unionists desire Northern Ireland
to remain a part of the powerful United

*Here Ashley
addresses an
assumption
that she believes
most readers
share about her
topic. It's not
that simple, she
suggests, and
then explains
why.*

Carvalho 5

Kingdom and separate from the Republic of
Ireland (McKittrick and McVea 26-28).

In 1968, the violence of the Troubles
began with several small sparks born from a
housing allocation dispute that soon became
a full-fledged conflagration, and Northern
Ireland's history was to be forever transformed (McKittrick and McVea 40-44). Over
the next three decades, violence raged in
streets and city centers throughout Northern Ireland, resulting in casualties of a
type and scale previously unseen in Northern Ireland's hospitals. In a setting where
only one murder had been recorded in the
preceding decade, Northern Ireland's hospitals were suddenly inundated with Troubles
victims as the civil conflict became a part
of daily life (D'Sa, "Symposium" 51). Over
the thirty-year period of the Troubles,
nearly 3,600 people were killed, and over
ten times that number injured as a result
of the violence (McKittrick and McVea
324-28). From a medical perspective,
numbers of this magnitude are difficult to
cope with in any capacity, and Northern
Ireland's hospitals had to quickly mobilize
the resources, personnel, and expertise to
face the violence of the Troubles head-on.

Carvalho 6

Fig. 2.  Royal Victoria Hospital, Belfast.

Dr. Colin Russell is not a super-hero, and he doesn't claim to be. As a surgeon who worked in Belfast's Royal Victoria Hospital (see fig. 2) during the peak of the Troubles, Russell witnessed almost daily the tragedy of lives left wrecked by human hands, but rarely does he lose his composure speaking about his memories. In fact, I can't help but smile along with him as he remembers not the horror but the exhilaration, the sheer thrill of playing a healing role in the Troubles. In the sitting room of his spacious, secluded South Belfast home, Russell and his wife, Pat, sit opposite me. "I would be dishonest if I denied that

*If you use figures or tables in your paper, make sure you refer to them in the text.*

Carvalho 7

there was an excitement about working
during the Troubles," Russell says, opt-
ing for a conversational interview rather
than a rigid question-and-answer session.
"At night, there was an almost wartime
atmosphere prevailing in the hospital. We
were only people, confined together, under pressure, and emotions ran high. But
us doctors, we were not immune to getting
upset" (Russell).

In his mid-seventies now, Russell's
face still retains a youthful quality, a
perpetual, boyish eagerness for education
and understanding. For Russell, the time
of the Troubles was a hands-on learning experience. He began his postgradu-
ate schooling not as a surgeon, but as
a dentist. After completing a five-year
dentistry course at Queen's University
Belfast, Russell realized as the course
progressed that the aspect of dentistry
that interested him most was surgery. Upon
gaining a post as a dental surgeon in the
Royal Victoria Hospital, Russell became
increasingly frustrated; with his dental
degree, he simply didn't have enough education and expertise to work in the hospital's surgical wards. So, in 1967, he
went back to Queen's University, this time

Carvalho 8

as a medical student. Graduating in 1971,
just as the brewing political turmoil began to froth and boil over, Russell was
appointed to the surgical house staff of
the Royal Victoria, and the bulk of his
surgical training and career was spent at
the Royal Victoria during the height of
the Troubles—specifically, the 1970s and
early 1980s.

The outbreak of the Troubles was a
critical moment, a point of no return,
not only for Russell but also for countless other medical trainees working in
Belfast's hospitals at the turn of the
decade. Speak to any of these individuals, and the odds are that they can pin-
point the exact moment when, for them,
everything changed. Siobhan,[1] a doctor at
both the Royal Victoria and Belfast City
hospitals, attributes her life-changing
moment to the introduction of internment.
On August 9, 1971, Northern Ireland's
prime minister demanded the large-scale
arrest and imprisonment, without trial,
of suspected IRA members in the hopes
that civil violence would lessen with the
IRA locked away. Siobhan, only a junior

1. Name has been changed at the request of the
interviewee.

Carvalho 9

doctor at the time, recalls what August
9, 1971, symbolized for her:

> I remember looking out from the
> second floor of the West wing of
> the Royal Victoria, where my bedroom
> was at that time, and seeing scores
> of troop carriers arrive silently,
> in the dead of night. One minute,
> Dunville Park across the road was
> as it ever was. The next moment,
> it was surrounded by a host of
> camouflaged vehicles, silently
> moving in and taking their places
> in a massed migration influx. My
> life, our lives, would never be
> the same again. Like seeing Kennedy
> shot, like seeing a man land on the
> moon, like seeing the Twin Towers
> falling, it was a salient moment
> in history, one which I will never
> forget.

*Quotations that are more than four lines are "blocked" by indenting one inch from the left margin. And, by the way, what a great quotation!*

As the largest and best-equipped
hospital in all of Northern Ireland, the
Royal Victoria experienced a recurring
influx of patients injured in riots,
and the hospital's proximity to the
Falls Road meant that it was often the
center of the riot zones. In the nearly
thirty years of violence, the Royal

Carvalho 10

Victoria accommodated victims of rioting
episodes almost nightly (Clarke 114-18).
These were peppered in between frequent
terrorist bombings, and the combination
of the two types of incidents produced a
steady stream of casualties. Secondly,
and equally problematic, was the need for
the hospital and its employees to remain
neutral throughout the conflict. This
proved difficult for some, particularly
during the many high-stress, emotionally
charged incidents the violence of the
Troubles produced. Many of the injured who
arrived in the hospital's Accident and
Emergency Department following a bombing
or shooting were friends or relatives of
the medical personnel. Still others who
sought medical care from the hospital were
paramilitaries or members of a wrongdoing
sectarian gang. Within the highly
politicized milieu of the Troubles, where
one's religious and political views could
be figured out just by learning one's
name (during the Troubles and even today,
a Gerald O'Callahan or an Aisling Murphy
would be categorized as a Republican Irish
Catholic while a Richard Carrington or an
Elizabeth Montgomery would be assumed a
Unionist Protestant), shrugging off the

Carvalho 11

shroud of politics and throwing on the
neutrality cloak [weren't] exactly easy.
But healthcare providers in Northern
Ireland sidestepped this difficulty
and continued to provide high-quality,
nonbiased healthcare to the injured.

In the hospital ward, medical
personnel looked after civilians,
terrorists, freedom fighters, innocent
bystanders, policemen, and soldiers
alike, curious but never aware of who
was who, or who fired the deadly bullet
or detonated the lethal bomb, or who
was Catholic or Protestant. In tense
situations, Siobhan focused on her work:
"I learned very early on to be apolitical
and to never, ever comment on any
political incident one way or another,
to my colleagues or to my patients. My
role was to care always and to cure if
possible."

The most catastrophic weapon appeared
on the stage of the Troubles at the end of
1971. Worried that the British army would
not be able to contain the IRA, and wanting to exercise their newfound strength,
the loyalist Ulster Volunteer Force (UVF)
in conjunction with the Ulster Defense
Association (UDA) placed a fifty-pound

Carvalho 12

bomb in a small North Belfast Catholic pub called McGurk's Bar. The explosion killed fifteen people and injured many more (McKittrick and McVea 75). This incident marked the debut of the bomb as a means for paramilitary organizations to influence Belfast's street politics.

Bombings provided a sizeable stimulus to Belfast's healthcare services in two ways: first, to develop a system that could provide comprehensive care to the sheer numbers of those injured in a bombing incident and, second, to create new methods of treatment to address the variety of injuries produced in a bomb blast. For example, the McGurk's Bar bombing resulted in a wide range of injury patterns, the worst of which included crush injuries, burn injuries, cranial injuries, lacerations from projectiles, and carbon monoxide poisoning (Gillespie 37-40).

*A sentence like this firmly reattaches the essay to its thesis much like a tack pins down loose fabric so that it keeps its shape.*

Regarded as the most violent year of the Troubles, 1972 saw an unparalleled level of violence, and the state of civil conflict in Northern Ireland closely resembled civil war. The events of this year placed a higher strain on Belfast's hospital services than any other year

Carvalho 13

of the Troubles, not necessarily because
the incidents of violence were the most
catastrophic, but because they occurred
with an unpredictable and terrifying
frequency. One month into the year, the
infamous Bloody Sunday in Londonderry
left thirteen dead and another thirteen
injured when British troops openly fired
upon a large illegal march. Enraged,
Republican supporters bolstered the IRA
with money, guns, and men, and violence
was loosed upon the streets throughout
Northern Ireland (Coogan 674-75). Riots,
shootings, and bombings began to occur
with alarming regularity. On March 4th,
the IRA slipped a six-pound bomb inside
one of the shopping bags carried by two
sisters. Having decided to stop for tea,
the girls, unknowingly carrying the
bomb, entered the Abercorn, a popular
restaurant in Belfast city center. The
girls were killed immediately and at
least one hundred others were injured
(Gillespie 47-49). For the first time in
its history, the Royal Victoria used a
documented disaster plan to care for the
masses of the injured (McKittrick and
McVea 78).

Carvalho 14

Bomb injuries presented an entirely
new set of challenges to Belfast's
hospitals. Colin Russell, who worked in
the Royal Victoria that day, recalled
that mass casualty on this large a scale
was an entirely new experience, one
that the hospital and its staff weren't
totally ready for. "There were horrific
injuries," Russell remembers. Making
matters worse, this particular bomb was
designed to explode outward, rather
than upward as most bombs do, and the
shockwaves from the blast careened along
the Abercorn's wooden floors. Trying to
contain my horror, I winced inwardly as
Russell showed me some slides containing
photographs of the horrific injuries that
came into the Royal that day: a chair leg
shot through someone's thigh, pieces of
amputated limbs placed on green towels in
the surgical wards, unable to be reunited
with the bodies of their owners, faces
charred beyond recognition. But none of
this prepared me for the emotional shock
that came next from Russell's memories:
"I remember the senior anesthetist who
was on call at the time, working on one
of the victims of the bombing in the
operating room. He was completely unaware

Carvalho 15

of the fact that the two sisters who were carrying the bomb and who were killed in the blast were his daughters" (Russell).

The medical progress made in Northern Ireland's hospitals during the Troubles speaks to the remarkable ability of the medical personnel to rise to the challenges posed by the civil violence. Developments in disaster planning, triage, and organization in Northern Ireland's hospitals went hand-in-hand with the creation of specific medical treatments to address the needs of civil violence victims. Throughout the Troubles, paramilitary violence generated casualties that varied greatly in the type and pattern of injury as well as in the numbers of injured, calling attention to the need for a comprehensive, all-encompassing system of treatment. In Northern Ireland's hospitals, the seamless joining of the methods of disaster planning and the methods of medical treatment enabled these hospitals to meet the demands of mass casualty terrorist incidents head-on throughout the decades of civil violence.

The innovation of Belfast's medics is clearly seen in the treatment of punishment injuries. These injuries were

*This paragraph is a typical example of how well Ashley reports information from her research but finds her own way of saying things (e.g., "in a bizarre twist of vigilante justice") and characterizing them.*

Carvalho 16

different from other types of injury seen
during the Troubles because they were
completely nonsectarian; in a bizarre
twist of vigilante justice, Protestants
would shoot Protestants, and Catholics
would shoot Catholics, usually for some
sort of wrongdoing on the victim's part. A
certain subset of punishment injury termed
"kneecapping," whereby the victim was shot
from close range in the back of the legs,
is unique to Northern Ireland and, as such,
necessitated a unique form of surgical
treatment (Nolan and McCoy 405-06). If an
individual were suspected of a serious
crime, such as rape or murder, he would be
punished with gunshots through the elbows
and ankles in addition to the knees—the
proverbial "six pack"—although this type of
punishment was much less common.

Throughout the thirty-year period of
violence, some 2,500 people in Northern
Ireland sustained a kneecapping injury
(Williams 79). The high prevalence of
this type of injury and the severe
destruction of knee vasculature that it
caused presented a host of challenges
to trauma surgeons during the Troubles,
and it wasn't long before they developed
effective methods of treatment. Belfast's

Carvalho 17

trauma surgeons learned to reconnect
the damaged blood vessels in the knee
using an ingenious system of shunts and
vein grafts, and toward the end of the
Troubles most kneecapping injuries were
repaired successfully and quickly, the
victim up and walking within a matter of
months (D'Sa, "Decade" 38-39).

But however clever Belfast's trauma
surgeons proved to be, the paramilitary
organizations tried to be more clever. In
response to the surgical developments made
by trauma surgeons during the Troubles, the
IRA changed its methods of kneecapping in
order to cause further damage and to hinder
surgeons in repairing the knee vasculature,
which in turn prompted surgeons to again
reinvent treatment methods in reaction.

The method created in Belfast to
restructure severely fractured skulls might
be the most resourceful of all medical
developments during the Troubles. This
method was created in the mid 1970s and was
the brainchild of a dental surgeon, George
Blair, and a neurosurgeon, Derrick Gordon,
in the Royal Victoria. Skull fractures like
the ones seen during the Troubles posed a
real challenge to neurosurgeons, not least
because of the bony defects that resulted

Carvalho 18

in the skull, but also the fact that pieces
of the skull were often lost, leaving the
underlying brain layers completely exposed.
Gordon and Blair devised a method of
treatment in which a material used to make
impressions of the teeth called alginate
was poured into a light metal cap, which
was placed on the patient's head to make
an impression of the fractured skull.
Then, titanium metal was poured into the
impression to make a plate, which was
fitted into the patient's skull. Titanium,
as a fairly light yet inert metal, was
perfect for the job. Later research showed
that the success rate for this procedure
was at least 90 percent (Roy 544). Today,
this treatment method is used in hospitals
worldwide.

Even today, the tension isn't
completely gone from Belfast's streets. It
will still take another couple of genera-
tions for the emotional sting of the
Troubles to lose its poignancy and for the
painfully sharp memories of the violence
to soften around the edges. But even now,
the hope of Belfast's overwhelming
majority is one of peace, of moving away
from a violent, harrowing past and toward
a brighter future. In terms of the

Carvalho 19

Fig. 3.  Rainbow in a Troubled Sky, Belfast.

developments and progress in medicine
achieved by Northern Ireland's healthcare
workers, Northern Ireland's medics left a
legacy of tenacity, determination, and
strength of spirit. Just as the mural-
painters fought the Troubles by expressing
themselves through art, the medics fought
the Troubles in their own way: by patching
up Belfast and healing the city. In
finding a silver lining within the black
stormclouds of the Troubles, placing a
rainbow (see fig. 3) in Belfast's perpetu-
ally grey skies, and creating good from
bad, these medics are truly remarkable.

Carvalho 20

Works Cited

Bardon, Jonathan. *A History of Ulster.* Belfast:

    Blackstaff Press, 1992. Print.

Clarke, Richard. *The Royal Victoria Hospital*

    *Belfast: A History 1797-1997.* Belfast:

    Blackstaff Press, 1997. Print.

Coogan, Tim Pat. *The Troubles: Ireland's Ordeal*

    *and the Search for Peace.* New York:

    Palgrave, 1996. Print.

D'Sa, Airres Barros. "A Decade of Missile-Induced

    Vascular Trauma." *Annals of the Royal*

    *College of Surgeons of England* 64 (1982):

    37-44. Print.

---. "Symposium Paper: Management of Vascular

    Injuries of Civil Strife." *British Journal*

    *of Accident Surgery* 14.1 (1982): 51-57.

    Print.

Gillespie, Gordon. *Years of Darkness: The*

    *Troubles Remembered.* Dublin: Gill &

    Macmillan, 2008. Print.

McKittrick, David, and David McVea. *Making Sense*

    *of the Troubles.* London: Penguin, 2001.

    Print.

Nolan, P. C., and G. McCoy. "The Changing Pattern

    of Paramilitary Punishments in Northern

    Ireland." *Injury* 27.6 (1996): 405-06.

    Print.

*The Works Cited list begins on a new page at the end of your paper.*

Carvalho 21

Roy, Douglas. "Gunshot and Bomb Blast Injuries:
   A Review of the Experience in Belfast."
   *Journal of the Royal Society of Medicine*
   75.7 (1982): 542-45. Print.

Russell, Colin. Personal interview. Oct. 2010.

Siobhan. Personal interview. Sept. 2010.

Williams, John. "Casualties of Violence in
   Northern Ireland." *International Journal of
   Trauma Nursing* 3.3 (1997): 78-82. Print.

# APPENDIX C

# Guide to APA Style

The American Psychological Association (APA) style is, like MLA style, commonly used for documenting and formatting college papers. APA style is the standard for papers in the social and behavioral sciences as well as in education and business. In those disciplines, the currency of the material cited is often especially important. Therefore, APA style's author/date citation system emphasizes the date of publication, in contrast to MLA's author/page system.

## Checklist Before Handing in a Paper in APA Style

- My paper is double-spaced throughout, including the References list (see pages 311, 313, and 326).
- I have a running head (see pages 306–307) in the upper left-hand corner on each page, and a page number in the upper right-hand corner.
- I've cited page numbers in my paper whenever I've quoted a source.
- I've "blocked" every quotation that is 40 or more words (see page 310).
- Whenever possible, I've mentioned in my text the names of authors I cite and put the date of the appropriate publication next to their names.
- I've doubled-checked the accuracy of DOIs and URLs of electronic sources that I included in my References.
- The References list begins on a new page and is organized alphabetically by the authors' last names.
- In article and book titles cited, only the first words of titles and subtitles are capitalized; the remaining words are not capitalized unless they would always be capitalized.

I think you'll find APA style easy to use, especially if you've had some practice with MLA. Converting from one style to the other is easy (for some key differences between the two, see Table 1). Appendix C covers what you need to know about APA style, including how and when to cite sources in your essay (Part One) and how to assemble the References page (Part Three). The discussion of conventions for formatting your paper (Part Two) offers guidance on pagination, layout, and specifics of style.

**TABLE 1**   Key Differences Between MLA and APA Formats

| MLA | APA |
| --- | --- |
| Capitalizes most words in book and article titles on Works Cited page. | Capitalizes only the first word and proper nouns in book and article titles on References page. |
| Uses author's full first and last names on Works Cited page. | Uses author's last name along with first and middle initials on References page. |
| Uses the word "and" to combine authors' names in in-text citations and on Works Cited page if there is more than one author for a source. | Uses an ampersand (&) to combine authors' names in in-text citations and on References page if a source has more than one author. |
| In-text citations use author's last name and pages cited. | In-text citations use author's last name and date; page numbers aren't required except for quotations. |
| In-text citations use no punctuation between author's name and page number. | In-text citations use a comma between author's last name and date, and between date and page numbers. |
| Page numbers are listed simply as a number in in-text citations. | Page numbers are denoted with a "p." or "pp." in in-text citations. |
| There is no separate title page. | There is a title page with running head. |
| Running head contains author's last name and the page number, in the top right-hand corner. | Running head contains the first words of the paper's title (at left) and the page number (at right). |
| No subheadings occur within the paper. | Subheadings often occur within the paper. Paper often begins with an abstract. |
| Tables and figures are integrated into the body of the paper. | Tables and figures can be integrated or appear in an appendix. |

Finally, you can see what APA style looks like in a paper like the one you're writing (Part Four).

The *Publication Manual of the American Psychological Association*\* is the authoritative reference on APA style, and the sixth edition, published in 2010, features some updates, including some new guidelines for referencing electronic sources. The APA Web site now includes some free tutorials on the citation style, narrated by a guy who seems really excited about it. Though the information in the sections that follow should answer your questions, check the manual when in doubt.

## Directory of APA Style

\**Publication Manual of the American Psychological Association.* 6th ed. Washington, DC: APA, 2010. Print.

# Part One:
# Citing Sources in Your Essay

## 1.1 The APA Author/Date System

*The Basics of Using Parenthetical Citation*

The author/date system is pretty uncomplicated. If you mention the name of the author in your text, simply place the year her work was published in parentheses immediately after her name. For example:

```
Herrick (2006) argued that college testing was

biased against minorities.
```

If you mention both the author's name and the year in the text of your essay, then you can omit the parenthetical citation altogether. For example:

```
In 2006, Herrick argued that college testing was

biased against minorities.
```

If you don't mention the author's name in the text, then include that information parenthetically. For example:

```
A New Hampshire political scientist (Bloom,
2008) studied the state's presidential
primary.
```

Note that the author's name and the year of her work are separated by a comma.

**When to Cite Page Numbers.**   If the information you're citing came from specific pages (or chapters or sections) of a source, that information may also be included in the parenthetical citation, as in the example below. Including page numbers is essential when quoting a source.

```
The first stage of language acquisition is
called caretaker speech (Moskowitz, 1985, pp.
50–51), in which children model their parents'
language.
```

Or, if the author's name is mentioned in the text:

```
Moskowitz (1985) observed that the first stage
of language acquisition is called caretaker
speech (pp. 50-51), in which children model
their parents' language.
```

### 1.1.1 A WORK BY ONE AUTHOR

```
Herrick (2006) argued that college testing was
biased against minorities.
```

*or*

```
One problem with college testing may be bias
(Herrick, 2006).
```

### 1.1.2  A WORK BY TWO AUTHORS

When a work has two authors, always mention them both whenever you cite their work in your paper. For example:

```
Allen and Oliver (1998) observed many cases of
child abuse and concluded that maltreatment in-
hibited language development.
```

Notice that if the authors' names are given in a parenthetical citation, an ampersand is used:

```
Researchers observed many cases of child abuse
and concluded that maltreatment inhibited lan-
guage development (Allen & Oliver, 1998).
```

### 1.1.3  A WORK BY THREE TO FIVE AUTHORS

If a source has three to five authors, mention them all the first time you refer to their work. However, in any subsequent references give the name of the first author followed by the abbreviation *et al.* For example, here's what a first mention of a multiple-author source would look like:

```
The study found that medical students some-
times responded to an inquiry-based approach
by becoming more superficial in their analyses
(Balasoriya, Hughes, & Toohey, 2011).
```

Subsequent mentions use the abbreviation *et al.*:

```
Though collaboration is supposed to promote
learning, in one case it actually hindered it
(Balasoriya et al., 2011).
```

### 1.1.4  A WORK BY SIX OR MORE AUTHORS

When citing works with six or more authors, *always* use the first author's name and *et al.*

### 1.1.5 AN INSTITUTIONAL AUTHOR

When citing a corporation or agency as a source, simply list the year of the study in parentheses if you mention the institution in the text:

```
The Environmental Protection Agency (2007) is-
sued an alarming report on global warming.
```

If you don't mention the institutional source in the text, spell it out in its entirety, along with the year. In subsequent parenthetical citations, abbreviate the name. For example:

```
A study (Environmental Protection Agency [EPA],
2007) predicted dire consequences from continued
global warming.
```

And later:

```
Continued ozone depletion may result in wide-
spread skin cancers (EPA, 2007).
```

### 1.1.6 A WORK WITH NO AUTHOR

When a work has no author, cite an abbreviated title and the year. Place article or chapter titles in quotation marks, and italicize book titles. For example:

```
The editorial ("Sinking," 2007) concluded that
the EPA was mired in bureaucratic muck.
```

### 1.1.7 TWO OR MORE WORKS BY THE SAME AUTHOR

Works by the same author are usually distinguished by the date; these would rarely be published in the same year. But if they are, distinguish among works by adding an *a* or *b* immediately following the year in the parenthetical citation. The References list will also have these suffixes. For example:

```
Douglas's studies (1986a) on the mating hab-
its of lobsters revealed that the females are
```

```
dominant. He also found that the female lob-
sters have the uncanny ability to smell a loser
(1986b).
```

These citations alert readers that the information came from two works by Douglas, both published in 1986.

### 1.1.8 AUTHORS WITH THE SAME LAST NAME

In the rare case that you're using sources from different authors with the same last name, distinguish between them by including the first initials of each author whenever you mention them in your paper, even if the publication dates differ:

```
M. Bradford (2010) and L. S. Bradford (2008)
both noted that Americans are more narcissistic.
```

### 1.1.9 SEVERAL SOURCES IN A SINGLE CITATION

Occasionally, you'll want to cite several sources at once. Probably the most common instance is when you refer to the findings of several relevant studies, something that is a good idea as you try to establish a context for what has already been said about your research topic. When listing multiple sources within the same parenthetical citation, order them as they appear in the References (that is, alphabetically) and separate them with semicolons. For example:

```
A number of researchers have explored the con-
nection between Internet use and depression
(Sanders, Field, & Diego, 2000; Waestlund,
Norlander, & Archer, 2001).
```

### 1.1.10 INDIRECT SOURCES

If you discover, say, a great quotation or idea from someone who is mentioned in another author's book or article, try to track down the original source. But when you can't find it, signal parenthetically that you're using an indirect source with the phrase *as cited in*.

```
De Groot's study on chess expertise (as cited in
Kirschner, Sweller, & Clark, 2006) is....
```

The only source you'll include in your References list is the indirect source you used; you won't include the original source.

### 1.1.11 NEW EDITIONS OF OLD WORKS

For reprints of older works, include both the year of the original publication and that of the reprint edition (or the translation).

Pragmatism as a philosophy sought connection between scientific study and real people's lives (James, 1906/1978).

### 1.1.12 INTERVIEWS, E-MAIL, AND LETTERS

Interviews and other personal communications are not listed in the References at the back of the paper because they are not *recoverable data,* but they are parenthetically cited in the text. Provide the initials and last name of the subject (if not mentioned in the text), the nature of the communication, and the complete date, if possible.

Nancy Diamonti (personal communication, November 12, 1990) disagrees with the critics of *Sesame Street.*

In a recent e-mail, Michelle Payne (personal communication, January 4, 2011) complained that. . . .

### 1.1.13 A WEB SITE

When referring to an *entire* Web site, cite the address parenthetically in your essay. Do not include a citation for an entire Web site in your References list.

The Centers for Disease Control (http://www.cdc.gov) is a reliable source for the latest health information.

If you're quoting from a Web site, you should cite the date of online publication, if available, and the page number, if available. (When simply referring to a part of a Web site, just use the date, if available, not the page number.) However, most Web documents that aren't also available in print do not have page numbers. What do you do in that case? If you can, use a heading or short title from the source to help readers locate the part of the document where they can find the material you cited. Then add a paragraph number using the abbreviation *para.*

```
According to Cesar Milan (2010), it's essen-

tial that dog owners establish themselves as

"pack leaders" ("Why Does CDC Teach Wolf Pack

Theory?", para. 2).
```

# Part Two: Formatting Your Essay

## 2.1 Formatting the Essay and Its Parts

### 2.1.1 PAGE FORMAT AND HEADER

Papers should be double-spaced, with at least one-inch margins on all sides. Number all pages consecutively, beginning with the title page; using the Header feature of your word processor, put the page number in the upper right-hand corner. In the upper left-hand corner of each page, beginning with the title page, give an abbreviated title of the paper in uppercase letters. As a rule, the first line of all paragraphs of text should be indented five spaces or a half inch.

### 2.1.2 TITLE PAGE

Unlike a paper in MLA style, an APA-style paper usually has a separate title page. The title page includes the title of the paper, the author's name, and the author's affiliation (e.g., what university she is from). As Figure C1 shows, this information is double-spaced, and each line is centered. The upper left of the title page has the abbreviated title in uppercase letters, preceded by "Running head" and a colon, and the upper right has the page number.

### 2.1.3 ABSTRACT

Though it's not always required, many APA-style papers include a short abstract (between 150 to 250 words) following the title page. See Figure C2. An abstract is essentially a short summary of the paper's contents. This is a key feature because it's usually the first thing

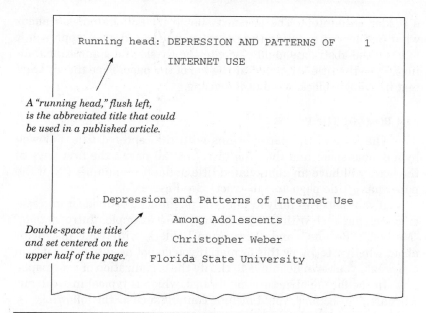

Running head: DEPRESSION AND PATTERNS OF     1
                    INTERNET USE

A *"running head," flush left, is the abbreviated title that could be used in a published article.*

Depression and Patterns of Internet Use

Among Adolescents

Christopher Weber

Florida State University

*Double-space the title and set centered on the upper half of the page.*

**FIGURE C1**    **Title Page in APA Style**

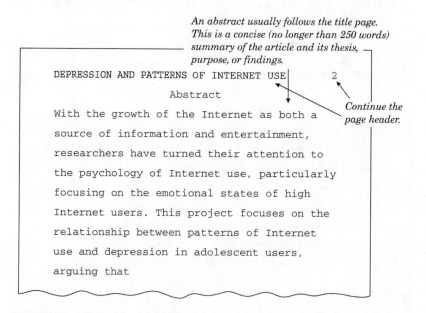

*An abstract usually follows the title page. This is a concise (no longer than 250 words) summary of the article and its thesis, purpose, or findings.*

DEPRESSION AND PATTERNS OF INTERNET USE     2

Abstract

With the growth of the Internet as both a source of information and entertainment, researchers have turned their attention to the psychology of Internet use, particularly focusing on the emotional states of high Internet users. This project focuses on the relationship between patterns of Internet use and depression in adolescent users, arguing that

*Continue the page header.*

**FIGURE C2**    **The Abstract Page**

a reader encounters. The abstract should include statements about what problem or question the paper examines and what approach it follows; the abstract should also cite the thesis and significant findings. Type the title "Abstract" at the top of the page. Type the abstract text in a single block, without indenting.

**2.1.4 BODY OF THE PAPER**

The body of the paper begins with the centered title, followed by a double space and then the text. Like all pages, the first page of the body will have an abbreviated title and a page number ("3" if the paper has a title page and abstract). See Figure C3.

If your paper is fairly formal, you might need to divide it into specific sections, each with its own heading—for example, "Introduction," "Method," "Results," and "Discussion." Check with your instructor about whether to follow this format. If you do not need to follow it, you can create your own headings to clarify the organization of your paper.

In the formal structure mentioned, which is typical in academic journals, the sections would include content such as the following:

- Introduction: Why does your research question matter? What has already been said about it? What is the hypothesis you'll be exploring?
- Method: How did you test your hypothesis? What you say here depends on the kind of study you did.

DEPRESSION AND PATTERNS OF INTERNET USE          3

Depression and Patterns of Internet Use Among

Adolescents

　　　　　　　　　　　　　　　　　　　　　　　*Center the title*
Before Johnny Beale's family got a new     *of the paper*

computer in August 2008, the sixteen-year-old   *and double-space*
*to begin the body*
high school student estimated that he spent    *of the text.*

about twenty minutes a day online, mostly

checking his e-mail. Within months, however,

Beale's time at the computer tripled, and he

admitted that he spent most of his time

playing games. At first, his family noticed

**FIGURE C3    The Body of the Paper in APA Style**

- Results: What did you find?
- Discussion: How do you interpret the findings? To what extent do they support—or fail to support—your initial hypothesis? What are the implications of these discoveries?

### 2.1.5 HEADINGS

If you use headings, the APA specifies the following hierarchy:

**Centered, Boldface, Uppercase and**

**Lowercase** (Level 1)

**Flush Left, Boldface, Uppercase and**   *Five levels*
                                          *of headings*
**Lowercase** (Level 2)

    **Indented, boldface, lowercase, ending with**
**period, running into paragraph.** (Level 3)

    ***Indented, boldface, italicized,***
***lowercase, ending with period, running into***
***paragraph.*** (Level 4)

    *Indented, italicized, lowercase, ending with*
*a period, running into paragraph.* (Level 5)

A paper, particularly a short one, will rarely use all five levels of headings. In fact, it's much more common for a student paper to use just two or possibly three.

### 2.1.6 HANDLING QUOTED MATERIAL

When you borrow words, phrases, or passages from another author, typically the material must be contained in quotation marks. Usually, it is smoothly integrated with attribution (*According to Ballenger, ...*), and parenthetical citation including page numbers, into your own sentences and paragraphs. For example,

> According to Ellison, Steinfeld, and Lampe
> (2007), Facebook and other social networking
> sites offer researchers an "ideal" chance to
> investigate "offline and online connection"
> (p. 12).

But if the quoted material is 40 or more words, it should be "blocked." Indent the entire quoted passage five spaces or a half inch from the left margin, and omit the quotation marks. For example,

> According to Perfetti's (2003) book on women in the Middle Ages and laughter,
>
> > Laughter is both a defense mechanism and a weapon of attack, essential to groups struggling to be taken seriously by the rest of society. But it is perhaps women, more than any other group, who have had the most complicated relationship with humor in Western culture. People of every religion, nationality, ethnicity, class, and occupation have at some time found themselves the butt of an offensive joke and told to lighten up because "it's just a joke." But it is women who have been told that their refusal to laugh at jokes made at their expense shows that they don't have a sense of humor at all. So a woman has to assert her right not to laugh at offensive jokes but simultaneously prove that she is capable of laughter or risk being seen as a humorless spoilsport: a balancing act requiring a quick wit. (p. viii)

Notice that blocked quotations are double-spaced and that the parenthetical reference is placed *after* the period rather than before it.

If you omit material from an original source—a common method of using just the relevant information in a sentence or passage—use *ellipsis points* (...). For example,

> The study (Lampe, 2010) noted that "student athletes in U.S. universities are highly

visible. . . . They are often considered to be representatives of the university, and may be the
most visible spokespeople for, in some
cases . . ." (p. 193).

### 2.1.7 REFERENCES LIST

All sources cited in the body of the paper are listed alphabetically by author (or title, if the source is anonymous) in the list titled
"References," as shown in Figure C4. This list should begin a new
page, and it is double-spaced throughout. The first line of each entry
is flush left; subsequent lines are indented a half inch. Explanation of
how to cite various types of sources in the References list follows (see
"Part Three: Preparing the References List").

### 2.1.8 TABLES AND FIGURES

Should you include a table, chart, or photograph in your paper?
Sure, if you're certain that it adds something to your discussion and
if the information it presents is clear and understandable. If you use
a table (and with programs like Excel and Word, tables are incredibly
easy to generate), place it in the manuscript as close as you can to
where you mention it. Alternatively, you can put your tables and figures in an appendix. Tables should all be double-spaced. Type a table

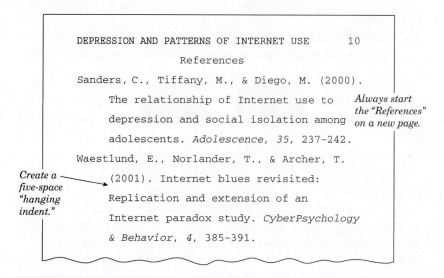

**FIGURE C4    The References Page**

number at the top, flush left. Number tables "Table 1," "Table 2," and so on, corresponding to the order in which they are mentioned in the text. The title, in italics, should be placed on the line below the number. Tables that you put in an appendix should be labeled accordingly. For example, Table 1 in Figure B2 in Appendix B would be numbered Table B1.

Figures (graphs, charts, photographs, and drawings) are handled similarly to tables. They are numbered consecutively beginning with "Figure 1." This figure number, below the figure itself, is followed by a title and, if needed, a caption (see Figure C5). Captions are often helpful in explaining a chart, photograph, drawing, or other figure. As with tables, insert figures in your paper as close as you can to where you refer to them or, alternatively, put them in an appendix.

### 2.1.9 APPENDIX

This is a seldom-used feature of an APA-style paper, though you might find it helpful for presenting specific material that isn't central to the discussion in the body of your paper: a detailed description of a device mentioned in the paper, a copy of a blank survey, a table, or the like. Each item, placed at the end of the paper following the References page, should begin on a separate page and be labeled "Appendix" (followed by "A," "B," and so on, consecutively, if you have more than one Appendix in your paper).

### 2.1.10 NOTES

Several kinds of notes might be included in a paper. The most common are *content notes,* or brief commentaries by the writer

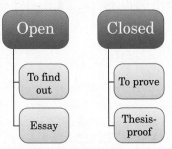

*Figure 1.* Two broad categories of writing assignments. Open-ended and more closed writing assignments each are characterized by a different motive and result in a different genre.

**FIGURE C5    Example of Format for a Figure**

keyed to superscript numbers in the body of the text. These notes are useful for discussion of key points that are relevant but might be distracting if explored in the text of your paper. Present all notes, numbered consecutively, on a page titled "Footnotes" (placed after the References page but before any appendixes) or at the bottom of the relevant page. Notes should be double-spaced. Begin each note with the appropriate superscript number, indented like the first line of a paragraph; subsequent lines of a note are not indented.

## 2.2 Some Style Considerations

### 2.2.1 USE OF ITALICS

The APA guidelines for *italicizing* call for its use when:

- Giving the titles of books, periodicals, films, and publications that appear on microfilm.
- Using new or specialized terms, but only the first time you use them (e.g., "the authors' *paradox study* of Internet users…").
- Citing a phrase, letter, or word as an example (e.g., "the second *a* in *separate* can be remembered by remembering the word *rat*").

Use quotation marks around the titles of articles or book chapters mentioned in your essay.

### 2.2.2 TREATMENT OF NUMBERS

Numbers 9 and below that don't represent precise measurements should be spelled out, and numbers 10 and above should be expressed as numerals. Any numbers that begin a sentence or represent a commonly used fraction (e.g., "one-quarter of the sample") should be spelled out.

# Part Three: Preparing the References List

Each parenthetical citation in the body of the paper should correspond to a complete source listing in the References list. The format for this section was described earlier in this appendix (see "References List" in Part Two).

## 3.1 Order of Sources and Information

### Order of Sources

List the references alphabetically by author's last name or by the first key word of the title if there is no author. This alphabetical principle has a few complications:

- You may have several sources by the same author. If these sources weren't published in the same year, list them in chronological order, the earliest first. If the sources were published in the same year, include a lowercase letter to distinguish them. For example:

  Lane, B. (2007a). Verbal medicine...

  Lane, B. (2007b). Writing...

- Because scholars and writers often collaborate, you may have several references in which an author is listed with several *different* collaborators. List these sources alphabetically using the second author's last name. For example,

  Brown, M., Nelson, A. (2002)

  Brown, M., Payne, M. (1999)

### Order of Information

A References list entry for a periodical or book includes this information, in order: author; date of publication; book title or, for articles, article title followed by periodical title; and publication information. Here are some basics about each of these entry parts; details and examples follow. Remember that all entries should be double-spaced and that the first line of each should begin flush left and all subsequent lines should be indented.

**Author or Authors.**    List all authors—last name, comma, and then initials. Invert all authors' names. Use commas to separate authors' names; add an *ampersand* (&) before the last author's name. End the list of names with a period. When citing an edited book, list the editor(s) in the author's place, and add the abbreviation *Ed.* or *Eds.* in parentheses after the last editor's name.

**Date.**    After the last author's name, in parentheses list the year the work was published. If the source is a magazine or newspaper, also include the month and day; for example, "(2011, April 4)." If a source doesn't list a date, use the abbreviation *n.d.* in parentheses. Add a period after the closing parenthesis.

**Book Title or Article Title.**    Use a period at the end of each title, and style titles as follows:

- **Book titles** are italicized. Only the first word of titles and subtitles is capitalized; all other words are lowercase unless ordinarily capitalized. For example:

  *The curious researcher: A guide to writing research papers.*

  *Sound reporting.*

- **Article titles** are given without italics or quotation marks. As with book titles, capitalize only the first word of the title and any subtitle.

  Student athletes on Facebook.

  Oyster apocalypse? Truth about bivalve obliteration.

**Periodical Title and Publication Information.**    Periodical titles are italicized, like book titles; unlike book and article titles, periodical titles use both uppercase and lowercase letters. Add the volume number (if any), also italicized and separated from the title with a comma. If each issue of the periodical starts with page 1, then also include the issue number in parentheses immediately after the volume number. End the entry, following a comma, with the page numbers of the article. For example, you might have *Journal of Mass Communication, 10*, 138–150. Use the abbreviation *p.* (for one page) or *pp.* (for more than one page) only if you are citing a newspaper.

**Publication Information for Books.**    List the city and state or country of publication (use postal abbreviations for states) and then, following a colon, the name of the publisher, followed by a period.

Bringing these elements together, a print book citation would look like this in APA style:

Blakeswell, S. (2010). *How to live or a life of Montaigne.* New York, NY: Other Press.

And a print periodical citation would look like this:

```
Alegre, A. (2011). Parenting styles and chil-
     dren's emotional intelligence. What do we
     know? The Family Journal, 19, 56-62.
```

**Digital Sources.**    In many ways, citing an electronic source is the same as citing a print one—you'll include author, title, and publication information. But there are also significant differences. Online material may appear in different versions—say, as a talk and as an article based on that talk—and because electronic sources may come and go, it's hard to be certain that readers will be able to find a particular source. APA has been making changes in an effort to meet the special challenges posed by online material. Basically, the organization recommends that you identify where the article or document is located using one of two methods:

1. Cite the DOI (digital object identifier).

*Or, if you can find no DOI,*

2. Include the URL of the home page (Web address).

The digital object identifier is a unique number that is assigned to an electronic document. Almost all journal articles these days have a DOI, which is often listed on the first page of a document. Because these numbers are stable and unique to each source, they are the preferred method of citing the location of an electronic source.

A journal article with a DOI would be cited like this:

```
O'Neil, J. (2011). The privatization of pub-
     lic schools in New Zealand. Journal
     of Education Policy, 26, 17-31. doi:
     10.1080/02680939.2010.493227
```

For example, here's a typical citation of an online document that has no DOI:

```
Perina, K., Flora, P., & Marano, H. P. (2011,
     January 1). Who are you? (And what do
```

you think of me?). *Psychology Today.*

Retrieved from http://www.psychologytoday

.com/articles/201012/who-are-you-and

-what-do-you-think-of-me

## 3.2 Citing Books, in Print and Online

### 3.2.1 A BOOK WITH ONE AUTHOR

Cite a print book like this:

Barry, J. M. (2004). *The great influenza: The*

*epic story of the deadliest plague in his-*

*tory.* New York, NY: Viking.

*In-Text Citation:* (Barry, 2004) *or* According to
Barry (2004),...

Cite a book that appears only electronically like this:

Burnheim, J. (2006). *Is democracy possible?*

*The alternative to electoral politics.*

Retrieved from http://setis.library.usyd

.edu.au/democracy/index.html

*In-Text Citation:* (Burnheim, 2006) *or* According to
Burnheim (2006),...

For an electronic book that is also available in print, include information in brackets about how it appeared digitally. For
example,

Gwynne, S. C. (2010). *Empire of the summer moon*

[iBook version]. Retrieved from http://www

.apple.com/us/ibooks

*In-Text Citation:* (Gwynne, 2010) *or* According to
Gwynne (2010),...

### 3.2.2  A BOOK WITH TWO AUTHORS

Glenn, J., & Hayes, C. (2007). *Taking things
     seriously*. New York, NY: Princeton
     Architectural Press.

*In-Text Citation:* (Glenn & Hayes, 2007) *or* According
to Glenn and Hayes (2007),...

### 3.2.3  A BOOK WITH THREE TO SEVEN AUTHORS

Belenky, M., Clinchy, B. M., Goldberger, N. R.,
     & Tarule, J. M. (1986). *Women's ways of
     knowing: The development of self, voice,
     and mind*. New York, NY: Basic Books.

*In-Text Citation:* (Belenky, Clinchy, Goldberger,
& Tarule, 1986) when mentioned first, and (Belenky
et al., 1986) thereafter.

### 3.2.4  A BOOK WITH EIGHT OR MORE AUTHORS

For a work with eight or more authors, give the first six authors
followed by an ellipsis (...) and the final author. For example,

Jones, B., Doverman, L. S., Shanke S.,
     Forman, P., Witte, L. S., Firestone,
     F. J.,...Smith, L. A. (2011). *Too many
     authors spoil the soup*. New York, NY:
     Oyster Press.

*In-Text Citation:* (Jones et al., 2011)

### 3.2.5  A BOOK WITH AN INSTITUTIONAL AUTHOR

American Red Cross. (2007). *Advanced first
     aid and emergency care*. New York, NY:
     Doubleday.

*In-Text Citation:* (American Red Cross, 2007)

### 3.2.6 A BOOK WITH NO AUTHOR

*The Chicago manual of style* (16th ed.). (2010).
Chicago, IL: University of Chicago Press.

*In-Text Citation:* (Chicago Manual of Style, 2010)

*or* According to the *Chicago Manual of Style*
(2010),...

### 3.2.7 AN ENCYCLOPEDIA ENTRY

Cite an article from a print encyclopedia like this:

Hansen, T. S. (2003). Depression. In *The
new encyclopaedia Britannica* (Vol. 12,
pp. 408-412). Chicago, IL: Encyclopaedia
Britannica.

*In-Text Citation:* (Hansen, 2003) *or* Hansen (2003)
defines depression as....

Cite an article from an online encyclopedia like this:

Diarrhea. (2008). In *Columbia encyclopedia* (6th
ed.). Retrieved from http://www.encyclopedia
.com/doc/1E1-diarrhea.html

*In-Text Citation:* ("Diarrhea," 2008) *or*
According to the *Columbia Encyclopedia*
(2008), diarrhea....

### 3.2.8 A CHAPTER IN A BOOK

Kuhn, T. S. (1996). The route to normal science.
In *The structure of scientific revolutions*
(pp. 23-34). Chicago, IL: University of
Chicago Press.

*In-Text Citation:* (Kuhn, 2006) *or* Kuhn (2006) argues
that....

### 3.2.9 A BOOK WITH AN EDITOR

Crane, R. S. (Ed.). (1952). *Critics and criti-cism*. Chicago, IL: University of Chicago Press.

*In-Text Citation:* (Crane, 1952) *or* In his preface, Crane (1952) observed that. . . .

### 3.2.10 A SELECTION IN A BOOK WITH AN EDITOR

McKeon, R. (1952). Rhetoric in the Middle Ages. In R. S. Crane (Ed.), *Critics and criticism* (pp. 260–289). Chicago, IL: University of Chicago Press.

*In-Text Citation:* (McKeon, 1952) *or* McKeon (1952) argued that. . . .

### 3.2.11 A REPUBLISHED WORK

James, W. (1978). *Pragmatism*. Cambridge, MA: Harvard University Press. (Original work published 1907)

*In-Text Citation:* (James, 1907/1978) *or* According to William James (1907/1978), . . .

### 3.2.12 A GOVERNMENT DOCUMENT

U.S. Bureau of the Census. (1991). *Statistical abstract of the United States* (111th ed.). Washington, DC: Government Printing Office.

*In-Text Citation:* (U.S. Bureau, 1991) *or* According to the U.S. Census Bureau (1991), . . .

## 3.3 Citing Articles, in Print and Online

### 3.3.1 A JOURNAL ARTICLE

Cite a print journal article like this:

Blager, F. B. (1979). The effect of intervention
　　　on the speech and language of children.
　　　*Child Abuse and Neglect, 5,* 91-96.

*In-Text Citation:* (Blager, 1979) *or* Blager (1979)
stated that. . . .

Include the DOI, if available:

Wang, F., McGuire, P., & Pan, E. (2010).
　　　Applying technology to inquiry-based learn-
　　　ing in early childhood education. *Early*
　　　*Childhood Education Journal, 37,* 381-389.
　　　doi:10.1007/s10643-009-0634-6

*In-Text Citation:* When first mentioned cite all three (Wang,
McGuire, & Pan, 2010) *or* Wang, McGuire, and Pan
(2010) argue that. . . . Subsequent mentions can use
*et al.:* (Wang et al., 2010).

For a journal article with no DOI, include the URL of the database or the online journal's home page:

Kaveshar, J. (2008). Kicking the rock and the
　　　hard place to the curb: An alternative and
　　　integrated approach to suicidal students in
　　　higher education. *Emory Law Journal, 57*(3),
　　　651-693. Retrieved from http://find
　　　.galegroup.com/itx/start.do?prodId=AONE

*In-Text Citation:* (Kaveshar, 2008) *or* According to
Kaveshar (2008), . . .

### 3.3.2 A JOURNAL ARTICLE NOT PAGINATED CONTINUOUSLY

Most journals begin on page 1 with the first issue of the year and continue paginating consecutively for subsequent issues. A few journals, however, start on page 1 with each issue. For these, include the issue number in parentheses following the italicized volume number:

Williams, J., Post, A. T., & Strunk, F. (1991).

The rhetoric of inequality. *Attwanata*,

*12*(3), 54-67.

*In-Text Citation:* (Williams, Post, & Strunk, 1991) *or* Williams, Post, and Strunk (1991) argue that. . . . When first mentioned, cite all three authors; subsequently you can use *et al.*: (Williams et al., 1991).

### 3.3.3 A MAGAZINE ARTICLE

To cite print articles, include the year, month, and (if present) day published.

Moore, Peter. (2003, August). Your heart will

stop. *Men's Health*. 142-151.

*In-Text Citation:* (Moore, 2003) *or* Moore (2003) observed that. . . .

Cite online articles like this:

O'Hehir, A. (2008). Beyond the multiplex.

Salon.com. Retrieved from http://www

.salon.com/ent/movies/btm/

*In-Text Citation:* (O'Hehir, 2008) *or* According to O'Hehir (2008), . . .

### 3.3.4 A NEWSPAPER ARTICLE

Cite print articles like this:

Honan, W. (1991, January 24). The war

affects Broadway. *The New York Times*,

pp. C15-C16.

*In-Text Citation:* (Honan, 1991) *or* Honan (1991) said that "Broadway is a battleground" (p. C15).

Cite online articles like this:

Englund, W., DeYoung, K., & Willgoren, D. (2011, February 4). Huge protests continue for 11th day as Obama administration weighs Egypt options. *The Washington Post*. Retrieved from http://www.washingtonpost.com

*In-Text Citation:* (Englund, DeYoung, & Willgoren, 2011) *or* According to Englund et al.,...

### 3.3.5 AN ARTICLE WITH NO AUTHOR

If there is no author, a common situation with newspaper articles, alphabetize using the first significant word in the article title. For example:

New Hampshire loud and clear. (1998, February 19). *The Boston Globe*, p. 22.

*In-Text Citation:* ("New Hampshire," 1998) *or* In the article "New Hampshire loud and clear" (1998),...

### 3.3.6 AN ARTICLE ON A WEB SITE

Note that this citation includes the abbreviation *n.d.* because the article did not include a date.

Lopez, M. (n.d.). Intellectual development of toddlers. *National Network for Childcare*. Retrieved from http://www.nncc.org/Child .Dev/intel.dev.todd.html

*In-Text Citation:* (Lopez, n.d.) *or* According to Lopez (n.d.),...

### 3.3.7 AN ABSTRACT

The growth of online databases for articles has increased the availability of full-text versions and abstracts of articles. While it is almost always better to use the full article, sometimes an abstract itself contains useful information. Typically, there are two situations in which you might choose to cite just an abstract: when you're working with an original print article or when you've culled the abstract from a database like *Biological Abstracts*. In the first case, include the term *Abstract* in brackets following the title and before the period.

For example,

Renninger, A. K. (2009). Interest and identity

    development in instruction: An inductive

    model [Abstract]. *Educational Psychologist,*

    *44,* 105–118.

*In-Text Citation:* (Renninger, 2009) *or* Renninger
(2009) claims that....

If the abstract was from a database or some other secondary source, include the name of that source. The term *Abstract* in brackets isn't necessary in this case. For example,

Garcia, R. G. (2002). Evolutionary speed of

    species invasions. *Evolution, 56,* 661–

    668. Abstract retrieved from *Biological*

    *Abstracts.*

*In-Text Citation:* (Garcia, 2002) *or* Garcia (2002)
argues that....

### 3.3.8 A BOOK REVIEW

Cite a review that's in print like this:

Dentan, R. K. (1989). A new look at the brain

    [Review of the book *The dreaming brain,*

    by J. A. Hobsen]. *Psychiatric Journal,*

    *13,* 51.

*In-Text Citation:* (Dentan, 1989) *or* Dentan (1989)
argued that....

Cite an online review like this:

Benfey, C. (2008). Why implausibility sells
     [Review of the book *Painter in a savage
     land,* by M. Harvey]. *Slate.* Retrieved from
     http://www.slate.com/id/2193254/

*In-Text Citation:* (Benfey, 2008) *or* Benfey (2008)
argued that. . . .

### 3.3.9 AN EDITORIAL

Egypt's agonies [Editorial]. (2011, February 2).
     *The New York Times.* Retrieved from http://
     www.nytimes.com/2011/02/04/opinion
     /04fr1.htm

*In-Text Citation:* ("Egypt's Agonies," 2011) *or The New
York Times* (2011) argued. . . .

### 3.3.10 A LETTER TO THE EDITOR

Hill, A. C. (1992, February 19). A flawed his-
     tory of blacks in Boston [Letter to the
     editor]. *The Boston Globe,* p. 22.

*In-Text Citation:* (Hill, 1992) *or* Hill (1992) complained that. . . .

### 3.3.11 A PUBLISHED INTERVIEW

Personal interviews are usually not cited in an APA-style
References list even though they are cited in your text. Published interviews are cited as follows:

Cotton, P. (1982, April). [Interview with J. Tule,
     psychic]. *Chronicles Magazine,* pp. 24–28.

*In-Text Citation:* (Cotton, 1982) *or* Cotton (1982)
noted that. . . .

## 3.4 Citing Other Sources

### 3.4.1 AN ENTIRE WEB SITE

If you're referring to an entire Web site in the text of your essay, include the Web address parenthetically. However, there is no need to include an entry for it in the References list. For example:

The Google Scholar search engine (http://scholar
.google.com) is considered excellent for academic
research.

### 3.4.2 A FILM, DVD, OR ONLINE VIDEO

Hitchcock, A. (Producer & Director).

(1954). *Rear window* [Film]. United

States: MGM.

*In-Text Citation:* (Hitchcock, 1954) *or* In *Rear Window*, Hitchcock (1954). . . .

Here's how to cite an online video:

Price, P. (Writer). (2008, April 4). *Researching*

*online: Five easy steps* [Video file].

Retrieved from http://www.youtube.com/watch

?v=Ylp9nJpGak4&feature=related

*In-Text Citation:* (Price, 2008) *or* In *Researching Online*, Price (2008). . . .

### 3.4.3 A TELEVISION PROGRAM

Burns, K. (Executive producer). (1996). *The*

*West* [Television broadcast]. New York, NY:

Public Broadcasting Service.

*In-Text Citation:* (Burns, 1996) *or* In Ken Burns's (1996) film, . . .

### 3.4.4 AN AUDIO PODCAST

Kermode, M. (2008, June 20). The edge of love. *Mark Kermode and Simon Mayo's movie reviews* [Audio podcast]. Retrieved from http://www.bbc.co.uk/fivelive/entertainment/kermode.shtml

*In-Text Citation:* (Kermode, 2008) *or* In his latest review, Kermode (2008) decried....

### 3.4.5 A BLOG

Shen, H. (2008, June 4). Does your password meet the test? [Web log post]. Retrieved from http://googleblog.blogspot.com/2008/06/does-your-password-pass-test.html

*In-Text Citation:* (Shen, 2008) *or* Our passwords are vulnerable, says Shen (2008), because....

### 3.4.6 A WIKI

How to use Audacity for podcasting. (n.d.). Retrieved from http://sites.google.com/a/biosestate.edu/podcasting-team/Home

*In-Text Citation:* ("Audacity," n.d.)

### 3.4.7 ONLINE DISCUSSION LISTS

These include listservs, electronic mailing lists, newsgroups, and online forums, with the method of citation varying slightly depending on the specific type of source. For example,

Hord, J. (2002, July 11). Re: Why do pigeons lift one wing up in the air? [Online forum comment]. Retrieved from rec://pets.birds.pigeons

*In-Text Citation:* (Hord, 2002) *or* Hord asks
(2002)....

Note that the citation includes the subject line of the message as the title and bracketed information about the source, in this case an online forum comment. For listservs, use "[Electronic mailing list message]."

### 3.4.8 A MUSICAL RECORDING

Wolf, K. (1986). Muddy roads [Recorded by E.

Clapton]. On *Gold in California* [CD]. Santa

Monica, CA: Rhino Records. (1990).

*In-Text Citation:* (Wolf, 1986, track 5) *or* In Wolf's
(1986) song,...

# Part Four:
# Student Paper in APA Style

Laura Burns' fascinating look at the 1978 mass suicide among followers of Jim Jones' People's Temple does what good writing should do: it challenges us to take a look at something we may have seen before and consider seeing it differently. She does not dispute that this was a tragedy or that Jones was, in the end, a madman. But Laura argues that to see only these things is to miss the admirable idealism that was once behind the People's Temple, an idealism that makes the tragedy even worse.

Looking for Utopia: The Men and Women

of the People's Temple

Laura Burns

State University

Looking for Utopia: The Men and
Women of the People's Temple

Even in mid-November, the air in
the Guyanese jungle was thick with heat.
The screams of spider monkeys pierced the
silence over the corrugated tin roof of a
pavilion. Fields of cassava, eddoes, and
pineapple lay abandoned, trailing off into
the vast green jungle (Hatfield, 1998).
And on the soft, spongy ground, circled by
plastic barrels dripping with red, lay the
bodies of over 900 people. Above the muddy
road leading into the settlement, a sign:
"Welcome to Jonestown."

The rise and fall of the People's
Temple, the Reverend Jim Jones, and the
cataclysmic mass murder/suicide at
Jonestown, Guyana, on November 18, 1978,
still haunt the American consciousness.
However, the further removed we are from
the devastating events of that day, the
less clearly we are able to see the
humanity of its victims. The tragedy at
Jonestown was not caused only by brain-
washing or coercion, but rather by a
more complex formula—it was the product
of the dream of a new group of liberal
idealists who, frustrated with their

*In most argumentative essays, the thesis is parked right up front in the piece, as it is here.*

disaffected society, came together to find solace in the hope of utopian possibility, no matter what the cost.

James Warren Jones, the man who was to become the Reverend Jim Jones, was born on May 13, 1931, in rural Crete, Indiana, and developed an interest in religion early on. At the young age of 21, Jones accepted a position as a pastor at the Somerset Southside Methodist Church in Indianapolis. He had a unique vision for a church, though—one that didn't mesh with what was happening in Indianapolis in the 1950s. Infuriated by the congregation's refusal to desegregate, Jones left and purchased a small building he called the Wings of Deliverance Church (Lattin, 2003). Later that year, the name of the church was changed to the People's Temple.

In developing a doctrine, Jim Jones focused his vision on racial equality and civil rights. This immediately appealed to the black community in Indianapolis, who flocked to the church to hear Jones's sermons: "What is God anyway?" he would ask the congregation, and then answer, "God is perfect justice, freedom, and equality" (Weston, 1981, p. 56). And Jones practiced what he preached.

LOOKING FOR UTOPIA                                    4

     In 1953, he and his wife, Marceline,
went to a local adoption agency, where
they witnessed a wealthy black doctor
refuse to take home a child, claiming
the boy was "too black." Furious, Jones
retorted, "Well, in that case, I'll take
him" ("Messiah," 1978). This was to be
the first of seven ethnically diverse
children the family would adopt. For many
black congregants, Jones was the first
white man who had ever showed kinship to
them and compassion for their struggle.
Through tithing and other support,
they could be a part of Jones's social
movement. In religious terms, Jones's
style of preaching and practice of
healings and psychic magic were aligned
with traditional Pentecostalism, a
familiar faith for many black congregants.
They felt right at home.

     In the early 1960s, Jones, like
many other Americans, became caught up in
nuclear paranoia. He decided a permanent
location change for the Church was needed,
and selected Ukiah, in Redwood Valley,
California. In 1963, Jones and his
family, along with over 70 members of the
Indianapolis People's Temple, relocated

to rural Ukiah. In California, the Temple recruited a new group of converts: white, middle-class intellectuals and idealists. The political landscape in America was in upheaval, and in California, the alienation experienced by many budding idealists led them to fringe religious groups, such as Hare Krishna, Scientology, and the People's Temple. Jones provided an opportunity for recruits of all races—his "rainbow family"—to join hands and work to make a utopia of equality and freedom.

Jones preached *apostolic social-ism,* which combines Christian doctrine with socialist goals. He quoted Bible verses, such as Acts 4:31-32, which advocates for common finances, and Acts 4:35, which speaks of the distribution of resources according to need (Wessinger, 2000). The People's Temple was engaged in a new kind of civil rights activism, pairing the Christian stance of Martin Luther King Jr. with the militarism of Marcus Garvey (Hall, 1987). Jones was vibrant and well-loved, and the Temple community was tight-knit and warm, and successfully broke down barriers of race, age, and gender (nearly all Temple

*Notice how Laura loops back to her thesis with the reference to the "utopian" dreams of early members of the Church. Imagine that a thesis statement is a tack that the writer drives into the material to keep it anchored to the controlling idea.*

LOOKING FOR UTOPIA                    6

leaders were women). This meant that even
when the doctrine got darker and their
leader grew more and more paranoid, the
congregants stayed put. Everything the
People's Temple was fighting against
lurked right outside the Church doors;
if they wanted to realize their dream of
utopia, they had to stick with Jones.

*Laura hammers in another tack, building support for her thesis.*

By the early 1970s, the Church
was already functioning as a standalone
socialist community, financially supported
by members' donations of Social Security
checks, paychecks, and the funds from
the sale of their private homes. However,
as his paranoia increased, Jones was
tightening the reins. He forced members to
prove their loyalty by signing blank power-
of-attorney forms and false confessions
of murder and child molestation, stating
that should they leave the Church, he
would turn these in to the police (Maaga,
1998, p. 13). The Diversions Committee,
a group comprised of Jones's most loyal
confidantes, was organized to push forth
the principles of the Temple and undermine
opposition in the public arena. He also
began to lay the groundwork for an exodus
from "capitalist America, racist America,

fascist America" (Chidester, 1988, p. 72)
to Guyana, a small nation in South America
that had granted Jones a lease in October
1973 (Weston, 1981). He preached the danger
of radioactive fallout and the threat of
the government and media, asserting that
he had "seen, by divine revelation, the
total annihilation of this country and
other parts of the world" (Appel, 1983,
pp. 28-29).

In 1977, *New West Magazine* published
an article by Marshall Kilduff that was
harshly critical of Jones and the People's Temple. It was a public relations
nightmare, and Jones panicked and moved
immediately to Guyana, enacting an emergency six-week egression. Most Temple
members followed him. A planned exodus
of this kind is not out of line with the
actions of similar groups, such as Marcus Garvey's Back-to-Africa movement, and
Guyana provided an opportunity to start
fresh. "I wanted my son to grow up in
a better place," remembered Vernon Gosney. "I wanted to help create this utopia
that Jim Jones had talked about, where
people would live in harmony and peace"
(Vandecarr, 2003, p. 38). Guyana was the

promised land, and Jones was going to
lead them there (Hall, 1987).

Once the members arrived in George-
town, the capital of Guyana, they were
transported by small passenger plane to
Port Kaituma. From there, they were driv-
en by truck for seven miles on muddy,
unpaved roads to the Jonestown Agricultural Commune. In the beginning, there
was little to see—merely a large, open-
air pavilion framed by fields of cassava, eddoes, and pineapple. Eventually,
thanks to the ceaseless hard work of the
Temple members, the commune would house a
sawmill, a 10,000-book library, a nurs-
ery, a hospital, a dispensary, ammunition
and equipment storage, a repair shop,
and a playground. On the walls of the
buildings hung signs painted with hope-
ful quotes: "Where the spirit of the Lord
is, there is liberty," "All that believed
were together, and had all things in common" ("What I Saw," 1978, p. 43). "It
was a harmonious, supportive community,"
recalled Vernon Gosney. "Everyone was
building beautiful buildings. Jim Jones
was a benevolent figure" (Vandecarr,
2003, p. 38).

Despite that early sense of harmony, the move to Jonestown only increased the intensity of the control Jones wielded over Temple members, and his paranoia was significantly worsened by his descent into prescription drug addiction. Jones enacted frequent emergency drills, or *white nights*, announced with sirens. Some white nights concluded with suicide drills. Members were given wine, which they were told was poisoned. If they didn't drink it immediately, they were berated until they did. They were told that in death, they would be transformed and live with Jones in a better world (Long, 1994). Although extreme, suicide drills were not unheard of in other radical movements. Jones's white nights followed the example of Black Panther Minister of Defense Huey Newton, who stated, "By having no family, I inherited the family of humanity. By having no possessions, I have possessed all. . . .By surrendering my life to the revolution, I have found eternal life" (Chidester, 1988, p. 14). "The white nights didn't seem real," recalled Vernon Gosney. "I should have seen it coming, but I didn't" (Vandecarr, 2003, p. 38).

*One sign of authoritative research writing is a paragraph like this one, which uses three different sources rather than relying on one.*

Gosney was not the only one who didn't seem to see the warning signs. While in the United States, Temple members didn't defect mostly for ideological reasons, but in Guyana, miles away from civilization, the reasons became more mortal. In Jonestown, Temple members were mentally and emotionally exhausted from constant fear of punishment, excessive work, and malnourishment. For many, despite the conditions, the community they were creating in Guyana was still the closest they had ever come to their idea of a societal utopia. The problem was that the "People's Temple at some point lost its ability to look self-critically at itself and to challenge the decisions of the leadership—not just Jim Jones," states the Rev. Mary McCormick Maaga, a Jonestown scholar. "And Jones lost his ability to lead because of drug addiction and mental illness" (Hatfield, 1998).

*Further evidence supporting the thesis: Despite the incredible hardship, the utopian dream was powerful enough that the residents of Jonestown endured.*

Shortly after Jones's exodus to Guyana, on November 17, 1978, a delegation of reporters, photographers, and concerned relatives of Jonestown residents, led by California Congressman Leo Ryan, arrived in Port Kaituma. The junket

spent that evening in Jonestown interviewing Temple members, who were effusive
about their love for Jonestown, and en-
joying entertainment and freshly prepared
food. Impressed, Ryan announced, "From
what I've seen there are a lot of people
here who think this is the best thing
that has happened in their whole lives"
(Neff, 1978, p. 41). However, before the
party left for the evening, a small note
was slipped to reporter Don Harris, who
later showed it to Ryan. It read: "Vernon
Gosney and Monica Bagby. Please help us
get out of Jonestown." The next day,
Ryan extended an open invitation to any
Temple members who wanted to leave with
him, and at around 11:00 in the morning,
16 defectors, including Vernon Gosney,
Monica Bagby, and last-minute addition
Larry Layton, departed for the airstrip
in Port Kaituma, where two planes waited
to take them back to the United States.
The smaller plane was boarded by Monica
Bagby, Vernon Gosney, Dale Parks, and
Larry Layton, who, upon the closing of the
doors, pulled out a gun, wounding Bagby
and Gosney. Simultaneously, a tractor and
two trailers belonging to the People's

Temple arrived on the airstrip and opened fire. Congressman Ryan, defector Patricia Parks, and reporters Greg Robinson, Don Harris, and Bob Brown were shot dead within seconds. Brown's camera, which was on, kept rolling even after he fell to the ground (Stephenson, 2005).

Meanwhile, Jones was preparing for the end of his own movement. As night fell, the familiar siren rang out over Jonestown: "This is a white night. Everyone to the pavilion." Jones instructed Dr. Laurence Schacht and others in his inner circle to prepare the concoction of Fla-V-or Aid, liquid cyanide, and Valium (which Dr. Schacht believed would cause painless death) in large white buckets. Slowly, carefully, Jones explained the drastic action. "Some months I've tried to keep this thing from happening," he said breathily into his microphone. "But now I see...it's the will of the Sovereign Being that this happen to us. That we lay down our lives in protest against what's being done." One woman, 60-year-old Christine Miller, interrupted Jones: "As long as there's life," she said, "there's hope." Kindly, Jones responded:

"Well, someday, everybody dies. . . . And I'd like to choose my own kind of death for a change" (Stephenson, 2005, pp. 131-136). Miller relented and joined the others, who walked willingly to the poison. Certainly, they had been prepared for this moment by the suicide drills and Jones's recent apocalyptic sermons, but more importantly, the Temple members didn't see their deaths as senseless. Their suicides fit in with the doctrine of the Temple, enacting a release from a corrupt society, revenge against capitalism and inequality, and a revolution against the degradation that they believed existed in American society (Chidester, 1988).

With the organization of Temple leaders, the children were lined up before the vats of Fla-V-or Aid, and with syringes, squirts of the red liquid were pressed into their mouths. Adults were given plastic cups with the poison, and after drinking, were told to lie down in the grass with their children. However, the mixture wasn't quite right, and the Valium didn't adequately dull the pain of the cyanide's work. Within minutes, Temple members began to convulse and sob, blood flowing out of their noses and mouths. Jones and his

LOOKING FOR UTOPIA                                    14

inner circle escaped this brutal fate, and
moved to Jones's private cabin, where they
shot themselves (Hall, 1987). Within about
an hour, 914 people, blood covering their
faces, tears staining their cheeks, arms
tightened about each other, lay dead.

"The people who died in Jonestown
were sweet, altruistic people," stated sur-
vivor Timothy Stoen. "One of the tragedies
of Jonestown is that people haven't paid
enough attention to that" (Hatfield, 1998).
It was not only Jones's sweet talking that
convinced the Temple members to "drink the
Kool-Aid." The people of Jonestown were
idealists building a utopia, following a
man they thought would lead them there.
They loved their children, and feared for
their futures. They cared for each other,
and stayed together, even in death. They
believed in a better world, and dedicated their lives, and deaths, to making
it a reality. "As a society we fail to
take seriously the very strong and powerful desire, or hunger, for community,
a community of people working for social change," stated Rebecca Moore, whose
sisters, Carolyn Layton and Annie Moore,
died in Jonestown. "At times I despair
we've learned nothing" (Hatfield, 1998).

*This is an end-
ing that not
only echoes
the thesis but
also poignantly
adds to it. The
last lines re-
mind readers
through the
voice of a sister
of Jonestown
victims that the
aftermath of
the tragedy led
to yet another:
The idealistic
motives of the
victims were
ignored and
misunderstood.*

## References

Appel, W. (1983). *Cults in America*. New York, NY: Holt, Rinehart and Winston.

Chidester, D. (1988). *Salvation and suicide*. Indianapolis, IN: Indiana University.

Hall, J. R. (1987). *Gone from the promised land*. Somerset, NJ: Transaction.

Hatfield, L. (1998, November 8). Utopian nightmare. *San Francisco Chronicle*.

Kilduff, M., & Tracy, P. (1977, August 1). Inside people's temple. *New West*.

Lattin, D. (2003, November 18). Jonestown: 25 years later. *San Francisco Chronicle*.

Long, R. E. (Ed.). (1994). *Religious cults in America*. New York, NY: H. W. Wilson.

Maaga, M. M. (1998). *Hearing the voices of Jonestown*. Syracuse, NY: Syracuse University.

Messiah from the midwest. (1978, December 4). *Time*.

Neff, D. (1978, December 4). Nightmare in Jonestown. *Time*.

Stephenson, D. (Ed.). (2005). *Dear people: Remembering Jonestown*. Berkeley, CA: Heyday.

Vandecarr, P. (2003, November 25). He lived to tell. *The Advocate*, pp. 37–39.

Wessinger, C. (2000). *How the millennium comes violently*. New York, NY: Seven Bridges.

Weston, J., Jr. (1981). *Our father who art in hell*. New York, NY: Times Books.

What I saw. (1978, December 4). *Newsweek*.

*Always begin the References on a new page.*

# Credits

## Photo Credits

**p. 30:** Where's Waldo image from Classic Media Distribution.
**p. 38–39:** Photos by Bruce Ballenger.
**p. 51:** "Three Fronts" image by Bruce Ballenger.
**p. 66:** *Nutrition Journal*, www.nutritionj.com
**p. 70:** "Looking for Patterns" image by Bruce Ballenger.
**p. 135:** USA.gov
**p. 139:** "Faces of Fear" image WDCN / Univ. College London / Science Source
**p. 277:** Graffiti, Peace Wall, Belfast. Ashley Carvalho
**p. 280:** Royal Victoria Hospital, Belfast. Ashley Carvalho
**p. 293:** Rainbow in a Troubled Sky, Belfast. Ashley Carvalho

## Text Credits

**p. 24–26:** Student samples reprinted with permission of Amanda Stewart.

**p. 56:** "Google Tips and Tricks" from Becca Ballenger.

**p. 105:** Carolyn A. (Biddy) Martin, "What is College For?" Chronicle of Higher Education, April 22, 2013. Reprinted by permission of the author.

**p. 113–14:** Excerpt from Bill Bryson, *At Home: A Short History of Private Life,* Anchor Books (a division of Random House), 2011.

**p. 115:** Excerpt "The Unending Conversation" from Kenneth Burke, *The Philosophy of Literary Form,* University of California Press, 1974.

**p. 117–22:** Thomas Lord, "What? I Failed? But I Paid for Those Credits! Problems of Students Evaluating Faculty," Journal of College Science Teaching, Nov/Dec 2008. Reprinted by permission of NSTA.

**p. 126, 129–30, 132:** Student samples reprinted with permission of Amanda Stewart.

**p. 139:** Reprinted from Acta Psychologica, 135/3, Holger Hoffmann, Henrik Kessler, Tobias Eppel, Stefanie Rukavina, Harald C. Traue, "Expression intensity, gender and facial emotion recognition: Women recognize only subtle facial emotions better than men," 278–83, Copyright November 2010, with permission from Elsevier.

**p. 144:** "Mandy's Dialogue with Dave" from Mandy Peterson.

**p. 192–93:** Student sample reprinted with permission of Amanda Stewart.

**p. 210:** "Active Verbs for Discussing Ideas," Cinthia Gannett. Reprinted with permission.

**p. 275–95:** Ashley Carvalho, "Patching Up Belfast." Reprinted with permission.

**p. 329–43:** Laura Burns, "Looking for Utopia." Reprinted with permission.

# Index